HISTORY IN THE MAKING
Series Editor: J. A. P. Jones

3 The
Early
Modern
World
1450–1700

# HISTORY IN THE MAKING

J. A. P. Jones

**First Deputy Head,**
**The Verdin School, Winsford, Cheshire**

# 3 The Early Modern World

## 1450–1700

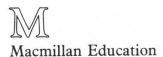

Macmillan Education

First published 1979
Reprinted 1981

Published by
MACMILLAN EDUCATION LIMITED
Houndmills Basingstoke Hampshire RG21 2XS
and London
Associated companies in Delhi   Dublin
Hong Kong   Johannesburg  Lagos  Melbourne
New York   Singapore and Tokyo

Photoset in Great Britain by
Fakenham Press Limited, Fakenham, Norfolk
Printed in Hong Kong

*British Library Cataloguing in Publication Data*

History in the making.
  3: The early modern world, 1450–1700.
  1. World history
  I. Jones, J. A. P.
  909        D21

ISBN 0-333-22305-5

*To Rachel*

# Series
# Preface

Changes in the teaching of history over the last decade have raised many problems to which there are no easy solutions. The classification of objectives, the presentation of material in varied and appropriate language, the use and abuse of evidence and the reconsideration of assessment techniques are four of the most important. Many teachers are now encouraging their pupils individually or in groups to participate in the processes and skills of the professional historian. Such developments are being discussed increasingly in the context of mixed ability classes and the need to provide suitable teaching approaches for them.

*History in the Making* is a new course for secondary schools intended for pupils of average ability. It is a contribution to the current debate, and provides one possible way forward. It accepts many of the proven virtues of traditional courses: the fascination of the good tale; the drama of human life, individual and collective; the need to provide a visual stimulus to the written word.

But it has built on to these some of the key features of the 'new history' so that teachers can explore, within the framework of a textbook, many of the 'new' approaches and techniques.

To this end each chapter in this volume has four major components.

1  **The text**  This provides the basic framework of the chapters, and although the approach is essentially factual, it is intended to arouse and sustain the interest of the reader of average ability.

2  **The illustrations**  These have been carefully selected to stand beside the written pieces of evidence in the chapter, and to provide (so far as is possible) an authentic visual image of the period/topic. Photographs, artwork and maps are all used to clarify and support the text, and to develop the pupil's powers of observation.

3  **Using the evidence**  This is a detailed study of the evidence on one particular aspect of the chapter. Did the walls of Jericho really come tumbling down? Was the death of William Rufus in the New Forest really an accident? What was the background to the torpedoing of the *Lusitania*? These are the sort of questions which are asked, to give the pupil the opportunity to consider not only the problems facing the historian, but also those facing the characters of history. Different forms of documentary evidence are considered, as well as archaeological, architectural, statistical, and other kinds of source material; the intention is to give the pupil a genuine, if modest, insight into the making of history.

4  **Questions and further work**  These are intended to test and develop the pupil's reading of the chapter, and in particular the *Using the evidence* section. Particular attention is paid to the development of historical skills, through the examination and interpretation of evidence. The differences between primary and secondary sources, for example, are explored, and concepts such as bias in evidence and its limitations. By applying the skills which they have developed, pupils may then be able to formulate at a suitable level and in appropriate language, ideas and hypotheses of their own.

*History in the Making* is a complete course in five volumes, to meet the needs of pupils between the ages of 11 and 16 (in other words up to and including the first public examination). However, each volume stands by itself and may be used independently of the others; given the variety of syllabuses in use in schools today this flexibility is likely to be welcomed by many teachers. *The Ancient World* and *The Medieval World* are intended primarily for 11–13-year-old pupils, *The Early Modern World* 1450–1700, for 12–14-year-old pupils, *Britain, Europe and Beyond* 1700–1900, for pre-CSE pupils and *The Twentieth Century* for CSE examination candidates.

It is our hope that pupils will be encouraged, within the main topics and themes of British, European and World History, to experience for themselves the stimulus and challenge, the pleasure and frustration, the vitality and humanity that form an essential part of History in the Making.

J. A. P. Jones

# Contents

# List of Maps

# The Sixteenth Century

# I The world beyond Europe

### The story of Marco Polo

One warm summer day in the year 1269 a young boy stood on the quayside of the rich port of Venice. He listened eagerly to the tales of a group of weather-beaten sailors about the Tartars, the conquering nomadic horsemen who now ruled the Asian lands to the east. The stories were also about the fabulous wealth of the great Khan, the ruler of the whole of Asia. The boy had already heard about Prester John, the Christian king, supposed to rule somewhere in the heart of Asia. The lands to the east obviously fascinated him.

The boy, Marco Polo, had a reason to be interested. Fifteen years earlier, just before Marco was born, his father Nicolo Polo and his uncle Maffeo had vanished into the east. They were jewel merchants and, after two years of wandering in Central Asia, they finally reached the court of the great Kublai Khan. They had received a magnificent welcome and had been sent back to the west on an embassy to the pope.

As Marco sat listening on the quay in 1269, none of this was known. Later that year, however, the two brothers returned to Venice and the young Marco was told at first hand about the wealth and customs of the East.

Two years later, the brothers decided to return to the khan, and Marco begged to go along too. The khan had requested that they take with them two Dominican friars to tell him about Christianity, but the friars heard that there were wars in Armenia and they refused to go

*Marco Polo sets sail from Venice in 1271*

*A fourteenth-century drawing showing Marco Polo's journey to China*

*The court of Genghis Khan*

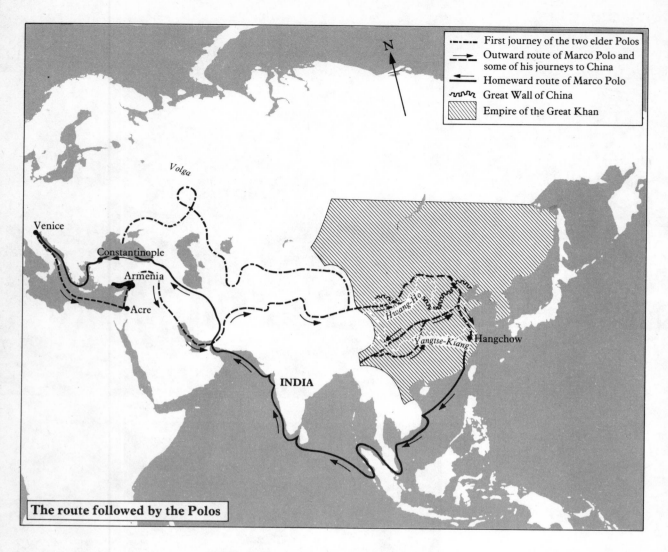

The route followed by the Polos

**Legend:**
- First journey of the two elder Polos
- Outward route of Marco Polo and some of his journeys to China
- Homeward route of Marco Polo
- Great Wall of China
- Empire of the Great Khan

farther. Thus the three Polos journeyed on alone, following the route shown on the above map. It took them three and a half years to reach the court of the Great Khan.

When they arrived, the khan was so impressed by Marco's intelligence that he made him a royal attendant. For the next seventeen years Marco served the khan as an ambassador and official, and he became highly respected throughout the whole of China. He made a number of journeys within the empire and even spent three years as governor of Hangchow, one of China's greatest trading cities. His uncle and father also served the khan, on one occasion building Venetian-type siege towers to help him capture a rebel town.

By 1292, however, the Polos were keen to return home again. The khan was old and many men hated the Venetians' wealth and influence. At first the khan would not let them go, but eventually he relented, and towards the end of 1295 the three men sailed back to Venice.

On their return, none of their old friends could recognise them, believing the real Polos must be dead. Also they found these three strangers, dressed in Tartar clothes, somewhat frightening. Only when they held a lavish banquet and produced 'an infinite treasure of jewels and precious stones, rubies, sapphires, diamonds, emeralds', did their friends and relations accept that they were indeed the Polos.

## The world beyond Europe

The Polos had shown that wealth and civilisation were not to be found in Europe alone. If you look at the map which now hangs in Hereford Cathedral (see below), you will see how churchmen of the thirteenth century saw the world: Christian countries were grouped around the

*The Tartar conqueror, Tamerlain the Great*

*The thirteenth-century map which now hangs in Hereford Cathedral*

Mediterranean and little was known of Africa and the Far East, nothing of America or Australia.

Even in the thirteenth century, however, Venetians and other Italian traders knew far more. One chronicler at that time wrote:

> The Venetians went about the sea, and in all places wheresoever water runs, and brought merchandise to Venice. Dalmatia, the Black Sea, Trebizond, the Holy Land and Egypt were the fruitful gardens wherein people found security and profit.

Since the time of the Crusades, the Venetians had travelled by ship and camel along the caravan routes in search of silks, jewels, gold and the precious spices that made so much difference to the taste of bad meat which had been salted during the autumn months. Their journeys were dangerous and many cargoes were lost, but the merchandise brought such high profits for small quantities that traders were keen to risk their lives and their fortunes.

### China

At the end of their journey the Polos found a great civilisation in the Far East, the court of the great emperor of all China, Kublai Khan. The capital city of the old Chinese Empire which Kublai conquered was Kinsai or Hangchow, 'the greatest and noblest city, and the finest for merchandise, in the whole world'. The city perimeter was 160 kilometres round. There were twelve great gates in the walls and, according to Marco Polo, there were 12 000 stone bridges. The city was famous for its market place, its beautiful women dressed in fine silks, and the pleasure gardens and palaces of the islands in the middle of 'Lake Prospect'. Merchants and traders came from all over the world to Hangchow.

Hangchow was the greatest city in a very large empire, which the emperor Kublai Khan ruled with a large civil service. His government was much better organised than the monarchies of Western Europe: China had paper money, printing presses, compasses for navigation, and gunpowder, long before these were developed in the West.

In the fourteenth century the great empire of Kublai Khan broke up and trading contact with Europe was ended. The merciless Turk, Tamerlain, built up an empire in Central Asia in the late fourteenth century and murdered any Christian merchants or missionaries – making huge mounds of their heads. In addition, in 1368 a new Chinese dynasty took over in Hangchow and they too hated Christians and Western churchmen. But although trade with the Far East stopped, there were two other parts of the world where wealthy empires had developed by this time: the Indies and South America.

### India and South America

The people of India were divided into many tribes and states, each under its own ruler. Much of their wealth came from spices and silks.

These were brought from China and the spice islands of the Far East; they were then sold to Arab merchants who took them to Egypt and the Holy Land, whence Venetians carried them to Europe.

India too had great cities: as one Portuguese writer described:

The size of the city I cannot describe, because it cannot all be seen from one point. I climbed a hill and what I saw seemed as large as Rome and very beautiful: there are many groves of trees in the gardens of the houses, and many streams and artificial lakes. The people are too numerous to count.

Indian art was decorative and colourful, and was largely inspired by the Hindu and Buddhist religions, which Christian merchants found so different from their own.

At the same time in South America, as yet unknown to Europe, were two other great empires: those of the Aztecs of Mexico and the Incas of Peru. The Aztec capital was Tenochtitlan or Mexico City, a huge complex of streets, rivers, markets, palaces and temples, containing nearly half a million people. In this and the other cities of the Mexico valley, men lived well-ordered lives, earning their living by farming and trading, and worshipping the Sun God. It was the sun, they believed, which gave them life and helped their crops to grow. To keep the Sun God happy they sacrificed a large number of human beings each year. Consequently, all prisoners of war and even many Aztecs themselves,

*Cortez defeats the Aztecs in battle. Why did the Spaniards have an advantage in battle?*

*Incas at their daily work*

were slaughtered by the high priest on the sacrificial altar with a knife. The victim's heart was cut out and dedicated to the Sun God.

The Incas of Peru also worshipped the sun. Their king, called the Inca, was himself a descendant of the Sun God, and he ruled his people completely. The members of his family acted as nobles, but they were all trained and given strict examinations before they could help the Inca to rule. The state was very well organised: every peasant worked for the state and therefore had no freedom, but in times of famine he was looked after by the government, and when he married he received a state pension or a piece of land to keep his family. He also served in the army or helped to build roads and bridges (vital because the Inca cities were built high in the Peruvian Andes). Cuzco and the famous lost city of Machu Picchu had to be built very carefully of stone to withstand the earthquakes so common in this area. The remarkable thing about this great Inca civilisation was that the Incas had no way of writing and had no machinery or iron tools!

### The Portuguese Empire in the East

If you look at the map on page 17 you will see the routes which Portuguese discoverers, under King Henry the Navigator, took down the west coast of Africa in the fifteenth century. In 1487 King John II sent Bartholomew Diaz on a daring adventure to find the route around the south of Africa to India. Three little caravels (see page 20), one of

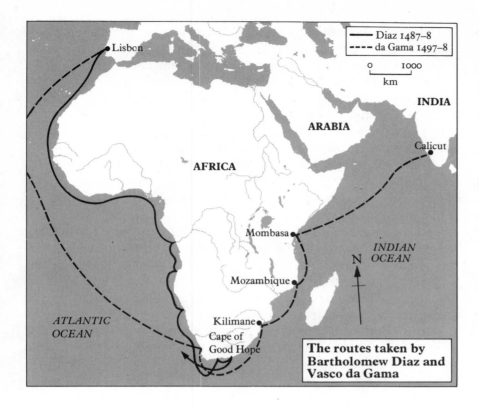

0    1000
km

INDIA

ARABIA

Lisbon

AFRICA

Calicut

Mombasa

INDIAN
OCEAN

N

Mozambique

ATLANTIC
OCEAN

Kilimane
Cape of
Good Hope

**The routes taken by
Bartholomew Diaz and
Vasco da Gama**

them a store-ship, journeyed for many days out of sight of land until
they rounded what is now the Cape of Good Hope.

In 1497 John II's successor, Manuel, sent a much larger expedition
under Vasco da Gama. He rounded the Cape and sailed north up the
east coast of Africa. He used an Arab pilot who knew the waters, and
sailed due east to Calicut in India. India's wealth could now be brought
directly to the west by sea. Portuguese trading settlements, known as
factories, were soon established in Java and the rich spice islands.

### The Spanish Empire in the West

The king and queen of Spain watched the success of the Portuguese
with some jealousy. In 1492 they received a visit from a Genoese sailor
called Christopher Columbus: now they saw a chance to compete with
their rivals. Columbus was a much-travelled sailor who did not believe
that the world was flat or that a ship which sailed too far would fall off
the edge. He believed the world was round and that if he sailed west he
would eventually reach the wealthy lands of China and India.

King Ferdinand and Queen Isabella agreed to finance a voyage of
discovery. They provided three ships and their crews. Two of the ships,
the *Pinta* and the *Nina* were small caravels, the other was a larger *nao*
called the *Santa Maria*. On 3 August 1492 they set sail and their historic
voyage is recounted at the end of this chapter. Altogether Columbus
made four voyages of discovery, and by his death in 1506 Spain had

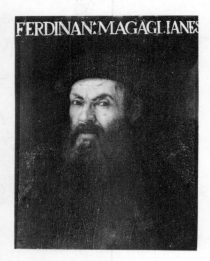

*Ferdinand Magellan*

taken possession of most of the Caribbean Islands.

A number of other explorers then began to add parts of the South American mainland to the Spanish Empire. In 1529 a Portuguese sailor called Ferdinand Magellan, financed by Spain, set sail on a voyage round the world. He himself was killed by natives in the spice islands, but three years after he set sail, one of his ships, the *Victoria*, sailed back to Spain, the first vessel to sail around the world.

Then two Spanish soldiers, Hernan Cortes and Francisco Pizarro, added the greatest lands to the Spanish Empire. Cortes set out with a small army in 1519 to defeat the Aztecs. He had two great military advantages: firstly, the Aztecs had never seen guns or horses in battle before, and secondly, they had a number of enemies among the neighbouring cities. After brutally defeating the cities of Tlaxcala and Cholula, Cortes approached Tenochtitlan. Montezuma, the Aztec emperor, decided to invite the Spaniards to enter his realm in peace, but the Spaniards began to taunt the Mexicans at one of their religious festivals. When Cortes asked Montezuma to speak to the rioting Aztecs, the chief was killed by a stone hurled by one of his own subjects. The Spaniards fled and narrowly escaped with their lives.

In the following year, however, Cortes returned with a huge force of Spaniards and Tlaxcalans. He captured and looted Tenochtitlan and then rebuilt it. The Spanish Empire in Mexico was established.

It took just one day for Francisco Pizarro to capture the Inca Empire in 1532! He had a small force of 183 men and twenty-seven horses, but his forces, like those of Cortes, possessed the advantage of guns and horses. A Spaniard called de Soto was asked by the Incas to show off his horsemanship. During his exhibition he charged his horse full speed at one part of the crowd, and all the Incas turned and ran. Fifteen of them were executed for cowardice. Pizarro invited Atahualpa, the chief Inca, to a meeting. The Inca was offered a Bible and listened politely as a Spanish priest preached a sermon. At the end of it he quietly dropped the Bible on to the ground. Immediately the Spanish troops opened fire, killing 3000 Incas and capturing Atahualpa. In 1533 the holy city of Cuzco was looted by Pizarro's men, and Atahualpa was then executed. In establishing their empire, the Spaniards destroyed the civilisations of Mexico and Peru.

### How do we know?

Most of our evidence for the expansion of Europe comes from the journals kept and letters sent by the explorers themselves. At the end of this chapter you will see examples of Columbus' own logbook, and most of the explorers from Marco Polo onwards either wrote their own accounts or had clerks to write them for them. Few statements survive from the conquered peoples, although several Aztec accounts record the horror and brutality of Cortes' conquest.

However, the great civilisations of China and South America have left their own evidence. Their art, buildings and city life, can all be judged

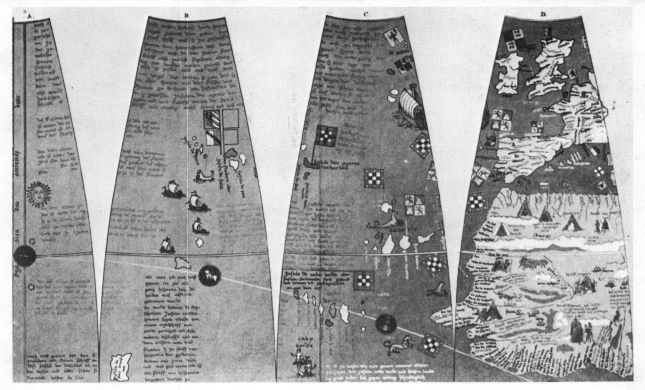

from objects and buildings which still survive. Spanish Christians condemned the Aztecs for their worship of the sun and their human sacrifice; yet how primitive was Cortes' behaviour when in 1519 he lured 2000 Aztecs from Cholula into a courtyard, and watched while his Spanish artillery mercilessly shot them down.

*Part of a globe showing the world in 1492. Can you identify the countries on the eastern side of the globe? There were many tales of weird fish and monsters in the Atlantic Ocean. Notice how these are depicted in the drawings*

| 1271 | Marco Polo set out for China |
| 1487 | Bartholomew Diaz sailed round South Africa |
| 1492 | Columbus' voyage to America |
| 1497 | Vasco da Gama sailed to India |
| 1520 | Cortes conquered the Aztec Empire |
| 1532 | Pizarro conquered the Inca Empire |

## Using the evidence: Columbus' first voyage to America, 1492

On 3 August 1492, Christopher Columbus set sail with his three ships, the *Nina*, the *Pinta*, and the *Santa Maria*. In the early days of September he passed the Canary Islands and headed west, for the open sea. After a further six weeks, he landed on the island of Haiti in the West Indies.

We know about his voyage from a number of sources. He and his men wrote letters and accounts after their return. He kept a detailed logbook for every day of the voyage. The book itself no longer exists, but a copy was made by a man called Las Casas. We also have several 'official' histories written after Columbus' death. One was by Oviedo, the royal historian of the kings and queens of Spain. He wrote in 1547.

This is how Columbus himself described parts of the voyage as they sailed:

(1) *Friday, 7 September* All day the ships were becalmed.
*Sunday 9 September* He sailed fifteen leagues [about 100 kilometres] that day, but decided to call it a smaller amount so that the crews should not take fright or lose courage if the voyage was a long one. In the night he went 120 miles which is thirty leagues, at ten miles an hour. The sailors steered badly, falling off to west by north and even to west-north-west; the Admiral rebuked them many times for this. . . .
*Tuesday 25 September* Much of this day was calm, but later there was wind and they followed their western course until night. The admiral shouted over to Martin Alonso Pinzon, captain of the *Pinta*, about a chart which he had sent to Alonso three days before, and on which were drawn certain islands supposed to be in that sea. . . . At sunset Alonso went up to the poop of his ship and called happily to the admiral, claiming a present because he sighted land. The whole crew of the *Nina* climbed the mast and rigging, and agreed that it was land.
*Wednesday 26 September* He followed his course westward until midday, until they discovered what they had taken for land was not land but cloud. . . .
*Monday 1 October* He kept on a westward course. They sailed twenty-five leagues, but he told the men twenty. They ran into a great storm of rain. . . . By dawn they had sailed 707 leagues, but the admiral had told the men it was 584. . . .
*Thursday 11 October* He sailed west-south-west. They saw petrels and reeds. The men of the *Pinta* picked up a small stick, apparently shaped with an iron tool. At such signs all breathed again and rejoiced. The *Pinta*, sailing ahead of the admiral, now sighted land and gave the signals which the admiral had commanded. The first man to sight land was a sailor called Rodrigo, who afterwards claimed the reward Columbus had promised. However he claimed in vain, for the admiral pocketed the money himself.

In his logbook Columbus also described why he sailed:

(2) In that same month of January, your highness commanded me to go with an adequate fleet to those parts of India and instruct those peoples in the holy faith. . . . In return you granted me great favours, giving me the title of High Admiral of the Ocean and making me viceroy and perpetual governor of such islands and mainland as I should discover and conquer.

Columbus' story is a primary source. It was written by a man who was present at the scenes and events he describes. Document 1 was written, from memory, at the end of each day. Document 2 was written at the end of the voyage.

Oviedo wrote his story fifty-five years after the voyage. Here he describes Columbus:

(3) I have heard from a number of Italians that Christopher Columbus was a native of Genoa. . . . He was a man of decent life and parentage, handsome and well-built, of more than average height and strength, with bright eyes and chestnut brown hair. He was well spoken, cautious and extremely intelligent, a man of great geographical knowledge. He was charming when he wished to be, but very irritable when annoyed. He had a mind for great adventures.

There is a story that a caravel, sailing from Spain to England with a cargo of provisions and wine, was overcome by violent winds and was forced to run west for many days until it sighted the Indies. A landing was made on one of the islands, wood and water were taken aboard, and, when the winds died down, they sailed back to their original course. The voyage was long and dangerous, lasting four or five months, and almost all the ship's crew died, but the pilot and three or four sailors survived to reach Lisbon.

Now this pilot was a close friend of Columbus and just before he died, he secretly marked on a map for Columbus the position of the lands he had discovered.... Whether these events took place or not, we do not know for certain.

In the next part of his *History*, Oviedo tells why he thinks Columbus sailed on his first voyage to America:

(4) Not content with their holy victory against the Moors in Spain, King Ferdinand and Queen Isabella decided to send an expedition in search of this new world and spread the Christian faith there, for they devoted every hour to the service of God. It was under their command that Columbus' great adventure began, and without their Christian zeal and support the enterprise would not have succeeded.

Oviedo's *History* is also a primary source. He lived in Spain and could talk to men who knew Columbus. He could also read their accounts. But, in addition, Oviedo is a secondary source, because he was not there himself. Like any historian today, he collected evidence by reading and listening and then told his story.

## Questions and further work

1 Make a list of the difficulties which Columbus said he encountered on the voyage.
2 Which of the following statements (from Document 3) are fact and which are opinions?
   (a) 'Columbus was a native of Genoa'
   (b) 'He was ... irritable when annoyed'
   (c) 'He was ... cautious and extremely intelligent'
   (d) 'He ... was handsome and well built'
3 (a) How did Oviedo know these things? (We can check Oviedo's statements by reading Columbus' own story.)
   (b) Which of Oviedo's statements are supported by Document 1? Which are not?
   (c) What opinion would you form of Columbus from reading Document 1?
4 List three reasons, from Documents 2, 3, 4, why Columbus made the voyage.
5 Oviedo wrote, 'It was under their [Ferdinand and Isabella's] command that Columbus' great adventure began, and without their Christian zeal and support the enterprise would not have succeeded.' In this sentence, which words tell you Oviedo's opinion about (a) the voyage, (b) the reason for its success? Why did Oviedo express this opinion, do you think?

*Columbus explains his plans to Ferdinand and Isabella. This painting was done long after the event*

*A modern reconstruction of Columbus' flagship, the* Santa Maria

# 2 The Renaissance

### Leonardo da Vinci (1452–1519)

Leonardo da Vinci was an 'all-round' genius. He once wrote this about himself in a letter to the duke of Milan:

I have a method of making bridges that shall be light, strong, and easy of transport. . . . I can make mortars, that can fling a storm of stones and blind the enemy with smoke. I can make ships to resist the heaviest naval guns. . . . I can lay mines, even under a river. . . . I can design buildings to equal the work of anyone, and I can divert water from one place to another. . . . I can make sculptures in marble, bronze and clay, and paint pictures as well as any other.

Leonardo wrote this letter to try to get a job with the duke. But, incredibly, everything he said was true – and he left out his ability in engineering and science!

He spent much of his life in the city of Florence, a place through

*A detailed drawing of the human organs by Leonardo da Vinci*

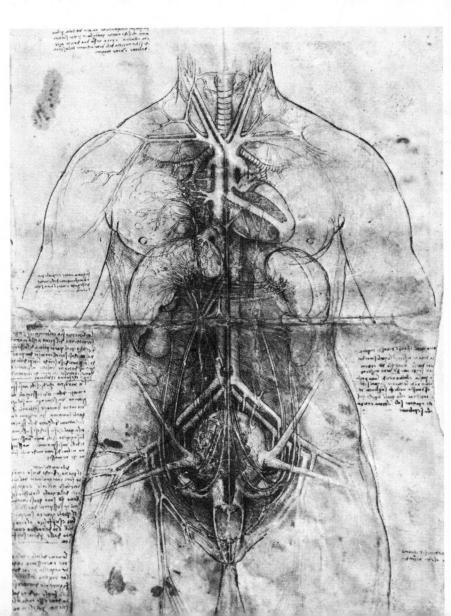

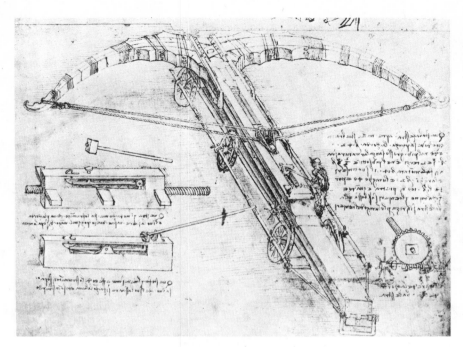

which many foreigners passed. Men admired its wonderful buildings and its beautiful paintings and sculptures. The place was alive and fascinating. Here Leonardo became interested in any problem which faced mankind. 'Men can do all things if they will' was his motto. His paintings, especially the *Mona Lisa* and *The Last Supper*, are well known.

In addition, Leonardo left 120 notebooks of drawings and sketches and comments. He considered most major problems of science, engineering and anatomy. He said, for instance, that he had cut up ten dead bodies to find out how the human body works. He wondered, too, why there were remains of sea shells surviving from past ages in the Italian mountains. He tried to make a submarine to support underwater divers and he badly wanted man to fly.

### Leonardo's dream

There is a story that, as a boy, Leonardo had a terrifying dream. In his dream, on a clear sunny day, he was looking up at the sun and the bright blue sky. Suddenly everywhere was darkness. He was in the shadow of a huge bird. The bird swooped down at great speed towards him, and brushed the whole of his body with the very tip of its tail before flying off.

For Leonardo, that dream was the start of another dream – that one day man would fly like a bird. He spent much of his time in the quest for the secret of flight. So much so, that he often bought caged birds in the market place and set them free, just for the pleasure of seeing their flight.

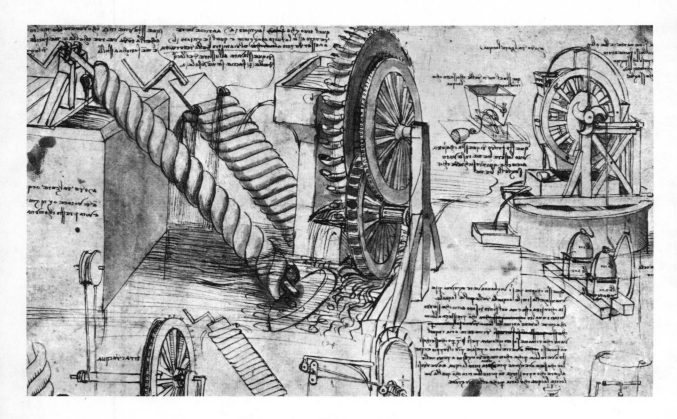

*Some design drawings by Leonardo. On the left is an Archimedean screw; in the centre is a water mill*

## Using the evidence: Leonardo's study of birds

Leonardo began a careful study of birds. 'A bird,' he wrote, 'is an instrument which works by mathematical laws. Men should be able to copy all its movements, though not with the same strength.'

Secondly, Leonardo studied the air in which birds fly. 'It is necessary first to give time to the science of winds, which we shall learn by means of the movement of water.'

He sat for many hours watching birds and came to the following conclusions:

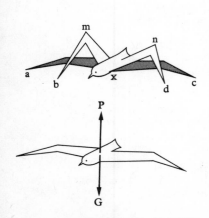

(1) The air is such that in places it may become very thick, or in others quite rarified. [The air must therefore be thick or condensed under a bird's wings to support it in flight.]

(2) When a bird shall be in a position *axc* and shall wish to rise, it will elevate the shoulders *m* and *n*, and will thus be in the position *bmxnd*. The air will be pressed between the sides and the points of the wings, so that it will become thicker and cause the bird to rise.

(3) [The weight of the bird presses down through its centre of gravity. The air presses up on the bird through its centre of pressure.] When, without the assistance of the wind, and without beating its wings, the bird remains steady in the air, then the centre of gravity and the centre of pressure are the same point.

(4) [The tail of the bird is vital.] Thus we may see a small movement of its rudder turn a ship of marvellous size and loaded with a very heavy cargo. . . . So, in those birds which can support themselves above the winds without

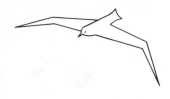

beating their wings, a slight movement of wing or tail suffices to prevent their fall. . . .

The speed of a bird is checked by the opening and spreading out of the tail.
(5) When a bird wishes to turn to the right or left by beating its wings, then it will beat lower with the wing on the side to which it wishes to turn . . . the bird beats its wing repeatedly on one side only when it wishes to turn round, as one wing is held stationary . . . like a man in a boat with two oars, who takes many strokes on that side from which he wishes to escape and keeps the other fixed.

1 Make a list, in your own words, of Leonardo's observations.
2 Look carefully at birds in flight, or think about how you swim. Which of Leonardo's observations are correct?
3 Leonardo made many other observations about how birds fly. Can you think of any important ones which are not included in your list? Again, it may help you to think about how you swim.

### Leonardo's own experiments

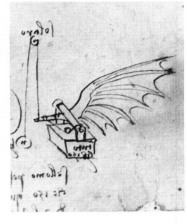

*Leonardo's artificial wing*

*Leonardo's parachute*

After many observations and much careful study, Leonardo tried to design a machine that would copy the birds, and fly. So far as we know, his ideas did not get beyond the drawing board. He never went into the Tuscan hills to try them out.

Leonardo's ideas went through four major stages of development.

(6) You will study the anatomy of the wings of a bird, together with the muscles of the breast which are the movers of those wings. And you do the same for man, in order to show that man could keep himself in the air by flapping [artificial] wings.
(7) If a man have a tent of densely woven linen, twelve braccia broad and twelve braccia high, he will be able to let himself fall from any great height without any danger to himself. [Braccia were units of measurement, one arm's length.]
(8) In two machines, flapping wings made of cane and starched taffeta should be added on to oars. The pilot lies, head facing downwards, strapped in by the belts. It is not clear how the wings should operate in one but in the second they are driven by crank handles. In the second, too, there is a rear-rudder operated by the pilot's neck muscles to steer the machine.

Leonardo said that both these machines should be tried out over a lake. And a hollow wineskin should be fitted.
(9) In a third design the man stands or sits upright. He drives two pairs of wings by a pulley system. For the first time mechanical power was being used to attempt flight. 'Make trial of the machine over water,' Leonardo wrote, 'so that if you fall you do yourself no harm.'

### Two modern opinions of Leonardo's attempts

(10) It is, of course, basic that since birds fly and men do not, the obvious procedure if man is to achieve flight is that he must somehow imitate the bird.

Leonardo's flying machines were designed to be worked by the muscles of the pilot's arms and legs – a muscle-power of from a fifth to a quarter of his total weight. But in the case of a bird the flying muscles account for as much as up to half the total weight. Added to which, the instinct of the species is to get up into and use the air, whereas the instinct of man is to keep his feet firmly on the ground. But when . . . we add the dead load of the weight of the wings and rest of the machine . . . the handicap becomes overwhelming. . . .

Any surface may be maintained in the air if it moves fast enough – but not alone by the supporting air pressure on the underside of the wing's surface.

I. B. Hart, *The World of Leonardo da Vinci*, 1961

(11) He studied the movement of water, built locks and harbours and drew the plans for a submarine, but he lacked the mathematics to put his ideas into practice. He drew birds in flight and designed both a helicopter and an aeroplane, but again lack of precise mathematics made these merely clever guesses.... He could never be a great scientist because he lacked the tools of the trade.

D. T. Witcombe, *Britain, Europe and the World*, 1974

4  Study Leonardo's sketches. Which of the observations you have listed in your answers to questions 1 to 3 are included in each of the sketches?

5  What criticisms are made by Hart and Witcombe of Leonardo's work? Which criticisms apply to each of the sketches?

6  What does the evidence tell you about Leonardo himself?

7  Is there any evidence to suggest whether or not Leonardo thought any of his machines would fly?

8  From the evidence in this section, what improvements would be needed before Leonardo's machines could fly?

## The New Learning

In Italy, and particularly in Florence, in Leonardo's time, there were many brilliant painters, architects, sculptors, writers and scientists.

*This sculpture of Cosimo dei Medici closely resembles the ancient busts of Roman emperors*

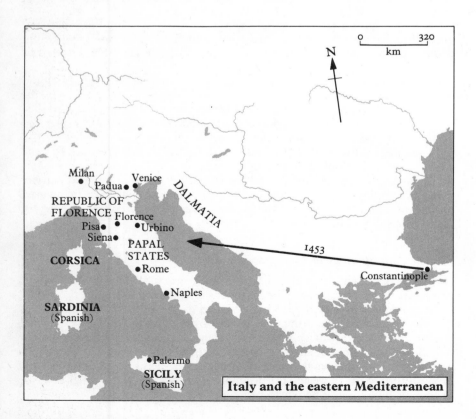

**Italy and the eastern Mediterranean**

The period is known as 'The Renaissance', which means 're-birth', and it indicates the rebirth or revival of interest in classical (that is, Roman and Greek) art and literature. Men began again to copy the styles of ancient Rome and Greece.

In Italy the large city states like Florence, Venice, Rome and Milan become great centres of learning. Artists and writers were paid by dukes like Cosimo and Lorenzo dei Medici in Florence, or the Visconti dukes of Milan or the Montefeltro dukes of Urbino. Others were supported by the popes at Rome, like Michelangelo when he painted the ceiling of the Sistine Chapel.

*The ceiling of the Sistine Chapel*

*An early printing press*

At the same time, interesting discoveries were made in European libraries. Many works by Greek and Roman writers were found, some on cracked parchment, covered in dust. Now they were published for scholars to read. Large new libraries were built to house them, such as the Medici library in Florence, or the Vatican library in Rome. And when Constantinople was captured by the Turks in 1453 many Greek scholars fled to Italy to add their knowledge to that of the West.

## Printing

One invention was necessary if this new learning was to spread quickly around Europe. In the Middle Ages books were copied, often by monks working by candlelight for long, tedious hours. 'Pray I to God', Chaucer once wrote, 'that none mis-write thee.' Much of the copying was inaccurate, and all of it was slow.

In the thirteenth century Europeans had learned from the Arabs how to make paper. They also discovered how to print, by using engraved wooden blocks. On one side of the block the printer would carve out letters and drawings; then he would damp the block on an ink pad and press it on to the paper. This too was a slow and cumbersome process.

Printers in the fifteenth century realised that it would be quicker if movable metal letters could be attached to the block to form words and sentences. In 1439 Johann Gutenberg, a German printer from Mainz, was known to be working on a 'secret process'. But soon the secret leaked out, and news spread like wildfire. In 1477 William Caxton established the first movable-type printing press in London and printed the first book. Altogether he published over a hundred books.

By 1500, there were seventy-three printing presses in Italy, fifty-one in Germany, thirty-nine in France and twenty-four in Spain. It is thought that 110 cities in Europe had presses. Many were built by German craftsmen from Mainz. Most of these presses set out to print the works of scholars. In Venice, for example, the famous Aldine Press was the first to print Greek works and was supported by Erasmus, perhaps the greatest scholar in Europe. The spread of knowledge was slow, but many more people could now read books for themselves because they were easier to get. More people could also learn to read. Lastly spellings became more standard: in England, for instance, London printing presses used similar spellings, so that local variations in spelling began to die out.

## Painting

Italy in the fifteenth century is particularly famous for its painting. Instead of the symbolic figures on stained glass or mosaic in medieval churches, Renaissance figures looked more human and as though they had been drawn from real life. The people portrayed were often clothed in Renaissance dress rather than in the clothes they would actually have worn. From Giotto (1267–1337) to Michelangelo (1474–1564) Italy had many great painters. But in Germany and other countries too,

Renaissance styles were copied by artists like Dürer (1471–1528).

The pictures below will help you to see how Raphael (1483–1520) came to paint *The Entombment* in 1507 in Florence.

1 What change did Raphael make between the first drawing and the final painting? Can you suggest any reasons for the changes?
2 What first catches your eye about the painting? Why do you think it does?
3 What do you notice about the clothes and the background scenery?
4 Look at the figure of Christ in the three drawings. Does any part of the body seem better in the drawings than in the painting?
5 Some people think that Raphael was better at drawing than painting. Would you agree or disagree with this?

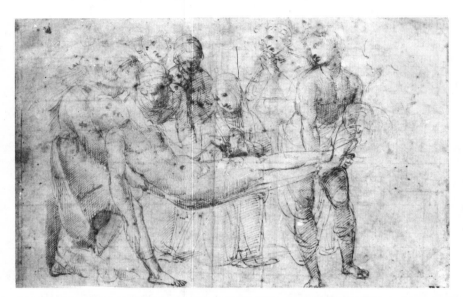

*Raphael was born in the mountain city of Urbino in Italy and his father was a painter. He learned his father's art and then at the age of twenty-five he went to seek his fortune in Florence and Rome. Here he was favoured by Popes Julius II and Leo X and received commissions for paintings and designs for buildings.*

## Sculpture

In fifteenth-century Italy many fine cathedrals were being built, adorned with stone and bronze sculpture. Some of the finest work was produced by Donatello (1386–1466). He was born in Florence and trained as a marble-sculptor in the cathedral workshop. Apart from ten years in Padua, he spent all his long life working in Florence.

Donatello was asked to show Salome bringing the head of John the Baptist to Herod. John had been placed in Herod's jail for criticising Herod's marriage to Herodias, his brother's wife. At a court banquet Salome, Herodias' daughter, danced and Herod promised to grant her any request 'up to half of his kingdom'. She took counsel with her mother and demanded John's head. Herod did not want to agree, but he had made the promise before his court. Salome, therefore, had her way.

Donatello received a commission for this work and an initial payment from Siena Cathedral in May 1423. Two years later the authorities wrote to him to complain about the delay and it took another two years before the bronze was in place.

*Donatello: Presentation of the Baptist's Head to Herod*

6 Which faces impress you most? What do you see in them?
7 Which other parts of the body show the most feelings of Donatello's subjects?
8 How does Herod seem to react to the head? What is the courtier to Herod's right doing?

## Literature, architecture and science

There were great writers, architects and scientists too. Dante (1265–1321), born in Florence, the son of a lawyer, wrote one of the greatest poems, *The Divine Comedy*, in Italian, not Latin. Boccaccio's short stories and Petrarch's love poems, written in the mid-fourteenth century, were also in Italian. Niccolo Machiavelli (1469–1527) was a diplomat and a politician, who was sacked by the Medici (the family who ruled Florence) and spent his long retirement writing books, like *The Prince*, a handbook for rulers.

> Jf it plese ony man spirituel or temporel to bye ony pyes of two and thre comemoraciōs of salisburi vse enpryntid after the forme of this presēt lettre whiche ben wel and truly correct, late hym come to westmonester in to the almonesrye at the reed pale and he shal

*The first English advertisement, the work of William Caxton in 1477*

Perhaps the greatest writer, however, was Desiderius Erasmus (1466–1536). He was born in Rotterdam, the illegitimate son of a priest. He became a wandering scholar, teaching and writing in turn in Paris, Cambridge, Basle and other university towns. He translated many Greek and Latin works and wrote a number of books himself. In one, *Julius Exclusis*, he described Pope Julius II at the gates of heaven where St Peter refused him entry. In another, *In Praise of Folly*, he had this to say about schoolteachers:

Surely a tribe whose lot would seem the most disastrous, the most wretched, the most godforsaken.... For they are afflicted not with five but with six hundred furies, always starving, ... on the treadmill and the rack among the hordes of boys. They grow grey with labour, deaf with noise, haggard with filth, yet they count themselves princes among men.... So they terrorise their flock with threats, cutting those wretched boys to pieces with cane and rod and whip and raging at their sweet will in all the ways they can think of....

Many new buildings were put up in this period. Filippo Brunelleschi (1377–1446) designed much of Florence singlehanded. He built the churches of Santo Spirito and Santo Lorenzo as well as the foundling hospital and the marvellous dome of Florence Cathedral. What Brunelleschi did in Florence, Michelangelo did in Rome.

In addition to Leonardo, two other figures stand out in science. Copernicus (1473–1543), a Polish astronomer, argued that the sun, not the earth was the centre of the universe. Vasalius (1516–64), a Dutchman educated at Padua, wrote a *Description of the Human Body* illustrated by clearly-drawn woodcuts to depict every aspect of the human body. Both these men were criticised for their observations, and Vasalius was forced to flee from Italy to Spain. But each helped later scientists to progress in their respective fields.

*Nicolas Copernicus*

# The Renaissance state

### King Louis XI of France (1461–83)

In the twenty years after his death in 1483, many terrible stories were told about King Louis XI of France. It was said that, during his last illness, he had drunk the blood of children. It was rumoured that he had many times delighted in the screams of tortured victims, that he had poisoned his young brother Charles, that he squeezed the people of France to satisfy his lust for money.

It is interesting to see how these stories arose. 'Never man feared death so much as he, nor tried so hard to find remedy against it,' wrote one of his courtiers. In his last illness in 1483 the king tried everything. He spent money on offerings to his favourite saints, he borrowed many famous relics from all over Europe, and he even sent three ships to the west coast of Africa. They brought back several great turtles. The turtles were killed and Louis washed his inflamed skin in their blood. This was thought to be a cure for leprosy, and Louis thought he had that disease. So bad was his skin, indeed, that he allowed no one but his closest servants to see him during the last month. Small wonder that men talked and rumours spread.

There is also some foundation for the stories of torture. The rack and branding with hot irons, were both used in Louis' reign. Cruel punishments were given to criminals. A thief might lose a hand, or be blinded, or be whipped so that he never walked again. A traitor might be hung, drawn and quartered, a witch might be burned at the stake, a forger might be boiled in oil. These were brutal days in France. But they were equally brutal elsewhere in Europe, and kings, before and after Louis, used these methods.

It is even more interesting to see why these stories spread. Why did Louis XI have such a bad reputation among Frenchmen? Stories were spread by word of mouth among nobles and peasants. The latter disliked Louis because he increased their taxes from a million livres to four-and-a-half million livres per year. An English writer who travelled in France said that the peasants lived on brown bread and water, dressed in canvas rather than cloth, 'Yet they dwell in the most fertile realm in the world.'

Rumours were also spread by the nobles and townsmen. Louis had done much to increase the power of France. When local Estates (assemblies of nobles and townsmen) met, they were asked simply to vote taxes. They were rarely asked their opinion in matters of state and Louis often collected more taxes than they offered him. In addition he allowed the Estates General to meet just once in his reign. It met a second time just after his death, and complained of his tyranny.

French historians at first believed these rumours and stories. Louis was described as a cruel tyrant. In the nineteenth century, novelists described his torture chambers in great horrific detail. Yet written evidence from his reign tells us a different story. Courtiers describe how he was always in the saddle, always ready to tackle a new problem, constantly showing himself and his court to the people. In his first

*King Louis XI*

*King Louis XI holds a council to plan war against his enemy the duke of Burgundy*

decade as king he energetically defeated a European conspiracy against him. He was respected by those who worked closely with him, and he rewarded them generously.

But Louis XI lacked the appearance and manners of a king. He dressed simply; his food was plain, the court often remained in one place while the king rode off with just a few of his friends. And when he died Louis left a son of thirteen as King Charles VIII, a boy of 'no money and less sense'. There was time for the tongues to wag.

## Renaissance kings

Between 1450 and 1600 a number of European rulers including the Tudors in England, increased both their own personal power and also that of the countries which they ruled. They did this in different ways. In Spain, Ferdinand and Isabella, Charles V and Philip II created what was known as the Golden Age – with the help of vast wealth brought back from the Spanish overseas empire. In Germany and central Europe, Maximilian and Charles V laid the foundations of a Hapsburg Empire, which was to survive until 1918. In France, Louis XI, Francis I and later Henry IV established a tradition of personal rule by the king: the basis of the *Ancien Régime* overthrown by the French Revolution in 1789.

Most of these rulers faced problems similar to those which confronted Louis XI. They had opposition from nobles, townsmen and peasants. They had to be decisive and ruthless, yet they needed to be popular. They had to secure the succession of an able son. They had to provide justice to punish the wrongdoer and deter the criminal. They had to be seen by their people as often as possible, and they had to look like rulers. It was no easy task. They needed money, armies, and above all, able and loyal advisers.

## Henry Tudor (1485–1509)

In England in the fifteenth century two families, York and Lancaster, had fought the Wars of the Roses. They fought to decide which family should have the throne. The wars ended in 1485 when a new ruler, Henry Tudor, won the battle of Bosworth Field and became Henry VII. Three months later he married Elizabeth, the fair-haired daughter of the Yorkist king Edward IV. Then he toured the country, showing himself to the people, and quelling riots and disturbances.

*King Francis I of France*

Portraits of King Henry show him as a serious, even sinister, man. It was said that he spent all his time in governing, that he kept his own accounts, that even when he attended a tournament he wrote official letters. Yet Polydore Vergil, an Italian living in London, said that 'his face was cheerful' and Bishop Fisher wrote that he was 'goodly and amiable'. He was a loving and gentle husband, for when their son Arthur died in 1502, Henry and Elizabeth consoled each other. When Elizabeth herself died two years later he 'privily departed to a solitary place, and would no man should resort unto him'.

Henry was also a very pious man. He attended Mass at least twice a day, visited many famous shrines and paid for a number of famous buildings, including the chapel of Westminster Abbey. He was generous in almsgiving, for he gave money to 'one that had his hand smitten off' and also 'for the healing of four sick men'. Yet again there was a lighter side to his nature: he was fond of hawking and hunting and he often gambled at cards. The king, said to be the meanest in English history, once lost forty-seven pounds in one evening of cards. Though he lived much of his life in hunting lodges like Woodstock, his court was magnificent and his clothing expensive and full of jewels. Henry knew that there were times when a king had to make a good impression.

*King Henry VII*

There were two major rebellions in Henry's reign and he dealt firmly with both. In 1487 Lambert Simnel, a boy of twelve from Oxfordshire, pretended to be the earl of Warwick, nephew to Edward IV. Henry had the real earl of Warwick under lock and key in the tower, but plotters flocked to Simnel. His army was poorly armed only with knives or knotted ropes for strangling. The royal army won an easy victory at Stoke, cutting down the 'dull and brute beasts' in the rebel army. Simnel was captured and admitted the pretence. But Henry showed mercy in victory: he put Simnel to work in the royal kitchens, and the boy served Henry well for many years.

A second pretender was not so lucky. Perkin Warbeck, a customs officer from Belgium, pretended to be Richard, duke of York, the son of Edward IV. Like Lambert Simnel, he secured help from Ireland and he married the cousin of the king of Scots whose armies crossed the border and ravaged the north of England. But Perkin himself was captured in a skirmish and promptly executed in 1499, along with the real earl of Warwick who had been involved in the plot.

Henry VII was very concerned about money. He knew that a full treasury made a king secure. 'The Kings my predecessors,' he said, 'weakening their treasure, have made themselves servants to their subjects.' He kept his own account books, signing every page himself. And he kept money in the Chamber, where he could keep an eye on it, rather than in the Exchequer with its complicated rules and procedures.

Henry was so careful that he did not need extra taxes. Each year he received a Parliamentary grant, customs duties on wool, and various fees paid by the aristocracy (for example, when a nobleman wanted permission for his daughter to marry). He also took 'forced loans' – he made his richer subjects give him money – and 'benevolences', which people paid to gain the king's good will. In addition, Henry worked hard to encourage trade. He built up the navy and made trade agreements with other states. The 'Magnum Intercursus' of 1496 secured the trade in wool between Britain and the Netherlands. The treaty of

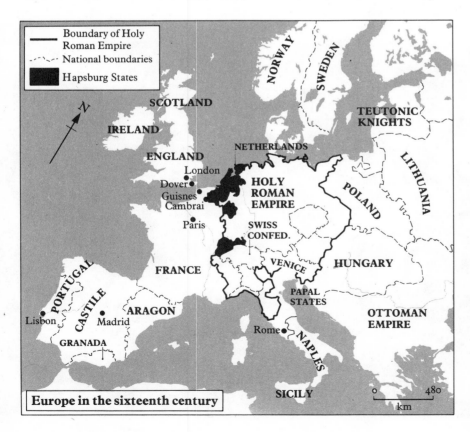

**Europe in the sixteenth century**

Medina del Campo of 1489 gave English and Spanish merchants equal rights in each other's countries.

This treaty was cemented by the marriage in 1501 of Princess Catherine of Aragon to Henry's son Arthur. But Arthur died soon afterwards and Catherine was betrothed to Arthur's younger brother, called Henry after his father. When Henry VII died in 1509 he was buried in a magnificent tomb at Westminster Abbey and his son Henry became king.

### King Henry VIII (1509–47)

One bright spring day in the year 1509 a herald stood at the gates of Richmond Palace. He commanded quiet and announced to the world, 'Henry VIII, by the grace of God, King of England, France and Lord of Ireland'.

The new king was as young and vital as that spring afternoon. On 11 June he married his beloved Catherine of Aragon. She was six years his senior, good-looking, with clear, bright eyes and a graceful manner. They were very much in love. They had much in common – dancing, music, the gaiety of the court – and, even though Henry's father had arranged the match, Henry said 'If I were free, I would still choose her for wife before all others'.

That same summer Henry was crowned king amidst lavish and expensive ceremonial. Wherever he went people celebrated by 'shoot-

*Armour presented to Henry VIII by the Holy Roman Emperor Maximilian I in 1514*

ing, dancing, wrestling, playing at recorders, flute and virginals and in setting of songs and ballads'. Court masks (or dances) were particular merry occasions. Guests were dressed 'in garments long and broad, wrought all with gold, with viziers and caps of gold. After the banquet was done, the maskers came in . . . and desired the ladies to dance'.

The queen watched Henry at tournaments. These were dangerous contests, so Henry did not fight often. But on some occasions, he appeared in armour and vizor, often with Catherine's initials on his coat and on the trappings of his horse. He named himself 'Sir Loyal Heart' and once knocked Sir William Compton, one of his courtiers, flying from his horse. One of the best tournaments was held on New Year's Day, 1511. Catherine had just had a baby boy and Henry was keen to celebrate the birth of his heir. But two months later the baby died suddenly. In the next three years three more children were born, all boys: all died at birth.

*Henry the man*

The king had a fine physique. He went hunting most days, often riding eight or ten horses to exhaustion. In tournaments he threw the javelin in competition, and he led the court in dancing and other entertainments. One writer described him in 1519:

His majesty was the handsomest prince that ever I saw. He is above the usual height, with an extremely fine calf to his leg, his complexion fair and bright, with auburn hair, combed straight in the French fashion, and a round face so very beautiful it would become a pretty woman, his throat being rather long and thick.

Now look at this portrait of Henry:

*King Henry VIII*

You will see that the account and the portrait agree on some points. But they differ on others. Why might this be? Here is a story about Henry, written by the Venetian ambassador in London in 1518:

His Majesty came into our garden, and addressing me in French, said, 'Talk with me a while. The king of France, is he as tall as I am?' I told him there was but little difference. He continued, 'Is he as broad?' I said, he was not. He then inquired, 'What sort of leg has he?' I replied, 'Spare.' Whereupon he opened his doublet, placed his hand on his thigh and said, 'Look here; and I also have a good calf to my leg. . . .' On hearing that King Francis wore a beard, he allowed his own to grow, and it is reddish, he has now got a beard that looks like gold.

In later years Henry became more irritable and cruel. Constant activity had worn his body out. Once in 1524 he was jousting with his brother-in-law, the earl of Suffolk. The crowd noticed that the king had not properly closed his vizor. They yelled a warning. But Henry took their yells for cheers. He rode faster at Suffolk. Suffolk's lance shattered on the king's shield and many splinters smashed into his face. It could have been a very dangerous accident. But Henry quickly recovered, and recklessly rode another six rounds. Similarly in 1525 he was out hawking. He tried to pole-vault a ditch. He failed and landed head-first in the

*Henry VIII on board his flagship at Dover. The ship is probably the* Henri Grace à Dieu

mud. He could have been drowned. Again, he recklessly carried on.

Yet throughout his life Henry was often a very sick man. He probably suffered from a disease called osteomyelitis. This may have been caused by an infection of his thighbone after a tournament. The disease causes the bones to splinter, and pieces come painfully to the surface of the skin. Horrible ulcers formed on both legs. At times Henry found the pain unbearable. Small wonder that he was irritable and unpredictable.

### Cardinal Wolsey, Lord Chancellor 1515–29

As a young man Henry was loath to spend his time in government. He preferred to spend his day hunting, hawking and jousting, and his evenings at banquets and dances. He had precious little time to write official letters and proclamations.

Indeed a man came to his notice who was able and willing to do these jobs for him. This was Thomas Wolsey. A hard-working lawyer, Wolsey was educated at Oxford and in 1507 became chaplain to Henry VII. In 1509 he was appointed King's Almoner and thereafter he did the king's paperwork while Henry enjoyed himself. He sent Henry a brief report of all he did, 'because it should be painful for your Grace to read the whole treaty'. Archbishop of York in 1514, Wolsey received a cardinal's hat and the chancellor's gown the following year. He was now the most powerful man in England.

Wolsey was a genius in diplomacy. Twice his allies in Europe, the Hapsburg Empire and Spain, cheated him when war was prepared against France. Yet twice, in 1513 and 1518, he beat them to make peace. In 1518, the Treaty of London between France, England and the new younger emperor, Charles V, was marked by a mass at St Paul's Cathedral and a magnificent royal banquet. Two years later Charles V came to England for talks with Wolsey and Henry – Henry arrived late and breathless after a hunting expedition to find Charles already gone to his bedroom!

Later that summer 5000 of the English aristocracy sailed from Dover to France dressed in the richest of velvets, satins and gold. At Guisnes near the French border 6000 workmen prepared a huge pavilion. King Francis I and his entourage were similarly prepared just over the hill. On the morning of 7 June, cannon thundered from both sides, but it was not another battle between England and France. The two courts moved towards each other. Facing each other they stopped. There was complete silence. Then a trumpet fanfare. Gently, Henry and Francis spurred their own horses forward. The rest remained still. The two kings met, embraced, dismounted and embraced again. For the next two weeks the two courts jousted by day and danced by night. The Field of the Cloth of Gold was magnificently staged by Wolsey, and he was now very firmly in power.

But his power did not last. In 1525 the Emperor Charles, with help from England, defeated and captured Francis at the battle of Pavia. Wolsey pushed the English armies into France. Now they could conquer French land and gain a real advantage. But Charles saw no reason to give England this advantage. He released Francis and France recovered. Moreover, when Wolsey started scheming with the pope against Charles, Charles attacked and plundered Rome itself in 1527. In the same year France and Charles made peace at Cambrai. Wolsey and England were out in the cold. Henry looked for the man responsible and blamed his chancellor.

Wolsey had his problems in England too. In 1523 he had tried to persuade Parliament to grant an extra tax. They agreed to half his request and stated that it must be spread over several years. Wolsey ignored them and tried to collect the whole. Rioting broke out all over the realm. In Kent and Essex there was armed rebellion. Henry looked into the matter, pardoned the rebels and gave Wolsey a rap over the knuckles.

To make matters worse, Henry was now anxious to divorce his queen, Catherine of Aragon. She had failed to provide his son and heir and he had fallen in love with one of her ladies-in-waiting, Anne Boleyn. The story of Catherine's divorce is told in the next chapter. What mattered to Wolsey was that he failed to engineer the divorce. In 1527 he set up a secret commission in his own home. He was the pope's legate. He hoped to secure the divorce, then negotiate the pope's agreement. But while the commission was sitting news came that the pope had been captured by Charles v, Queen Catherine's nephew.

Now Henry came out into the open. He told Catherine that he was determined to divorce her and marry Anne Boleyn. Catherine passed a message to Charles v. Charles was outraged and ordered the pope to tell Henry he could not do it. The king now took matters into his own hands. Wolsey was no longer trusted, and this story shows how Anne Boleyn disliked him:

*Thomas Wolsey*

And I heard it reported by them that waited upon the king at dinner, that Mistress Anne Boleyn was much offended with the king ... that he so gently entertained my lord (Wolsey), saying,

'Sir, is it not a marvellous thing to consider what debt and danger the cardinal hath brought you in with all your subjects?'

'How so, my sweetheart?' quoth the king.

'Forsooth,'quoth she, 'there is not a man within all your realm ... but he hath indebted you unto him.'

'Well, well, as for that, there is in him no blame.'

'Nay sir,' quoth she, 'what things hath he wrought in your realm to your great dishonour.... If my lord of Norfolk, or Suffolk, or my father or any other noble person had done much less, they should have lost their heads on this.'

'Why then, I perceive', quoth the king, 'ye are not the cardinal's friend.'

At this time the waiters had taken up the table, and so they ended their communication.

George Cavendish, *Life of Thomas Wolsey*, 1557

In the summer of 1530 Wolsey was summoned from York to London to stand trial for treason. A royal guard escorted him but the cardinal was sick. On 29 November he died in a Leicestershire abbey. 'If I had served God,' he said on his deathbed, 'as diligently as I have served my king, He would not have given me over in my grey hairs.'

*Anne Boleyn*

### Henry's wives and old age

Henry's marriage to Anne Boleyn and the changes it produced are described in the next chapter. But Anne was never popular with the people of England: 'There is little love for the one who is queen now or for her family,' said one French visitor. In the country there was a saying, 'A lady will destroy the kingdom.'

One day in 1529, Anne found a book of old sayings. One page was marked and she turned to it. On the page she saw three figures, marked H, Q and A. The woman marked A had been beheaded! Anne showed the picture to her maid. The woman was terrified: 'If I thought it true,' she said, 'though I thought him an emperor I would not marry him.' But Anne could only laugh: 'I think the book a bauble. I am resolved to have him whatever may become of me.'

Anne was safe so long as Henry loved her and so long as she bore him a son. But in this she was unsuccessful. Early in 1533 a daughter, Elizabeth, was born. Thereafter all the babies were stillborn. By 1536 Henry had lost patience. Anne was accused of treason and executed.

Henry wore white for mourning and the next day he was betrothed to Jane Seymour. She was a simple Wiltshire girl, one of Anne's ladies, 'full of goodness, of middle stature and of no great beauty'. Henry was first attracted to her gentle manner in September 1534. He wrote her long love letters but she would not open them. He sent her presents but she refused them.

Within a month of Anne's execution, however, they were married. A year later, at Hampton Court, Jane bore a child. Henry had left London

*(Above) Anne of Cleves*

*Jane Seymour*

*Catherine Howard*

because of the plague, but at the news of Jane's confinement he dashed back. He rushed into his wife's chamber and held her in his arms. 'Your Grace has a son,' he was told. Henry wept with joy. The boy was christened Edward.

But the joy turned to grief. Eight days later Jane fell ill. Infection had set in after the birth. Two days later she was dead. Again Henry wept – this time tears of sorrow. His heart was broken. He seems genuinely to have loved Jane. Now Thomas Cromwell decided to find him another wife to take his mind off her. Various foreign princesses were visited. Portraits were painted and brought to England, but none was suitable.

At last Cromwell found one. The duke of Cleves had two sisters and Cromwell wanted his friendship to stave off a war with France. Holbein painted both. Henry was interested in Anne. His ambassadors visited her, but found her covered in clothes 'so that they could see neither her face nor her person'. They asked her to allow them to see more, but the chancellor of Cleves replied, 'Would you see her naked?' and refused! One visitor sent Henry a favourable report, however: 'Every man praiseth her beauty, as well for the face, as the whole body.'

The wedding was fixed for autumn 1539. Henry, in great excitement, rushed to Rochester to meet his new bride. But when he saw her he was horrified. 'I am ashamed that men have praised her. I like her not.' But how could he be rid of her? He was desperate for friendship with Cleves so the marriage went ahead. Yet in six months it was annulled and Henry married the bright-eyed Catherine Howard, just nineteen years old.

She was the niece of the duke of Norfolk. For two years she entranced and delighted the increasingly irritable Henry. He gave her lands and jewels. The court became alive again. But in the autumn of 1541 he was told that she had had other lovers. Like Anne Boleyn, she was executed for treason.

Henry was now diverted, in old age, by his last war in France and his last marriage. Catherine Parr was thirty-one years old, twice a widow herself. She was devout, well-educated, intelligent. She was an ideal stepmother for Henry's children and she brought Henry some family life in his old age. When he died in January 1547, she survived him and kept the family together.

| | |
|---|---|
| 1485 | Henry VII won the battle of Bosworth |
| 1509 | Henry VIII crowned king |
| 1520 | Field of the Cloth of Gold |
| 1530 | Death of Wolsey |

*Catherine Parr*

## Using the evidence: the case of Sir Thomas More

Sir Thomas More (1478–1535) was trained as a lawyer and soon entered the service of King Henry VIII. The king enjoyed his quick wit and clever conversation. When in 1519 Henry published a book against Martin Luther, most of it was written by More. In 1529 More became Lord Chancellor. Throughout his life, he enjoyed European fame: his many writings, including *Utopia* in 1516, won him the respect and friendship of European thinkers like Erasmus.

Yet by 1535 Sir Thomas More was on trial for treason. King Henry had put aside his wife, Catherine of Aragon, and taken a new queen, Anne Boleyn. Parliament had passed the Act of Supremacy. This made Henry the head of the Church of England, and ordered all important people to take an oath to approve Queen Anne and condemn Catherine.

But Thomas More refused to take the oath. He said that the king and Catherine had been married by the Church; they could be divorced only if the pope agreed. The pope had not agreed and More said that the king had no right to take away the authority of the pope.

*How history is written*

The trial of Sir Thomas More has been described in three main ways:
1    Primary sources: writers who were alive at the time and wrote soon after the event. One of these was William Roper, More's son-in-law. He wrote a life-story of More about twenty years after his death. He could not always remember the exact words used at the trial, but his description is nevertheless very clear, and supported by the other evidence we have.
2    Modern historians: writers who read the primary sources, examine them carefully, and then try to provide an accurate account of what happened. R. K. Chambers wrote a biography of More in 1935.
3    Dramatists: writers of plays wish to inform their audiences in a dramatic and lively way. They often work from primary sources and secondary writers, but their main concern may not be to provide a historical account of the events.

*The trial*

More's trial was conducted by the Lord Chancellor, Lord Audeley. The evidence against More came from the Solicitor General, Sir Richard Rich. He asserted that on 12 June 1535, in the Tower, More had told him that the pope could not be deposed by Act of Parliament. Two other men were in the room at the time: Sir Richard Southwell and Master Palmer were packing up More's books.

(1) At his trial Sir Richard Rich was questioning More. 'Admit that there were an Act of Parliament that all the realm should take me, Richard Rich, for king; would not you, Master More, take me for king?'
'That would I,' said Sir Thomas, '. . . but take a higher case; how if there were an Act of Parliament that God should not be God?'
'That cannot be,' replied Rich, 'but I will put a middle case: you know that our king has been made Supreme Head. Why will you not take him as such, even as you would take me as a king . . .?
'If I were a man, my lords, that did not regard an oath, I need not, as is well known, in this place, at this time, nor in this case, to stand here as an accused

person. And if this statement of yours, Master Rich, be true, then pray I that I never see God in the face; which I would not say, were it otherwise, to win the whole world. In good faith, Master Rich, I am sorrier for your perjury than for my own peril. . . .'

Master Palmer, upon his deposition, said that he was so busy, about the trussing up of Sir Thomas More's books in the sack, that he took no heed to their talk. Sir Richard Southwell, likewise, upon his deposition, said that because he was appointed only to look into the conveyance of his books, he gave no ear unto them.

William Roper, Life of More, written about 1555

1 In the second paragraph, More is defending himself against Rich. What does he mean by 'How if there were an Act of Parliament that God should not be God?'
2 Explain, in your own words, More's argument in his defence in the fourth paragraph.
3 Does the evidence in the fifth paragraph help More's case? If so, how?

(2) Then, Rich asserted, More had replied that, though a king could be made by Parliament, and by Parliament deposed, it was not so with the head of the Church.

More denied the conversation. . . . He then gave his own version of what had passed. . . . He gave a scathing account of the character of Rich. Was it likely that he would utter to such a man the secrets of his conscience?

Rich called upon Southwell and Palmer, who had been present in the tower, to support his evidence. . . . Richard Southwell was a young man who two years before had been pardoned for complicity in a murder. It remains very much to his credit, and that of Palmer, that they would not support the evidence of Rich . . .

The jury, after an absence of quarter of an hour, found a verdict of guilty and Lord Audeley at once began to pass sentence. . . . More must speak now, or never. He interrupted Audeley.

R. W. Chambers, Thomas More, 1935

(3) More defended himself brilliantly in the trial scene, but, by dint of . . . accepting the perjured evidence of Sir Richard Rich, who deposed to having tricked More into speaking treason, the judges commissioned for the trial felt able to convict him.

G. R. Elton, England under the Tudors, 1955

(4) [In this play Norfolk is a friend of More.]
*Cromwell*: Now, Rich, on 12 March, you were at the Tower?
*Rich*: I was.
*Cromwell*: With what purpose?
*Rich*: I was sent to carry away the prisoner's books.
*Cromwell*: Did you talk with the prisoner?
*Rich*: Yes.
*Cromwell*: Did you talk about the king's supremacy of the Church?
*Rich*: Yes.
*Cromwell*: What did you say?
*Rich*: I said to him: 'Supposing there was an Act of Parliament to say that I, Richard Rich, were to be king, would not you, Master More, take me for king?' 'That I would,' he said, 'for then you would be king.'
*Cromwell*: Yes?
*Rich*: Then he said—
*Norfolk* (*sharply*): The prisoner?

*Rich*: Yes, my lord. 'But I will put you a higher case,' he said. 'How if there were an act of Parliament to say that God should not be God?'

*More*: This is true; and then you said—

*Norfolk*: Silence! Continue.

*Rich*: I said, 'Ah, but I will put you a middle case.' Parliament has made our king head of the Church. Why will you not accept him?'

*Norfolk* (*strung up*): Well?

*Rich*: Then he said Parliament had no power to do it.

*Norfolk*: Repeat the prisoner's words!

*Rich*: He said: 'Parliament has not the competence.' Or words to that effect.

*Cromwell*: He denied the title?

*Rich*: He did.

(*All look to More but he looks to Rich.*)

*More*: In good faith, Rich, I am sorrier for your perjury than my peril.

*Norfolk*: Do you deny this?

*More*: Yes! My lords, if I were a man who heeded not the taking of an oath, you know well I need not to be here. Now I will take an oath! If what Master Rich has said is true, then I pray I may never see God in the face! Which I would not say were it otherwise for anything on earth.

*Cromwell* (*to Foreman, calmly, technical*): That is not evidence.

*More*: Is it probable – is it probable – that after so long a silence, on this, the very point so urgently sought of me, I should open my mind to such a man as that?

*Cromwell* (*to Rich*): Do you wish to modify your testimony?

*Rich*: No, Secretary.

*More*: There were two other men! Southwell and Palmer!

*Cromwell*: Unhappily, Sir Richard Southwell and Master Palmer are both in Ireland on the king's business. (*More gestures helplessly.*) It has no bearing. I have their deposition here in which the court will see they state that being busy with the prisoner's books they did not hear what was said. (*Hands deposition to Foreman, who examines it with much seriousness.*)

*More*: If I had really said this is it not obvious he would instantly have called these men to witness?

*Cromwell*: Sir Richard, have you anything to add?

*Rich*: Nothing, Mr Secretary.

*Norfolk*: Sir Thomas?

*More* (*looking at Foreman*): To what purpose? I am a dead man. (*To Cromwell.*) You have your desire of me. What you have hunted me for is not my actions, but the thoughts of my heart. It is a long road you have opened. For first men will disclaim their hearts and presently they will have no hearts. God help the people whose statesmen walk your road.

*Norfolk*: Then the witness may withdraw.

(*Rich crosses stage, watched by More.*)

*Sir Thomas More*

*More*: I *have* one question to ask the witness. (*Rich stops.*) That's a chain of office you are wearing. (*Reluctantly Rich faces him.*) May I see it? (*Norfolk motions him to approach. More examines the medallion.*) The red dragon. (*To Cromwell.*) What's this?

*Cromwell*: Sir Richard is appointed Attorney-General for Wales.

*More* (*looking into Rich's face: with pain and amusement*): For Wales? Why, Richard, it profits a man nothing to give his soul for the whole world. . . . But for Wales—!

(*Exit Rich, stiff-faced, but infrangibly dignified.*)

*Cromwell*: Now I must ask the court's indulgence! I have a message for the

*Thomas More and his descendants. The picture was painted in 1593, long after More himself was dead*

prisoner from the king: (*Urgent.*) Sir Thomas, I am empowered to tell you that even now—

*More*: No, no. It cannot be.

*Cromwell*: The case rests! (*Norfolk is staring at More.*) My lord!

*Norfolk*: The jury will retire and consider the evidence.

*Cromwell*: Considering the evidence it shouldn't be necessary for them to retire. (*Standing over Foreman.*) Is it necessary? (*Foreman shakes his head.*)

*Norfolk*: Then is the prisoner guilty or not guilty?

*Foreman*: Guilty, my lord!

*Norfolk* (*leaping to his feet; all rise save More*): Prisoner at the bar, you have been found guilty of high treason. The sentence of the court—

*More*: My lord!

(*Norfolk breaks off. More has a sly smile. From this point to end of play his manner is of one who has fulfilled all his obligations and will now consult no interest but his own.*)

My lord, when *I* was practising the law, the manner was to ask the prisoner *before* pronouncing sentence, if he had anything to say.

*Norfolk* (*flummoxed*): Have you anything to say?

*More*: Yes. (*He rises: all others sit.*) To avoid this I have taken every path my winding wits would find. Now that the court has determined to condemn me, God knoweth how, I will discharge my mind ... concerning my indictment and the king's title. The indictment is grounded in an Act of Parliament which is directly repugnant to the Law of God. The King in Parliament cannot bestow the supremacy of the Church because it is a spiritual supremacy! And more to this the immunity of the Church is promised both in Magna Carta and the king's own Coronation oath!

Robert Bolt, *A Man for All Seasons*, 1960

## Questions and further work

1 Which of the following are the same in the play (Document 4) as they are in the accounts of Roper and Chambers (Documents 1 and 2)? Which are different?

(a) More's personal feelings for Rich

(b) The point at which More tells Rich he is sorrier for Rich's perjury than for his own peril

(c) The part played by Cromwell at the trial

(d) The evidence of Southwell and Palmer

(e) More's question about Rich's office as Attorney General for Wales

(f) The time which the jury took to reach a verdict

2 Where the points differ, it is the playwright who has deliberately chosen to avoid what really happened. Why do you think Bolt has done this?

3 Which is the key part of Rich's evidence in the play? How does Bolt show that the evidence is not reliable?

4 Elton (see Document 3) passes two opinions on the trial. What are they? Do the stories told by (a) Roper and Chambers, (b) Robert Bolt give the same opinions?

5 Divide your class into groups and act out the trial scene in *A Man for All Seasons*.

# 4 The Reformation

## The story of Martin Luther

Martin Luther was born in Saxony, the second son of a well-to-do copper-miner, Hans Luther. Hans wanted his son to become a lawyer and had sent him to study at Erfurt University. At the age of fourteen, though, Martin had been strangely influenced by Prince William of Anhalt. This prince was a wealthy man, who sold all his goods, gave his wealth away, and wandered the streets of the city of Magdeburg as a begging friar. Martin wrote, 'With my own eyes, I saw him carrying his sack like a donkey. He had so worn himself down by fasting and vigil that he looked like a death's head, mere skin and bone. No one could look upon him without being ashamed of his own life.'

This last sentence gives a clue to Luther's character. One friend described him as 'affable and friendly . . . vivacious . . . always cheerful and gay'. But underneath, he was unhappy with himself. 'I am dust and ashes and full of sin,' he said. He was afraid of the wrath of God, afraid that he would be punished for his sins, afraid that devils would drag him off to hell.

So Luther, at the age of twenty-two, became a monk. He hoped to lead a pure life, free from sin, and thus go to Heaven when he died. There was a well-known story of a certain Cistercian monk who was ill with fever. In his delirium he threw off his monk's habit and later died. When he arrived at the gates of Heaven, St Benedict did not know he was a monk and wouldn't let him in. He wandered round the walls looking inside, and only when other monks recognised him and spoke up for him was he allowed to enter.

At first Martin was happy in the Augustinian priory at Erfurt:

I was a good monk and kept the rule of my order so strictly, that if ever a monk got to heaven by his monkery it was I. . . . If I had kept on any longer, I should have killed myself with vigils, prayers, readings and other work.

Yet gradually Luther's doubts and worries returned.

One day his father came to visit him at the monastery. They were sitting to eat when Luther asked his father about the monastery. Was old Hans happy that his son had found a quiet and godly life?

Hans suddenly flared up. 'You learned scholar, have you never read in the Bible that you should honour your father and your mother? And here you have left me and your dear mother to look after ourselves in our old age!'

In 1510 Luther went to Rome, the centre of the Christian Church. There he climbed the 'Santa Scala', the twenty-eight steps which were said to come from Pontius Pilate's palace. He climbed up on hands and knees, kissed each step and said the Lord's Prayer. This was thought to gain pardon for sins. Yet when Luther reached the top he stood up, wondered for a moment, and said, 'Who knows if it is really so.'

The following year he was made a professor at Wittenburg University. On certain days in the year the people of this town could visit Duke Frederick of Saxony's collection of holy relics. These included a piece of

*The young Martin Luther*

JOHANNES TECELIUS PIRNENSIS
Dominicanus, Nundinator Romani Pontificis, anno
1517. à μιχαλαϸϸεν LutHero territus & in fugam versus,
uti talis ejus effigies visitur in templo Pirnensi.

Jesus' swaddling clothes, a thorn from the crown which Christ wore before his Crucifixion, and one of the nails driven into his hands on the Cross. They could then put money in a box and the Church said that their sins would be pardoned.

> When the coin in the coffer sings
> Then the soul to Heaven springs.

The chief seller of these indulgences or pardons was a Dominican friar called John Tetzel. When Tetzel entered a city,

all the priests and monks, the town council, schoolmasters, scholars, men, women and children went out to meet him with banners, songs and processions. Then all the bells were rung. He was conducted into church, a red cross was erected in the midst of the church and the pope's banner displayed. In short God himself would not have been welcomed with more honour.

Luther was furious. Many people were giving money to Tetzel. They would be better giving it to the poor. He wanted to protest. So he wrote out ninety-five theses or arguments and nailed them to the door of Duke Frederick's Castle Church. Scholars read them and translated them for the poor to understand. In them Luther dared to criticise the Roman Catholic Church to which all Christians in Europe belonged.

### The Roman Catholic Church

The pope was bishop of Rome and head of the Church. Archbishops and bishops were his representatives in different countries. They made or ordained priests in local parishes. Monks lived, like Luther, apart from the world in enclosed monasteries.

### The effects of Luther

News of Luther's stand quickly spread throughout Germany. Because the Church was in places unpopular, he gained many supporters. Some of these were important men, like the knight Ulrich von Hutten. He wrote this poem:

> To Martin Luther wrong is done –
> O God, be thou our champion.
> My goods for him I will not spare
> My life, my blood, for him I dare.

Luther himself wrote many pamphlets and books to attack the pope. One of these, the *Address to the German Nobility*, gained even more support.

It was fortunate that Luther had this help. The pope sent learned scholars to Germany to dispute with Luther. He also secured the aid of

Es ist ergriffen die Bestia vñ mit yr d falsch prophet der du sie zeychen than hat do mit er vorfurdt hat/ die so seynt zeychen von yme genommen /vnd sein bilde angebet seynt versenckt die teuffe des fewirs vnd schweffels vnd seynd getodt mit d schwerdt des der do reydt vffm weyssen pferdt/ das auß se maruel gehet. Apocal:19. Danne wirdt offenbar werden schalckhafftige born wirdt der herr Jesus toeten mit dem a seyns mundes vnd wirdt yn sturzen durch die glori seyner kunfft. 2. ad Tessa.2.

*The pope cast down with devils into Hell. What does this picture tell you about its German author, Lucas Cranach the Elder?*

**Central Europe in the sixteenth century**

POLAND

NETHERLANDS

Magdeburg
•Wittenburg
Erfurt  •Leipzig
HESSE  •Schmalkalden
SAXONY

Mainz
•Worms

BAVARIA
•Augsburg

HUNGARY

FRANCE

SWISS CONFEDERATION

VENICE

OTTOMAN EMPIRE

•Rome PAPAL STATES

N

0    100
km

Euangelium Suer am xvi Cap.

the young emperor, the mighty Charles V. Copies of Luther's books were publicly burned in Germany and Italy, though when the torch-bearer in Mainz turned to the people and asked, 'Shall I burn these books?' they shouted back 'No!' with one voice and he stepped down.

At last, in April 1521, Luther was summoned to a meeting with Charles V in the city of Worms. He attended accompanied by German knights. The pope's agents asked him if he would change his opinions. But Luther refused:

I do not accept the authority of popes.... My conscience is captive to the scriptures. I cannot and will not recant anything.... Here I stand, I cannot do otherwise. God help me. Amen.

The next day Luther left Worms. Fortunately he had good friends. He was sheltered by Duke Frederick of Saxony in the castle–fortress of the Wartburg. Here he wrote many books and pamphlets. He translated the Latin Bible into German so that the ordinary people could read it. He wrote hymns, like the carol 'Away in a Manger' and the powerful hymn 'A Mighty Fortress is our God'.

Thus he influenced many others to criticise or protest about the Catholic Church. Such critics became known as 'Protestants'. Some of these were German, but others came from farther afield, like the Swiss theologian John Calvin and the Scot John Knox.

In 1525 Luther at last set the seal on his life. Though he had been a priest and a monk, he decided to marry. His wife was 'Katie', Katherine von Bora. They were married in Wittenburg church and a banquet and dance followed. Luther paid no heed to his vows of chastity.

*A satirical drawing of Calvin, 1566*

## 'The King's Great Matter'

In England Luther's ideas were at first rarely heard. As soon as King Henry VIII heard of Luther's ninety-five theses, he called his advisers together and wrote his own book, *The Defence of the Seven Sacraments*, to attack Luther. A magnificent leather-bound copy was sent to the pope. Leo X was delighted. In 1521 he gave Henry the title *Fidei Defensor* (Defender of the Faith), still to be seen on English coins.

In the years which followed the Diet of Worms, there was growing criticism of churchmen in England. Monks were lazy and greedy, it was said, and many had wives. Parish priests were uneducated and often absent from their parishes. And many saw the pope as an Italian, interested in England only because she paid a regular tax called Peter's Pence to Rome.

*A service at a Calvinist Church in Lyons in France in 1564. The Church was very bare and the pulpit was in the centre*

Yet, as we have seen, Henry VIII ruled England firmly and supported the pope. One major problem caused him to change his mind though, and to break away from Rome. Henry's wife Catherine of Aragon was Spanish, the aunt of the emperor, Charles V. She had first been married to Henry's elder brother Arthur, but on his death she married Henry.

Now Henry was desperate to have a son. Catherine became pregnant soon after their marriage. Henry was overjoyed. But the baby, a girl, died at birth. A year later Catherine produced a healthy son, but he became ill and soon died. In the next three years she had three more sons, and all died soon after birth. Henry was distressed. Was there some curse on him? Why did his sons not live? In 1516 a baby girl called Mary did survive. 'We are both young,' said Henry. 'If it was a daughter this time, by the grace of God the sons will follow.'

But they didn't. Catherine had no more children. Henry read in the Bible that 'If a man shall take his brother's wife, it is an unclean thing. . . . They shall be childless.' This worried him, and soon Henry was looking elsewhere for someone to bear him an heir. His eye fell on a vivacious dark-haired lady-in-waiting, Anne Boleyn. Anne's great attractions were her eyes – 'black and beautiful', said the Venetian ambassador – and her manner. She had been in the French court and she knew how to attract men. Henry was completely infatuated by her.

But Anne was clever. She retired from court to her father's house in Kent. Henry wrote, pleading with her to return, vowing his love. She said she would not be his mistress, only his wife!

In 1527 Henry asked Wolsey if his marriage to Catherine could be

*Left: Thomas Cranmer*
*Centre: Thomas Cromwell*

annulled. When Pope Clement VII would not agree, Henry had to find another way. He needed a son, and he needed Anne. To work it out, Henry promoted two new men. Thomas Cranmer, a Cambridge scholar, was made Archbishop of Canterbury in 1533, and Thomas Cromwell, a tough soldier–politician, was made Chancellor of England instead of Wolsey.

In 1532 it was learned that Anne was pregnant. Henry was overjoyed. Arrangements had to be quickly made. In January 1533 he secretly married Anne, and Cranmer held a court which said that Henry's marriage to Catherine had never been lawful; finally Anne was crowned queen in May. In September her baby was born – another daughter, the future Queen Elizabeth I.

After Cranmer it was Cromwell's turn. In 1534 he persuaded Parliament – the 'Reformation Parliament' – to ban the pope's taxes in England and to pass the Act of Supremacy which made Henry 'supreme head of the Church of England'. Men had to swear an oath to accept this title. Some, like John Fisher, the saintly bishop of Rochester, and Sir Thomas More, one of the great scholars of the age, refused to swear. They were cast into the Tower and given a last chance to recant. Neither took the chance.

Fisher was led out first. Old and white and thin, he staggered to the block. 'Truly,' said one friend, 'of all bishops that we have known in our days, it may best be said that this bishop hath well lived.' His head was put on a pike on London Bridge, but a friend took it down that night.

Then it was More's turn. His daughter, at his side in the Tower, pleaded with him to recant. 'Too late, daughter,' he said. He walked steadily to the block, confident in God's mercy, and before he was settled on the block, he moved his long white beard clear of the axe, 'for

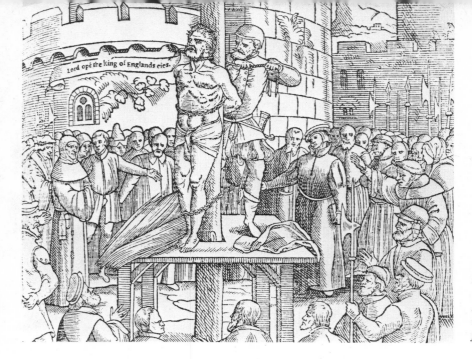

*William Tyndale was a leading English Lutheran. He fled abroad in 1524 to translate the Bible into English. He was executed for heresy in 1536. (Note he was strangled first, then burned.)*

it had never committed treason'. His last words were, 'I die loyal to God and the king, but above all to God.'

## The Dissolution of the Monasteries

In the medieval Catholic Church, monks and monasteries were very important. In England in 1530 there were 825 religious houses and over 9000 monks and nuns. It was said that churchmen owned one-third of all the land in the realm, and some abbeys like Glastonbury had an income of over £2000 per year, as much as the greatest earls.

Many monasteries and nunneries were founded in the Middle Ages. Monks and nuns wanted to be alone, away from the sins of the world, to think about God and to pray. In addition they sometimes kept schools, gave alms to the poor, looked after the sick, and gave hospitality to travellers. Later, rich people founded monasteries and placed monks in them. They asked the monks to pray for the souls of dead members of their families.

When Henry VIII broke away from the Roman Catholic Church, he had two main reasons for wanting to dissolve or close down these houses. Firstly, it was said that they were corrupt and that they were not doing the job they were founded to do. Secondly, Henry wanted their wealth.

So, in the summer of 1535, Thomas Cromwell chose a number of local commissioners and they catalogued the wealth of all churches, monasteries and nunneries in a document called the 'Valor Ecclesiasticus'. Then in the same year, a small group of hand-picked men visited all houses to investigate them. The visitor asked a number of questions: What meals did the monks eat? How did they dress? Did women ever come into the monastery?

The visitors made a great many notes; from Maiden Bradley in Wiltshire, Richard Layton wrote,

I send you relics such as God's coat, our Lady's smock . . . part of God's supper. . . . There is an holy father prior who hath but six children.

William Thirsk, the abbot of Fountains, was called a 'miserable idiot', accused of theft, sacrilege and keeping women in the house. The abbot was, in fact, forced to resign. Then from Ramsey Abbey came this report:

Many of the monks devote themselves to hunting and other sports . . . and sometimes some of them shoot arrows in the fields in unbecoming attire. . . . The prior is frequently drunk.

Many similar reports came through. Yet how true were they? Bear the following points in mind when you consider this:

1 The visitors were hand-picked by Thomas Cromwell.
2 The visitors knew that Henry VIII and Cromwell wanted to close the monasteries.
3 A hundred and twenty of the northern houses scattered throughout Northumberland were visited by Richard Layton and Thomas Legh between 22 December 1535 and 28 February 1536.
4 They did not physically visit each house. But they did ask questions about them of people who lived no more than ten miles (about sixteen kilometres) from each.
5 Local bishops had often visited monasteries before 1535. Their records show that improvements could be made, but they do not often agree with the findings of 1535–6.

Thomas Cromwell was told that monks were corrupt. In 1536 he encouraged Parliament to pass an Act to close or dissolve 243 smaller monasteries.

The opening of the 'Valor Ecclesiasticus'

## The Pilgrimage of Grace

In the north of England, many people were horrified. Ugly rumours spread everywhere: the king's agents were to take all jewel and plate to London; churches were to be closed; taxes were to be increased, and even placed on food.

The small town of Louth in Lincolnshire was normally a quiet and peaceful place. The people were proud of their parish church, with its newly built spire. Then in September 1536 they heard that a registrar from the bishop was to arrive on 2 October to check on their local priest. Again, rumours were rife. Why was he really coming? Many gathered together under one Nicholas Melton, a shoemaker, nicknamed Captain Cobbler. When the registrar arrived, they seized him, burnt his papers and made him swear an oath to support them. Within two weeks an army of 3000 men had marched on Lincoln.

At the same time 10 000 Yorkshire rebels, led by an able and popular

*Glastonbury Abbey in Somerset*

lawyer, Robert Aske, had captured York. Their banner showed Christ's bleeding wounds on the Cross. 'We are pilgrims,' said Robert Aske to one of the king's men.

Here is a list of some of the things the 'pilgrims' wanted:

1 The pope should be restored as head of the Church.
2 Abbeys which had been closed should be reopened and be given their lands back.
3 Thomas Cromwell, 'the subverter of the good laws of the realm', should be punished.
4 Richard Layton and Thomas Legh should be punished 'for their extortions . . . under bribes by them taken'.
5 Other reforms, such as a better system of taxes.

Against these rebels King Henry was nearly powerless, as he had no proper army of his own to face them. He began by issuing dire warnings of severe punishments and ordering the duke of Suffolk to move with a small force to Stamford. The Lincoln rebels, just sixty-four kilometres away, dispersed.

But in York spirits were high and hot-heads wanted to march on

London and seize the throne. Robert Aske held them back. The king would listen, he argued. They should send him their petition.

Henry tricked them. He did listen. He promised a free pardon and said he would heed their requests. Aske was delighted; he took off his badge of the wounds of Christ, and said, 'We will wear no badge or sign, but the badge of our sovereign lord.' The pilgrims went home and Aske and other leaders went to see the king in London.

Too late they found it to be a trick. They were arrested and tried, found guilty of treason and sent home to be executed before their own people. The earl of Shrewsbury marched into Cumberland and hanged seventy peasants on trees in their own villages for their wives and children to see. The monks of Sawley Abbey, reopened by the pilgrims, were 'hanged on long pieces of timber'.

### The end of the monasteries

At his trial Robert Aske said this about the monasteries of the north:

The abbeys of the north parts gave great alms to poor men and laudably served God.... The people were greatly refreshed by the said abbeys, where now they have no such succour.... Also the abbeys were one of the beauties of this realm.

How did Aske's opinion disagree with that of Richard Layton and Thomas Cromwell? When Aske was executed, there was little support left for the monks. In 1539 Parliament passed a second Act to dissolve all remaining monasteries and nunneries. There was very little opposition. Henry VIII and Thomas Cromwell had got what they wanted.

## Using the evidence: St Werburgh's Abbey, Chester

(1)

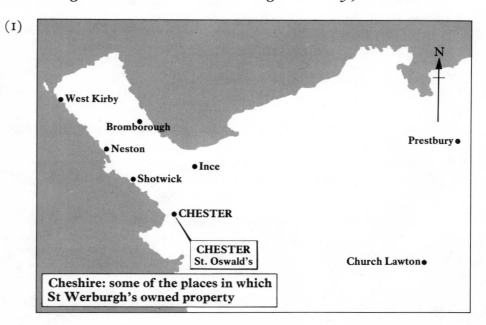

Cheshire: some of the places in which St Werburgh's owned property

## (2) The 'Valor Ecclesiasticus' for St Werburgh's:

### INCOME EACH YEAR

*Temporalities*

| | £ | s | d |
|---|---|---|---|
| Rents from 57 Cheshire manors | 554 | 15 | 0 |
| Rents from Chester city | 71 | 10 | 5½ |
| ,, ,, Derby county | 89 | 7 | 1 |
| ,, ,, Stafford county | 3 | 0 | 0 |
| ,, ,, Lancaster county | 2 | 0 | 0 |
| | 720 | 12 | 6½ |

*Spiritualities*

N.B. Tithe was a payment to the Church of one-tenth of a man's income; glebe was church land.

| | £ | s | d | £ | s | d |
|---|---|---|---|---|---|---|
| Prestbury | | | | 100 | 0 | 0 |
| Neston | | | | | | |
| Tithes of grain (average) | 9 | 10 | 5 | | | |
| ,, of lambs and wool | 4 | 5 | 0 | | | |
| Offerings to the abbey | 15 | 1 | 3 | | | |
| Glebe | 7 | 1 | 1 | 35 | 17 | 9 |
| Shotwick | | | | | | |
| Tithes of grain (average) | 18 | 0 | 2 | | | |
| ,, of lambs, wool and hay | 1 | 1 | 8 | | | |
| Quarterly roll | 2 | 0 | 0 | | | |
| Offerings (average) | 2 | 5 | 2 | 23 | 7 | 0 |
| Bromborough | | | | | | |
| Tithes of grain (average) | 59 | 13 | 4 | | | |
| Offerings | 1 | 15 | 8 | 61 | 9 | 0 |
| St Oswald's | | | | | | |
| Tithes of grain (average) | 56 | 12 | 2 | | | |
| Offerings | 7 | 13 | 7 | | | |
| Quarterly roll and small tithes | 8 | 6 | 10 | 72 | 12 | 7 |
| Ince | | | | 5 | 14 | 4 |
| Pensions | | | | 14 | 4 | 11 |
| Bordland tithes | | | | 13 | 8 | 8 |
| Worcestershire | | | | | | |
| Chipping Camden tithes | | | | 26 | 0 | 0 |
| | | | | 352 | 12 | 3 |
| | | | *Grand total* | £1073 | 4 | 9½ |

## EXPENDITURE EACH YEAR

|  | £ | s | d |
|---|---|---|---|
| To Otwell Worsley (the abbey's clerk) | 11 | 6 | 8 |
| To bailiffs' fees | 15 | 13 | 4 |
|  | 27 | 0 | 0 |

*Payments*

|  | £ | s | d |
|---|---|---|---|
| Rents paid to the king for land in Rudheath and Asthull | 8 | 18 | 8 |
| To the rector of Church Lawton for water course |  | 7 | 0 |
| To divers persons for land in Chester | 2 | 6 | 0½ |
| To the late prioress of Shene for land at West Kirby | 1 | 10 | 0 |
| To the king for 'a way called Spounden Way' |  | 6 | 8 |
| For maintaining a lamp in the church of Aston (Derbyshire) |  | 2 | 0 |
| Rent paid to Robert Woodhouse 'for land called Collys land in Westchester' |  | 2 | 0 |
|  | 13 | 12 | 4½ |

*Spiritual procurations*

|  | £ | s | d |
|---|---|---|---|
| Fees paid to the archdeacon of Chester | 3 | 3 | 0 |
| To the chaplain celebrating mass for the soul of Robert son of Jordanis de Worth | 4 | 6 | 8 |
| To ditto for the soul of William formerly bishop of Chester |  | 13 | 4 |
| To ditto for the soul of John Coly | 4 | 13 | 4 |
|  | 12 | 19 | 4 |
|  |  |  | (sic) |

*Alms*

|  | £ | s | d |
|---|---|---|---|
| Alms distributed to the poor on Maundy Thursday for the souls of the kings of England, founders of this monastery | 14 | 0 | 0 |

*Pensions*

|  | £ | s | d |
|---|---|---|---|
| Pension paid to Richard Dawes, vicar of St Oswald's | 1 | 13 | 4 |
| Ditto paid to Peter Brereton, minor canon of St John's, Chester | 1 | 6 | 8 |
|  | 3 | 0 | 0 |
|  | 70 | 11 | 8½ |

*Net total* £1003 5s 11d. *A tenth of which is* £100 6s 7½d.

The report of Thomas Cromwell's two visitors in 1536 runs as follows:

(3) St Werburga's, Chester. Immoral men 8; 3 seek release. [There were perhaps 28 monks altogether.] Founder the king. Rent £800: debt £100. Here

*Fountains Abbey in Yorkshire, as it can be seen today*

is buried the body of St Werburga, and they have the girdle of that Saint, in great request by lying in women.

(4) How did the two visitors find out about St Werburgh's? In the chapter house, they interviewed each monk alone. They asked seventy-four set questions. Each monk's answers were written down. When all monks had been interviewed, the above report was written. No monk was given the chance to defend himself against any accusation.

The Preamble to the Act of Suppression, 1536, includes the following:

(5) Forasmuch as manifest sin, vicious, casual and abominable living, is daily used among the little abbeys. . . . Where the governors of such houses . . . spoil and . . . waste . . . their churches . . . lands . . . and goods, to the high displeasure of Almighty God, slander of good religion, and the great infamy of the King's Highness. . . .

## Questions and further work

1 What does Document 2 tell you about the wealth of St Werburgh's? How much profit did the abbey make in one year? Where did it get its income from? What did it spend the money on?
2 What was Robert Aske's opinion of the work in monasteries? Does the evidence in Document 2 support his view?
3 What criticisms did the two visitors of 1536 make of St Werburgh's in their report (Document 3)?
4 Given the evidence in this chapter, do you think their criticisms were based on firm evidence?
5 From the evidence, why do you think Henry VIII wanted to close down St Werburgh's? What was the reason he gave in Document 5?

# The Catholic Reformation

### The story of Ignatius Loyola

In 1521 a French army marched across the Pyrenees into Spain and invaded the province of Castile. Their march was blocked by the town of Pamplona. One of the defenders was a thirty-one-year-old Castilian knight called Ignatius Loyola. This is his account of what happened:

I was in a fortress besieged by the French. All my companions wanted to surrender if their lives would be spared. They knew that defence was impossible. . . . But they took heart when they saw I was prepared to fight. In the attack a cannon ball struck one of my legs and shattered it completely. . . . Immediately the others surrendered to the French.

After lying for twelve days in Pamplona, I was carried on a litter to my father's castle where I became very ill. The leg would not heal. The French surgeons must have set it wrongly. Doctors were called in and began again to butcher my leg. My condition worsened. Doctors said that if I did not improve by midnight, I would die. . . . But it pleased our Lord that, the next day being St Peter's day, at midnight I began to feel much better, and within a few days I was out of danger.

Thereafter Ignatius lay for many long days and nights unable to walk. His mind wandered. He thought of many things. He learned to read many books, particularly on religion. Gradually he came to walk again but the leg never properly healed and he always walked with a limp. He would never be a soldier again. Instead, he turned his mind to St Peter and devoted his life to God.

After a pilgrimage to Jerusalem he went to Paris to continue his studies, and there he joined six other men who had similar ideas. They lived and studied in the city for six years.

Then, one August morning in 1534, the sun rising, the air becoming warm, Paris still asleep, the seven companions met in the centre of the city. They walked in peace in the early warmth of the morning, to Montmartre, to the chapel of St Denis. After they had said Mass, they all took solemn vows to be priests and to spend the rest of their lives working for God. Later they picnicked happily in the sun outside. Ignatius Loyola and his six friends had taken vows which were the start of the Society of Jesus.

*Ignatius Loyola, the founder of the Jesuit order*

### The Jesuits

Although King Henry VIII and others had decided to break away from the Catholic Church of Rome and form their own Protestant churches, many Catholics were determined to fight back. People like Erasmus and Sir Thomas More wanted to improve the Catholic Church and make it strong.

In 1535 Loyola and his friends left Paris for Italy. They hoped to reach Venice, form an army and sail to capture Jerusalem from the Moslems. But Venice was at war with the Turks, so no ships were available.

Instead they went to Rome, preached to the people, and tended the poor and sick in the terrible winter of 1538–9. Conditions were indeed very difficult:

*Father Pierre Lefèvre gives Mass to Loyola and his brothers at Montmartre in 1534*

It happened that three of the companions went to the same hospital. The beds offered them had been much used and were very dirty, the sheets were foul and covered with blood. Nevertheless, two of them, one with his clothes on, the other stripped, were not afraid to get in. The third, kept back by the horror of the filth, sought another spot. But, as he went, he thought about what he had done, and grieved greatly that he had shirked in the battle. . . .

But when he . . . arrived at the hospital of another village, the matron told him that there was no bed except one, which had been occupied the previous day by a man who had died of the horrible disease. . . . The sheets were thick with great big lice. . . . The brother seized his chance. He took off all his clothes and jumped quickly into the bed. The lice crawled all over him, pricked and stung him all night long. The brother had won a victory over himself.

Their work in plague-ridden villages won Loyola and his companions many friends. The next year Pope Paul III gave them a charter and the Society of Jesus, or Jesuits, was formed. It was to be a society of regular priests who worked to spread the faith by preaching, by education, by works of charity. All members vowed to obey the pope and their general. The first general was Ignatius Loyola.

## The work of the Jesuits

The Jesuit mission was an immediate success. Loyola stayed in Rome, but his six friends all went in different directions. They preached to the thronging masses, and were cheered by people who valued the good works they did. At Belluno there was a huge bonfire of Protestant

*The treatment of some Jesuit martyrs in Japan*

*Matteo Ricci, the first Jesuit missionary to China, with one of his early converts*

books. Everywhere schools and colleges were set up to educate future Jesuits and laymen into the Catholic faith. In 1550 the 'Collegium Romanum' was set up in Rome. Above all, the Jesuits were enthusiastic preachers and teachers. One Spaniard was described by a friend as a 'penniless rustic, under-sized, swarthy, entirely uneducated, vile and despicable in the eyes of men'. Yet his heart burned with a desire to preach and he quickly won respect as a man of God.

The Jesuit mission went outside Europe too. In 1540 the king of Portugal needed someone to go to the East and Francis Xavier took up the offer. He travelled across Asia and reached Japan in 1549. Everywhere, he preached to European traders, he taught native people in their own languages, he baptised people in their thousands, and he set up churches for Europeans and natives. Many of his converts were persecuted as in Japan in 1597 and again in 1622. St Francis Xavier died in 1552 of exposure and exhaustion when he was on the point of starting

a mission to China. Perhaps typical of his bravery and determination is the story of his 500-kilometre march to Kyoto in Japan. In places he walked barefoot up to his waist in snow.

*The painting of the Council of Trent by Titian*

## The Council of Trent

The popes, too, wanted to strengthen the Catholic Church. Pope Paul III ordered all bishops and many other priests to meet in 1545 in a great Church council in the Alpine city of Trent.

The meetings of the council lasted eighteen years, to 1563. In them the bishops reconsidered the beliefs of the Catholic Church; they condemned the heresy of men like Luther, they disciplined bishops and priests who did not do their jobs properly, and above all they decided that without doubt the pope was the leader of the Catholic Church.

When the council began, there was much disagreement among bishops. By the end, according to one eye-witness, 'many of the most

*King Henry VIII with his three children, Mary, Edward and Elizabeth. The lady on Henry's left is Catherine Howard, his fifth wife*

grave prelates weep for joy, and those who had treated each other as strangers, embrace with profound emotion'.

### Mary Tudor 1516–57

In October 1537 Princess Mary Tudor was much in the public eye. On 12 October, the queen, Jane Seymour, gave birth to Henry VIII's long-awaited son, and the following Sunday, Mary was godmother as the baby was christened Edward at Hampton Court. After the ceremony Mary held the baby's train as the procession left the chapel.

Twelve days after the birth, Jane Seymour died 'through the fault of them that were about her that suffered her to take great cold'. Her body was carried in state from Hampton Court to Windsor. Mary was chief mourner and rode on a horse draped in black velvet immediately behind the corpse.

On both these occasions Mary was clearly a leading member of the royal family and of the king's court. Yet just a few years before, Mary had feared for her life. She and her mother Catherine of Aragon were both kept in confinement while King Henry courted and finally married Anne Boleyn. There is a story that, one day, Mary overheard some ladies talk of her execution for treason. How could she prevent it or escape? Just then her old tutor came to see her. She could not talk to him privately, but she knew that her ladies understood no Latin. She therefore asked the tutor to test her Latin and he agreed. In Latin she then said to him, 'The king is thinking to cut off my head. Tell the emperor's ambassador.' The tutor told her that her Latin was very poor and hurried off to see the ambassador.

The Lady Mary after Queen.

Yet in spite of her fears Mary survived. In fact when Jane Seymour became queen she and Mary became friends and Mary was restored to Court. In July 1536 her father gave her a valuable diamond and 1000 crowns 'for her little pleasures'. Mary became 'the first after the queen and sits at table opposite her, a little lower down, after having first given the napkin for washing to the king and queen'.

Look at the picture of Mary. The French ambassador described her in 1541 as of medium height, with big bones and no fat. 'Her beauty is mediocre,' but she was very athletic, regularly taking a five-kilometre morning walk. She was a master of French and Latin and skilled at music and embroidery.

Like her mother, Mary was a Catholic. She attended regular Catholic Masses and wanted the English Church to be reunited with Rome. When Henry died, Mary's nine-year-old brother became king as Edward VI. Mary was very fond of him but he was a Protestant and the court was Protestant. So Mary spent most of his reign (1547–53) on her Norfolk estate at Kenninghall. In 1549 Parliament passed the Act of

Uniformity: a prayer book was published and all church services had to follow it. It was against the law to attend a Catholic mass, with a ten pound fine for first offences and life imprisonment for the third offence. Mary was allowed as a special privilege to hold mass in her own household, but she feared for the many Catholic people in England who could not. England was turning away from what she thought was the true faith.

Then in 1553 Edward, always a sickly youth, died. Mary became queen of England. She began negotiations to marry Philip, the Catholic king of Spain. She cancelled her father's and brother's Acts of Parliament and returned England to the Roman Catholic Church. Her problem was simple: how could she ensure that England remained a Catholic country? Three factors weighed on her mind:

1 Mary had no child and she was now thirty-seven years old.
2 If Mary died, the next ruler would be Elizabeth, the Protestant daughter of Henry VIII and Anne Boleyn.
3 There were many Protestants in England.

*Mary Tudor with King Philip II of Spain*

Mary's advisers included Bishop Stephen Gardiner, who 'condemned and burned several great and learned men, presuming that these examples would deter any in future from speaking against the popish religion'. In April 1554 Parliament passed an Act under which Protestants could be burned at the stake.

Some men gave other advice, however. Simon Renard, the Spanish ambassador, wrote to King Philip after a Protestant had been burned in London:

A certain Rogers was burned publicly yesterday. Some of the onlookers wept, others prayed to God to give him strength to bear the pain, others threatened the bishops. . . . Although it may seem necessary to apply punishment during Your Majesty's visit here, I think Your Majesty would be wise to abhor firmness. . . . Otherwise I foresee that the people may cause a revolt. . . . Your Majesty will also consider that the lady Elizabeth has her supporters, and that there are Englishmen who do not love foreigners. . . .

What was Renard's advice? Why does he take this view?

## Mary's persecutions

In spite of Renard's advice, Mary decided that her only hope was to make a public example of large numbers of Protestants. Only thus would Catholics be safe in future. John Foxe, a Protestant minister from Lincolnshire, recorded their numbers in his *Booke of Martyrs*.

The whole number burned during the reign of Mary amounted to 284. Nearly 400 fell a sacrifice on these sad occasions including those who died by imprisonment or famine. There were burnt 5 bishops, 21 divines, 8 gentlemen, 84 artificers, 100 husbandmen, servants and labourers, 26 wives, 20 widows, 9 girls, 2 boys, 2 infants.

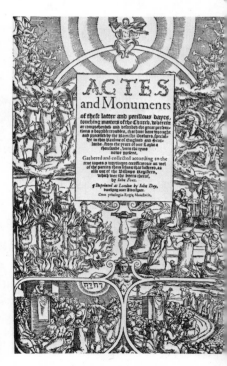

*The title page of John Foxe's* Booke of Martyrs

We can compare those burned by Mary with those by other Tudor monarchs:

| Ruler | Length of reign | Number of victims |
|---|---|---|
| Henry VII | 24 years | 10 |
| Henry VIII | 38 | 81 |
| Edward VI | 6 | 2 |
| Mary | 4 | 284 |
| Elizabeth | 44 | 5 |

In his book *The English Reformation* A. G. Dickens wrote this about the list of Mary's victims: 'It includes a surprisingly high total of more than fifty women ... and a very large proportion of people in their twenties or late teens.' (What else is surprising about Foxe's list above?)

## Using the evidence: the burning of Latimer and Ridley

In the reign of Edward VI, Hugh Latimer had been bishop of Worcester and Nicholas Ridley had been bishop of London. In 1555 they were tried and condemned as heretics. In October they were burned together at the stake.

(1) This picture shows how one man saw it.

John Foxe, who wrote his book about Protestant martyrs at the end of Mary's reign, described the event thus:

(2) So they came to the stake. Dr Ridley, entering the place first, earnestly holding up both his hands, looked towards heaven. Then, shortly after, seeing

Mr Latimer, with a cheerful look he ran to him and embraced him, saying, 'Be of good heart, brother, for God will either assuage the fury of the flame, or else strengthen us to abide it.'

He then went to the stake, and, kneeling down, prayed with great fervour, while Mr Latimer following, kneeled down also and prayed with like earnestness. After this they arose and conversed together, while Dr Smith began his sermon to them. . . . They were then commanded to prepare immediately for the stake. They obeyed with all meekness. Dr Ridley gave his gown to his brother in law. . . . He likewise made presents of other small things to gentlemen standing by, divers of whom were weeping pitifully. . . . Happy was he who could get the least rag for remembrance of this good man. Mr Latimer quietly suffered his keeper to pull off his apparel which was very simple. . . . Then the blacksmith took a chain of iron and placed it about both their waists; and, as he was knocking in the staple, Dr Ridley took the chain in his hand, and, looking aside to the smith, said, 'Good fellow, knock it in hard.'

Then Dr Ridley's brother brought him a bag of gunpowder and tied it about his neck. Dr Ridley asked him what it was. He answered, 'Gunpowder.'

Then said he, 'I will receive it. Have you any for Mr Latimer?'

'Yea, sir, that I have,' said he.

'Then give it him.'

So his brother went and carried it to Dr Latimer.

Then they brought a lighted faggot and laid it at Dr Ridley's feet. Upon which Mr Latimer said, 'Be of good comfort, Mr Ridley, and play the man! We shall this day light such a candle, by God's grace, in England, as I trust never shall be put out.'

When Dr Ridley saw the fire flaming up towards him he cried out with an amazing loud voice, 'Into thy hands, O Lord, I commend my spirit.'

Mr Latimer cried as loudly, 'O Father of Heaven, receive my soul,' after which he soon died, with seeming little pain.

But Dr Ridley, owing to the bad arrangement of the fire, was put to such exquisite pain (the faggots being green and piled so high, that the flames were kept down by the green wood and burned fiercely beneath) that he begged them for God's sake to let the flames come unto him. Which his brother in law heard, but did not very well understand . . . so he heaped faggots upon him, so that he quite covered him . . . that it burned all Ridley's lower parts before it touched his upper. . . . Yet in all his agony and torment, he did not forget to call upon God, 'Lord, have mercy upon me'. . . . In which pains he laboured till one of the bystanders pulled the faggots from above with a hook, and where Ridley saw the fire flame up, he leaned himself to that side. As soon as the fire touched the gunpowder he was seen to stir no more. . . . The dreadful sight filled almost every eye with tears.

## Questions and further work

1 Can you identify the man in the very top right-hand corner of the picture on page 67?
2 Make a list of the points in the Document which are the same as those in the picture.
3 Are there any differences in the Document?
4 What can you learn about John Foxe from the Document on Latimer and Ridley and from the other material in the chapter?

# The Great Powers of Europe

# 6 . Conflict in France

In 1559 disaster struck France. Her king, the intelligent and forceful Henry II, died suddenly. He and his father Francis I had ruled France sensibly for forty-four years. But now the crown was in danger. The new king, Francis II, was a pale and sickly youth of just fifteen years old. He was placed under the care of his mother, a foreign princess, Catherine dei Medici. So sickly was he that he died within a year, to be followed by his even younger brother Charles IX.

At this time, too, there was danger for the royal family. Two great and important families began to plot and scheme to take the crown. One was the House of Bourbon, the Huguenot or Protestant kings of Navarre. The other was the House of Guise, the great Catholic family from Lorraine.

These two families found support from many people. For the next forty years they were to battle for the French crown in the 'Wars of Religion'.

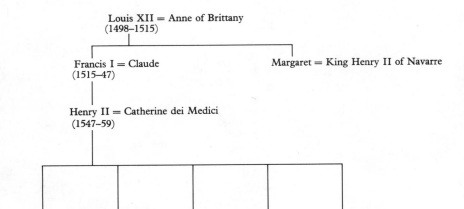

The French royal family tree

Louis XII = Anne of Brittany
(1498–1515)

Francis I = Claude          Margaret = King Henry II of Navarre
(1515–47)

Henry II = Catherine dei Medici
(1547–59)

| Francis II (1559–60) | Charles IX (1560–74) | Henry III (1574–88) | Francis, Duke of Alençon (died 1584) | Margaret = Henry of Navarre (later Henry IV 1589–1610) |

## Huguenots and Catholics, 1559–72

In 1560 Francis II was taken ill. His doctors thought it was serious and they said he should be taken to the country for fresh air and rest. So the whole court moved to the royal palace at Amboise in Blois.

The Huguenots decided that this was a good time to strike. Their leaders, the duke of Coligny and the count of Condé made a plan to capture the king and his mother, banish the Guise family from France, and take control themselves. All was ready.

But many Huguenots knew of the plot and several let out the secret. The Guises were put on their guard. Their spies were everywhere. On 13 March a troop of Huguenot horsemen were captured in a wood not far from Amboise. They were questioned and confessed that a rebel army of 40 000 was prepared.

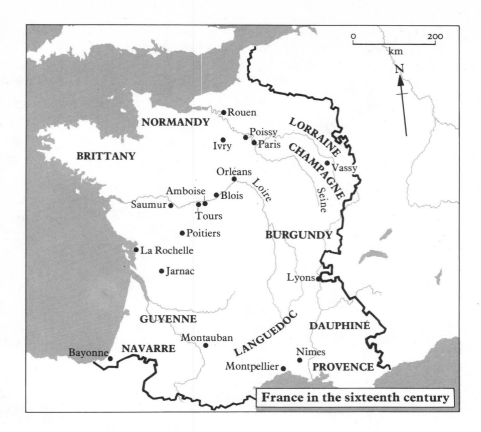

France in the sixteenth century

Shortly afterwards the Huguenots decided to act boldly. A band, over 150 in number, rode up to the gates of the palace and hammered on the door. They were quickly surrounded and captured. Mass executions followed: they were drowned in the moat and then beheaded. Their heads were placed on spikes on the castle walls as a warning to other plotters.

The duke of Guise was delighted at his success. He brought the young king and his brothers to see some of the executions. Only the duke's wife was unhappy. 'I have just seen', she said, 'the most piteous tragedy, the cruel shedding of innocent blood, the blood of the king's loyal subjects.'

Civil war was now raging between the two sides throughout France. In 1561 Catherine dei Medici brought Guise and Bourbon together to Poissy to try to make peace. It was agreed that there was to be no Huguenot preaching in French cities. Yet within a year Huguenot pastors were preaching openly. On Sunday 1 March 1562 the duke of Guise rode into the town of Vassy. He knew that the Huguenots were holding a service there.

There were 1200 Huguenots in the town. They hastily put up barricades to defend themselves. But the duke ordered his 200 dragoons to charge. Their muskets, pistols and swords cut down the Huguenots, armed only with knives and stones. The attack became a massacre.

Seventy-four were killed, hundreds injured, women and children as well as men.

The wars now spread all over France. For ten years the country was ravaged. Armies of mercenaries (paid soldiers), beggars and thieves, were all anxious to get rich by plundering their own countrymen. There was intense hatred on both sides, and both leaders were assassinated, the duke of Guise in 1563 and the duke of Condé in 1569.

### The events of 1572

By 1572 although many men had died there was still no end to the war. If anything, the Huguenots were gaining the upper hand. Coligny was now the king's chief adviser. In August, many leading Huguenots came to Paris for the wedding of the young Bourbon prince, Henry, to the king's sister, Margaret.

Four days after the wedding, 23 August 1572, a hired assassin shot and wounded Coligny in the street. He was carried back, in great pain, to his quarters. It was reported to him that the assassin had been hired by Catherine dei Medici.

The same night Catherine dei Medici went to her son, King Charles IX, and told him that Coligny and the Huguenots had been plotting to murder him and put Prince Henry on the throne. That was why they were all in Paris.

Charles didn't know what to think. How could he be safe? At last, in the early hours of the morning he gave the order Catherine wanted: all Huguenots in Paris were to be killed. By dawn the cry of 'Kill, kill the Huguenots!' was everywhere in the city. Nearly 10 000 Huguenots may have been killed in the massacre. The young duke of Guise broke into Coligny's quarters and put his own sword into the admiral. This was sweet revenge, for Coligny had been involved in his father's murder in 1563.

## Using the evidence: who caused the massacre?

There are a number of questions still unanswered in the story of the events of 1572. Who hired the assassin to shoot Coligny? Was it Catherine's own idea to visit the king on the night of 23 August? If it was, why did she go? Had the Huguenots really come to Paris to murder the king?

The central figure is Catherine. It was she who finally persuaded King Charles to give the order to massacre the Huguenots. But why? We have no direct evidence, we have no eye-witness account of their conversation that evening.

Instead we must turn to indirect evidence and ask certain questions:

*What sort of woman was Catherine?*

This description of her was written by a Venetian ambassador in 1570:

*The massacre of Huguenots at Vassy in 1562*

(1) Her Majesty is now fifty-one years of age. Her years, however, are not attended by the signs of feebleness and old age. She has a strong and vigorous constitution and there is no one in the court who can keep pace with her when walking. She takes a great deal of exercise, which gives her an appetite. . . . As princess, she is benevolent, courteous and affable to all, making it her business to see that none leave her dissatisfied, at least as far as words are concerned. Her knowledge of affairs is great. No step, however unimportant, is taken without her. . . . Yet she is beloved by no one in the land, or at least by few. The Huguenots say that she has given them fine words and mock welcomes, while all the time she has been treating with the Catholics. The Catholics, on the other hand, declare that she has favoured the Huguenots. Moreover, this is an age in France where men ask for all they can get. As she is a stranger, though she would give all, they would still say she gave nothing.

## What did Catherine herself say about the event?

Catherine wrote this letter to the French ambassador in Venice about a month after the massacre:

(2) I understand from your letter that certain people believe that what happened to the Huguenots was instigated by me and my son. . . . I think you should know therefore that I have never done or permitted anything but what

*Above left: The siege of Chartres in 1568. Notice the methods of defence and attack. The cannon have obviously devastated the central walls of the city.*

*Above right: The town schoolmaster*

*Catherine dei Medici*

honour, duty and love for my children commanded me, because the admiral, since the death of my husband, has shown by his deeds and bearing that he desired the overthrow of this kingdom and the usurpation of my son's crown.... Furthermore the admiral has so grievously conspired against the persons of the king and his brother and my own person.... The king is greatly troubled that, in the heat of the moment, certain other Huguenots were slain by Catholics, who remembered infinite evils, robberies and other wicked acts committed upon them during the troubles. Now at last all is peaceful, so that there is only one king.

## What did other people say about the event?

The following is an extract from the *Memoirs* of Gaspard de Tavannes. He died in 1573 and this extract was in fact written by his son, Jean. Interestingly, Catherine allowed Jean to inherit none of his father's offices or titles.

(3) The Queen mother hurries to see the king at Montpipeau. She shuts herself in a room with him. She weeps many tears and says, 'I took so much trouble to help you get on. I preserved for you the crown which the Huguenots and Catholics wished to take from you. I made many sacrifices and took many risks. And yet you have given me little thanks. You keep away from me – your

mother – and take advice from your enemies. You lean on those who wish to assassinate you. I know you and Coligny have secret plans. . . . You make me so unhappy. . . . Give me leave to return to the place of my birth.'

The following was written by King Henry IV, the prince who finally won the civil war:

(4) But I ask you, I ask you, what could a poor woman do, left by the death of her husband with five little children on her arms – and two families in France who were trying to grasp the crown – ours and the Guises? Did she not have to deceive first one, then the other? She had to guard her sons. . . . I am surprised she never did worse.

1  Document 2 was written soon after the massacre. What opinion does Catherine express about:
   (a)  Coligny (the admiral)
   (b)  His Huguenot followers
   (c)  Her own duty to her son and the French crown
   (d)  Her own part in causing the massacre
2  Document 1 was written about the same time. What opinion does it express about Catherine's duty to the crown? What evidence suggests that she may have been responsible for the massacre? What evidence suggests that it would be easy to blame her for it even if she were innocent?
3  Documents 3 and 4 were written by men who had good reason to dislike Catherine. On what opinions does Document 3 agree with Document 2? On what opinion does Document 4 agree with Document 1?
4  Is there enough evidence to convict Catherine of causing the massacre? If not, where would you try to search for more?

## The Massacre

This is part of the account written by Princess Margaret, the new wife of the Huguenot prince of Navarre:

(5) So the night passed without a wink of sleep. At daybreak my husband said he was going to play tennis. . . . He left my room, and all his gentlemen with him. Seeing that it was daylight and thinking that the danger of which my sister had spoken was now past, and overcome by sleep, I told my nurse to shut the door so I could sleep quietly. An hour later when I was fast asleep, there came a man beating at the door with his hands and feet, crying 'Navarre, Navarre!' The nurse, thinking it was my husband, ran quickly and opened the door. It was a Huguenot gentleman with a sword wound in his elbow and another from a halberd in his arm. He was chased by four archers who pursued him into my room. To save his life he threw himself on to my bed. I dragged myself into the space behind my bed, and him after me, holding me all the time in front of his body. . . we both shrieked and each was as frightened as the other. At last, thank God, the captain of the guard came up, and finding me in such a position, could not help laughing. He got rid of the archers and granted me the life of the poor man who was holding on to me.

One of the few Huguenots who escaped the massacre was a thirteen-year-old nobleman who later became duke of Sully:

(6) I made up my mind to try to reach the Collège de Bourgogne where I was a student, although it was far from my lodgings. The distance made it dangerous. I put on my student's gown and, taking a large breviary under my arm, went downstairs. As I turned out into the street I was horrified. There were madmen running to and fro, smashing down doors and shouting, 'Kill, kill, massacre the Huguenots.' Blood spattered before my eyes and doubled my fear. I ran into a clump of soldiers who stopped me. They plied me with questions and began to jostle me about when luckily they saw my breviary. That served as my safe-conduct. Twice again the same thing happened and twice again I escaped. At last I reached the college but there greater danger awaited me.

The porter refused to let me in. I remained out in the street at the mercy of the madmen who kept increasing in numbers. I thought to ask for the principal of the college, a good man who was very friendly to me, and by the aid of a little money, I persuaded the porter to let me in. The principal took me to his room, where two inhuman priests tried to get me out of his hands, saying that the order was to kill all Huguenots, even babies at the breast. The principal locked me up in a hidden closet, where I stayed for the next three days.

*The 1572 massacre of Huguenots in Paris*

1  What picture do Documents 5 and 6 paint of the massacre? Why do you think they give this view? Consider (a) the experience of the authors, (b) the beliefs they had at the time.
2  Why would these authors want to describe their experiences in such detail?

Within the illustration: *Henricus Rex Galliæ* · *Monsigneur Cognat* · *Henr̃ de Lorraine dux de Guise* · *1588* · *23 Decemb.*

*The assassination of the Duke of Guise, 1588*

## The end of the wars, 1574–89

The new king, Henry III, was very unpopular. 'He usually dressed as a woman,' wrote one critic, 'with a low-cut collar which showed his throat hung with pearls.' He taxed the people heavily, but gave much of the money away to favourites or *mignons*.

> They wear their hair long, artificially curled, and with little velvet bonnets on top. Their shirts are long and loose, so that their heads look like St John's on the platter. . . . Their occupations are gambling, blaspheming, quarrelling and following the king everywhere.

With such a king, Catholics and Huguenots again fought for power. Their leaders were Henry, duke of Guise – a brave dashing leader with a sabre-scar across his cheek, the son of the duke murdered in 1563 – and Henry, king of Navarre, the bridegroom of 1572.

In 1588 the crisis came to a head in the War of the Three Henrys. Henry of Guise invaded Paris and bribed the city mob.

> Immediately all took arms, went into the streets, took the chains and barricaded the corners. The artisan left his tools, the merchant his deals, the university its books, the lawyers their hats. . . . Everywhere there were frightened cries and seditious words to arouse the people to fury. The duke of Guise sent his partisans to each quarter to encourage the people who were

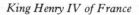
*King Henry IV of France*

rebellious, but disorganised, to barricade and defend themselves well.

The mob captured the royal palace but, just in time, King Henry fled to Blois. He had just one hope left – to murder the duke of Guise. 'He would not dare!' said Guise when he heard of the plot. But King Henry did dare and an assassin stabbed Guise to death on 23 December 1588.

The king felt the murder was necessary. The Catholics were horrified. Eight months later they got their revenge.

A young Dominican friar betook himself to St-Cloud. On arrival he told the guard that he had a message for the king. The king ordered that he could deliver his message on the following day. . . . The next day the monk was led to the king's chamber. As there were several persons present the monk demanded that the king should receive him alone. The two men then went into the royal cabinet where the king looked through the documents which the monk handed him. The king then asked if there were any more. The monk replied 'Yes' and in place of a script he drew forth from his sleeve a short knife, the width of two fingers, which he thrust into the king's stomach.

Two days later the king died. Two Henrys were dead. The third, the Huguenot Henry of Navarre, now became king of France, and after nine more years he persuaded all Frenchmen, Catholics and Huguenots, to support him.

# 7 The Golden Age of Spain

### The kingdoms of Spain

In the middle of the fifteenth century, Spain was divided into several Christian kingdoms: Castile, Aragon, Navarre and Valencia were the main ones. Each had its own rulers, its own customs, its own way of life. And to the south, in Granada, the Moslems or Moors still retained their own civilisation and religion.

One parish priest wrote of the horrors of life in Castile:

> For there was no justice in the land: common people were murdered, royal taxes and lands seized, men were robbed not only in the open fields but in cities and towns, priests could not live in safety, women were raped, and all men had the freedom to commit any crimes they wished.

At this point, in 1474, a young woman called Isabella, aged only twenty-three, became queen of Castile. She was determined to put things to rights. She married the young King Ferdinand of Aragon and together they set about restoring law and order and unifying the country. They destroyed the fortified castles of great nobles who broke the law. They improved the Spanish army under a brilliant new general, Gonsalvo de Cordoba. They provided a company of archers in each city to arrest criminals. And they increased their wealth by creating new taxes and enforcing payment. Together they were called the 'Most Catholic Kings' and given rights by the pope over all Catholics in Spain. Ferdinand's last achievement in 1515 was to add Navarre to Castile and Aragon and Granada.

*El Cid*

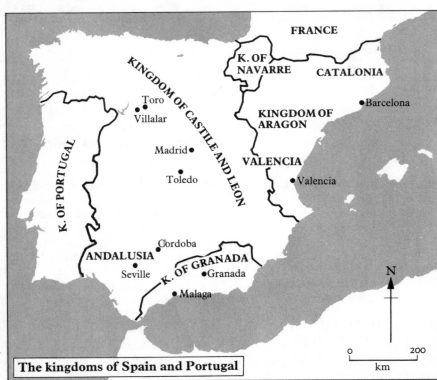

The kingdoms of Spain and Portugal

## The 'Reconquista', 1492

In the Middle Ages Moslem art and culture had flourished in Spain. But from the thirteenth century onwards the Moslems had been driven farther and farther south by the Christian kings of Castile and Aragon. In 1236 Cordoba with its magnificent mosque had been captured; in 1248 Seville was taken. By the fourteenth century only the small kingdom of Granada was left to the Moors.

In 1476 Queen Isabella demanded taxes from the Moslem king of Granada. He defiantly refused: his mints 'no longer coined gold but steel'. Isabella bristled with anger. In 1483 an army under the Grand Master of the Order of Santiago drove south into the mountains of Granada. They aimed to take the city of Malaga, but they got bogged down in the hills north of the city. The Moslems saw their chance, routed the Castilian army and captured most of its weapons, armour and horses.

*Isabella of Castile*

Only treason in the Moslem ranks enabled the Catholic kings to take Granada. Boabdil, nicknamed 'the Unlucky', the son of the Moslem ruler, was captured by Ferdinand in a skirmish. He was offered freedom on two conditions: that he turn traitor to his father and help the Christians, and that any lands he captured should be turned over to Ferdinand. Boabdil was freed, and in 1484 he helped Ferdinand to capture the province of Ronda and in 1487 the city of Malaga. Ferdinand decided to make an example of the citizens: many had to pay huge ransoms, some were deported, others sold into slavery.

Meanwhile in 1486 Boabdil's father had died and he had captured the city of Granada itself. Ferdinand demanded that he hand it over as they had agreed. But Boabdil realised that now he alone could protect the Moslems. He garrisoned the city and refused to surrender.

In 1491, therefore, Ferdinand besieged the city with a huge army of 40 000 foot and 10 000 cavalry. The Moslems tried to break out several times, but without success. Despite the danger, one Moslem crept out to set fire to the Christian tents: the flames spread quickly. But not even this could break the determination of Ferdinand and Isabella, and by the end of the year the city was starved into submission. They entered in triumph.

*Ferdinand of Aragon*

What was to happen to the Moslems now? They were given a choice: either they could sell their goods and property at a fair price and go safely into exile, or they could remain as loyal subjects of the Catholic kings in Spain. They were not to be forced to become Christians.

But Isabella was a very pious Catholic and she now appointed a new archbishop of Toledo, Cardinal Ximenes. Ximenes was angry that so few Moslems became Christian:

So as to preach to them and make them Christians, he named certain persons for the job, particularly one called 'The Lion', a man who lived up to his name, for those who fell into his hands were so roughly treated that, after being at his mercy for four or five days, they emerged saying that they wished to be Christians.

Three thousand Moslems were quickly converted, Moslem mosques were changed into Catholic churches and in 1502 an edict said that all Moslems must be converted or go into exile. The edict was issued in February and Moslems had until April to choose. It was an impossible choice. Those who accepted Christianity and stayed were known as Moriscoes.

Isabella and Ximenes later became even harsher. Decrees forbade the wearing of Moorish clothes, the use of Moslem books, even the Arabic language. Finally, a century later in 1609, all Moriscoes were expelled and their property confiscated. As many as 300 000 were forced to flee. Many died from disease, and few found decent homes. The 'Catholic Kings' treated the Moslems with unnecessary brutality.

### The Emperors Charles V and Philip II

*A wood carving (in relief) in Granada Cathedral. It shows the surrender of Granada to Ferdinand and Isabella. The figure in the front is probably Cardinal Ximenes*

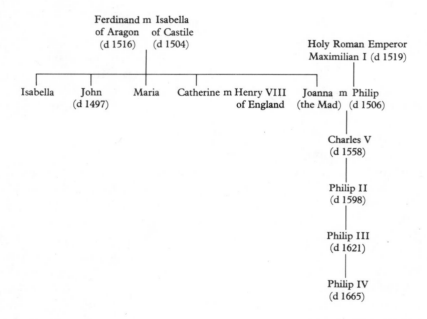

Charles V was the grandson of Ferdinand and Isabella. Before he died in 1516 Ferdinand named Charles as his successor on the throne of both Castile and Aragon. Two years later his other grandfather, Maximilian, died. So Charles became Holy Roman Emperor too. Thus at the age of nineteen, Charles ruled the most powerful empire in the world (see map on page 35).

But he was soon unpopular in Spain. He had been brought up in Burgundy and he spoke no Spanish. And, when he came to Spain, he brought foreign nobles with him and gave them Spanish offices and wealth. Revolts broke out. It took a year before the rebels were beaten in battle at Villalar in 1521.

Charles ruled Spain for forty-four years. Yet he spent no more than sixteen of them in Spain. The rest were spent in the Netherlands, Italy and Germany. Yet Charles always came back to Spain. Firstly, he needed it to provide money. 'I cannot be sustained,' he once wrote, 'except by my kingdoms in Spain.' But secondly, Charles came to love Spain for itself. In the 1520s he learned the Castilian language. Thereafter he would use no other. One French bishop once told the king he could not understand him. 'Do not expect', Charles replied, 'to hear from me any language but Spanish, which is so noble it deserves to be known by all Christian peoples.' After Charles retired from governing his huge empire in 1556, he went to Spain and it was there that he died.

It was Charles v who built up the Spanish Empire in South America. Chapter 1 tells how Cortes and Pizarro conquered the Aztec and Inca empires. South American gold and silver flowed back to Spain. In 1545 the famous 'silver mountain' of Potosi was discovered and loads of precious ore were shipped to Spain. At the same time, Catholic missionaries took ship for the New World. Some converted the native Indians by brute force. But others, like Las Casas, tried to treat the Indians as human beings with rights of their own.

In the reign of Charles' son, Philip II, Spain became the greatest state in Europe. She had a huge empire, including the Netherlands, parts of Italy, South America and the Philippines in the east. And she was seen to be the champion of the Catholic Church. Philip married Mary Tudor, the Catholic queen of England. But perhaps his greatest triumph came in the eastern Mediterranean.

**Spanish possessions in the New World in the sixteenth century**

*Las Casas in his book* The Destruction of the Indies *tried to show the cruelty of the Spaniards toward the Indians*

*King Philip II of Spain by Titian*

## The Turkish threat

The Ottoman Turks had long been a threat to Spain. In 1522 a Turkish fleet captured the island of Rhodes and forced the Knights of St John to seek refuge in Malta. Then in 1534 Khaireddin Barbarossa, the great corsair or pirate-leader from Algiers, joined forces with the Turks and became Grand-Admiral of their fleet. He led many attacks on Spain. One Spaniard wrote:

They have utterly ruined and destroyed Sardinia, Corsica, Sicily, the neighbourhood of Naples, Rome and Genoa, all the Balearic Islands and the whole east coast of Spain. Here they feast as they think fit, welcomed by the Moriscoes who live there, who, because they are zealous Moslems, tell the pirates all they need to know.

In 1535 Barbarossa led a brutal attack on Valencia. This made Charles determined to root him out and defeat him. He prepared a huge fleet, but fierce storms broke it up, and the raids continued for a further twenty years.

But when Philip II became king, he set out to stop the Turks for good. First, he needed money. He raised some from the pope, more from the Cortes of Castile. He used it to build ships in the docks of Catalonia and South Italy. In 1563 Spain had just thirty-seven ships; by 1570 she had over a hundred.

Most of them were galleys, over 45 metres long and 12 metres wide. They had three masts; the forecastle, raised above the deck, carried musketeers and 40-pound (18 kg) cannon. Each galley was driven by oars more than 4 metres long, each pulled by three to six men. Oarsmen were usually slaves, Turks or pirates captured in battle. One described his experiences:

Think of six men chained to a bench, naked, holding an immensely heavy oar, bending forwards towards the stern with arms at full reach to clear the back of the rowers in front. A galley oar sometimes pulls thus for ten, twelve, or even twenty hours without a moment's rest. The boatswain puts a piece of bread, steeped in wine, in the wretched rower's mouth to stop fainting, and then the captain shouts the order to redouble the lash. If a slave falls exhausted upon his oar (which often happens) he is flogged till he is taken for dead, and then pitched unceremoniously into the sea.

Philip had other preparations to make too. A hundred ships were not enough to defeat the Turks. In 1570 he sent ambassadors to the pope and to Venice to try to form a league against the Turks. He also tried to get France to join but she refused. 'They would be happy to lose an eye,' said the Spanish duke of Alva, 'so long as we lost two.'

At last, in September 1571, a combined fleet sailed from Messina in Sicily. At the same time, a large Turkish force was ready in the gulf of Lepanto. The Spanish commander was Don John of Austria, a half-brother to King Philip. Don John never felt that his brother trusted him. This was his chance to show his loyalty and courage. He was determined to fight.

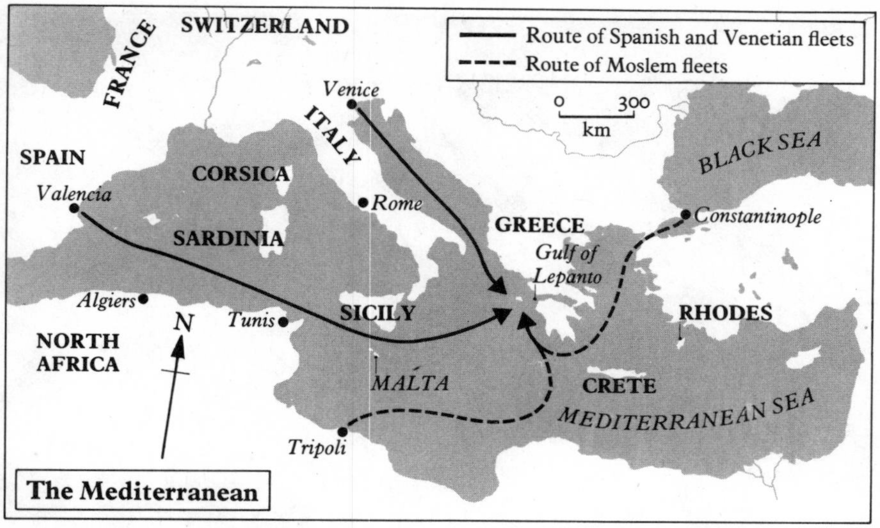
SWITZERLAND
FRANCE
Route of Spanish and Venetian fleets
Route of Moslem fleets
Venice
ITALY
0 300
km
BLACK SEA
SPAIN
CORSICA
Valencia
Rome
Constantinople
GREECE
SARDINIA
Gulf of
Lepanto
Algiers
N
Tunis
SICILY
RHODES
NORTH
AFRICA
MALTA
CRETE
MEDITERRANEAN SEA
Tripoli
The Mediterranean

The Turkish admiral, Ali Pasha, agreed. 'I will never give the impression,' he said, 'that my fleet is in retreat before the Christians. Captain, give the order to form a line of battle.' At sunrise on Sunday 7 October the fleets came face to face. One report said that the Turks had 230 ships, the Spaniards 208, but the latter had better guns and ammunition.

It was a clear sunny morning, with not a cloud in the sky. The Turkish right attacked first. They sailed towards the Venetian galleasses, but they were forced on to the rocks by the destructive weight of the Venetian shot. Many Turks leapt overboard, but Venetian ships pursued them, to kill as many as they could.

Then came the highlight of the battle. The two flagships, *Real* and *Sultana* crashed into each other. Four hundred soldiers fought a hand-to-hand duel for over two hours. Slowly Spanish muskets gained the upper hand. Ali Pasha was wounded. There is a story that Ali offered a bribe to a young Spanish officer to help him escape. The officer refused, cut off Ali's head, dived into the sea and brought it to Don John. The admiral rebuked him for murdering a prisoner of war. There were many stories of valour that day. The prince of Parma was said to have leapt alone into a Turkish galley. He fought his way single-handed through the soldiers until he seized the captain and forced him to surrender. The writer Cervantes, wounded in battle, said it was 'the greatest fight that past and present ages have ever seen'. Two hundred Turkish galleys were taken or sunk; 30 000 Turks were said to have been killed and a further 3000 captured; 15 000 galley-slaves were freed from Turkish ships. For their part the Spanish lost ten ships and 8000 men. Several witnesses said that the sea was red with blood.

The battle achieved King Philip's aim. 'Turkish supremacy', said one historian, 'had been broken.' The pope's comment, when he heard the news, was, 'There was a man sent from God whose name was John.' (What did he mean? Which John did that statement originally refer to?)

*The battle of Lepanto*

### The Jews and the Moors

In many parts of the world today, there are people who dislike or oppose others who are in some way different from themselves: in background, religion, or race, for example. Spaniards in the sixteenth century were like that. They were Christians; they would not tolerate Jews and Moors. They wanted *'limpieza de sangre'*, purity of blood, in Spain. Above all they hated Jews. One Christian friar wrote this about them:

[The Jews] have taken over all the tasks of artisans, and business dealings and likewise they serve as day labourers; and since their wages are low – for they are so tight-fisted they neither eat nor drink nor clothe themselves – Christian workers find no one to employ them. Even if a Christian finds a job, the pay is so low that he cannot live.

In 1391 mobs attacked the Jewish *aljamas* or ghettos in Toledo, Cordoba, Seville and Barcelona. Many Jews were killed. In addition,

Christians tried to convert Jews to their beliefs. Converts had to wear special clothes and hairstyles, and certain jobs were forbidden them. Moreover, no Jew could marry a Christian. One Jewish girl who wanted to marry a young Spaniard had her nose cut off.

Things came to a head in 1491. A vicious rumour was spread that a Christian boy had been hung on a cross by some Jewish fanatics near Toledo. Christian anger was aroused. Twelve Jews were captured and buried alive.

Ferdinand and Isabella decided to act firmly. In 1492 a decree stated that Jews should either go into exile or become Christians. They were given just four months to decide. Many were wealthy, but if they chose exile they had to leave 'gold, silver, money, horses and weapons' behind. Perhaps as many as half a million Jews left the country, but many were hard-working businessmen and craftsmen. Spain could ill afford to lose them.

### The decline of Spain

The reign of Philip II saw Spain's 'Golden Age'. But it also saw the beginning of her rapid collapse. The magnificent Armada was humbled by the English fleet in 1588; Spanish treasure ships were robbed by Drake and other English pirates. The Dutch rebelled, and, with English help, Holland and other northern provinces secured their freedom from Spanish control. And all these wars cost money. Taxes on the Spanish people were increased.

In addition, bad harvests and a series of severe plagues hit the people between 1599 and 1610. Philip's successors were too weak to deal with the crises. France captured several Spanish fortresses in the Thirty Years War, and revolts in Catalonia in 1639 and Portugal in 1640 finally weakened the monarchy. Spain's Golden Age was over.

| | |
|---|---|
| 1469 | Marriage of Ferdinand and Isabella |
| 1492 | Columbus discovered the New World |
| 1571 | Battle of Lepanto |
| 1588 | Defeat of the Armada |
| 1598 | Death of Philip II |

## Using the evidence: the methods of the Spanish Inquisition

The Spanish Inquisition was begun by Ferdinand and Isabella in 1478. Special priests were to check that no Spaniard held beliefs of which the Church did not approve. At first it was unpopular: it punished by fines and all its methods were secret. But in 1485 it was directed at the Jews and from then on many Spaniards supported it.

Once a person was brought before the Inquisitors, a case was made out. The person was arrested and imprisoned. Sometimes he stayed in

*Don John of Austria*

jail for years with no trial. Sometimes he might be tortured to confess his guilt. He was never told who betrayed him or why he was arrested. Only at his trial was he accused; but he could not defend himself. He had a lawyer, one of the Inquisitors, but he could not cross-examine witnesses. If he was found guilty, punishment followed.

The Inquisition had three occasions to use violence on its victims: the period in prison; torture before the trial, and the punishment. How brutal were the Inquisitors?

*Primary evidence*

Here is the evidence of one prisoner about the jails:

(1) The gaoler addressed to me a little sermon, recommending me to serve in this respectable house with great propriety; stating also that I must make no noise in my room, lest I disturb the other prisoners in theirs. My cell was 3.6 metres by 2.4 metres with a door leading to the passage. . . . In it were a wooden frame without feet, whereon lay a straw mattress, which was to be my bed; a small water pot and another utensil for various purposes, which was only to be emptied every eight days, when I was allowed out to go to mass in the prisoners' chapel. This was the only fresh air I had. . . . The cell floor was of brick, the walls of stone and very thick. The place was consequently very cold in winter and so damp that frequently gates were covered with drops of water. And my clothes were always wet. I stayed in this prison for three years.

(2) Torture was regularly used to extract confession. One Dutchman was placed on the rack in 1597. He was given three turns of the cord: 'On being given these he said first, "Oh God!" and then, "There is no mercy". After the turns he was warned and said, "I don't know what to say. Oh dear God!" Then three more turns of the cord were ordered to be given, and after two of them he said "Oh God, oh God, there's no mercy, Oh God, help me".' After three more turns of the cord, he confessed.

A woman who was being tortured was clearly very confused.

She said, 'I don't remember, take me away, I did what the witnesses say.' She was told to tell in detail what the witnesses said. She said, 'Senor, as I have told you, I do not know for certain. I have said that I did all that the witnesses say. Senores, release me for I do not remember it.'

(3) Punishments for those convicted varied. At a public ceremony, many were forced to 'declare their faith'. They wore the 'San benito', a garment of disgrace. The worst punishment was burning alive, though some victims were mercifully strangled beforehand. Between 1575 and 1610 the following decisions were made in Toledo:

| | | | |
|---|---|---|---|
| San benito | 186 | Slavery in the galleys | 91 |
| Confiscation of property | 185 | Burning at the stake | 15 |
| Imprisonment | 175 | Burning in effigy | 18 |
| Exile | 167 | Reprimand | 56 |
| Scourging | | Acquitted | 51 |
| (whipping in the streets) | 133 | Case dismissed | 128 |

*Some punishments imposed by the Inquisition.*

*The tortures of the Inquisition, as engraved for a seventeenth-century manuscript. Note that a scribe is writing down details of any confession*

*Some other factors*

(4) In making up their minds, historians must consider the following points.

(i) Torture was very common in sixteenth-century trials, except in England.

(ii) In 1561, the Inquisitors were instructed to 'take care that the sentence of torture is justified by law, reason and conscience'.

(iii) One historian estimated that in Toledo between 1575 and 1610 only 32 per cent of those who could legally have been tortured actually were.

(iv) All confessions under torture had to be repeated in court the next day.

(v) One eighty-year-old man defended himself successfully by saying he lost his memory. One thirteen-year-old girl, who was tortured, did not confess and was acquitted.

One judgement on the brutality was written in 1599 by an Englishman in Barcelona.

(5) Not far from the cathedral and next to the episcopal palace is the palace of the Inquisition. It is an enormous building and very high, with a facade ornamented with large beautiful windows. Each time that I passed this building my thoughts turned to the cruelties which are committed there, and which are described in the great book of *Martyrs*. Any man who is suspected by his conduct or his speech of . . . not finding everything perfect that is Catholic, is at once denounced to the Jesuit inquisitors and promptly incarcerated in this palace, charged with heresy. After a few days, or a few months, as the fathers think fit, one of them comes to interrogate him on the reasons for his detention, or to acquaint him with them, if he does not know. If he says that he is a Catholic, they ask him his age and where he was born, and where he made his last confession and his last communion, and his answers are at once checked by the spies whom the Jesuits have everywhere. If the prisoner has lied, or if he contradicts himself during the inquiry, without further ado he is burned alive as a heretic, for having misled the Holy Office.

## Questions and further work

1  How many victims were found guilty between 1575 and 1610 in Toledo? How many were acquitted or dismissed? What percentage of those tried were punished? What percentage of those tried were burned at the stake? What percentage of those tried were punished by some violent means?

2  In the list of five points, which ones suggest that the Inquisition was not particularly brutal? Why?

3  What is the author's judgement in Document 5? Which words or phrases tell you?

4  Write an essay to argue either (a) that 'The Inquisition was a brutal office that protected Catholics by violent means', or (b) that it was not.

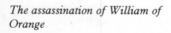

# 8 The Netherlands

### The murder of William the Silent

One Sunday evening in March 1582, the prince of Orange led his family and a few intimate friends from the table after their evening meal. They walked over to admire a new tapestry on the wall of the antechamber. Behind them, the prince's bodyguard kept their distance. The prince insisted on this, so that the crowds who thronged the antechamber could see him.

Suddenly a young Frenchman pushed his way violently through the crowd. He ran quickly towards the prince, drew a pistol and fired. Within seconds the assassin was dead, butchered by the swords of the bodyguard. But fortunately the prince survived. The bullet passed upwards through his mouth and out of his cheek. Within a week he was fully recovered.

The prince of Orange was named William. He was shaken by his ordeal, but this was not the first attempt on his life, and he suspected others would follow. With great determination, he did not hide himself.

On Tuesday, 10 July 1584, William again led his family away from the dinner table, this time in the royal palace at Delft. Again an assassin approached, an apprentice cabinet-maker called Balthazar Gérard who had bought a gun with money he had been given by William. The aim this time was more careful. The bullet pierced William's stomach and lungs. He died almost immediately.

In spite of recent events, William was not prepared for death. He had made no will. 'My Lord always thought', wrote Maria, his eldest daughter, 'that there was no hurry.' William's last words were 'My God, have pity on my poor people.' He was buried at the New Church in

*The assassination of William of Orange*

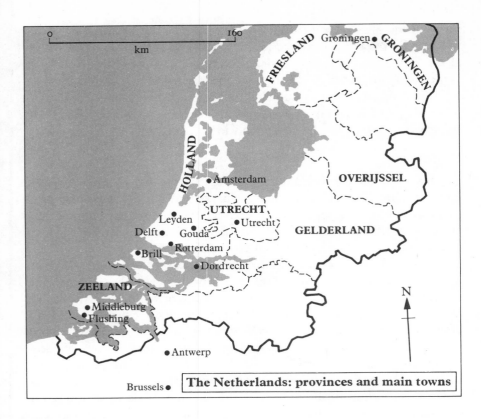

The Netherlands: provinces and main towns

Delft. On his tomb is the following inscription: 'William of Nassau, Father of the Fatherland, who valued the fortunes of the Netherlands above his own.' Public grief at his death was great. Gérard was tortured most brutally before his execution.

Who was William of Nassau, prince of Orange? Why did men want to murder him? Why did his death bring such sorrow to the Dutch people?

## William's early life

'Juliana von Stolberg, Countess and Lady of Nassau, between two and three in the morning, but nearer to three, gave birth to an infant of the male sex: he shall be called William.' These words were written by William's father, the count of Nassau, in 1533. He was forty-six, his wife just twenty-six.

Tradition has it that, at the birth, the count had his son's fortune told. The forecast was amazing. The child was to amass great wealth, face many problems in middle age, and die a violent death. No one believed it. To begin with, the family was poor: the count lived simply in his castle at Dillenburg and managed his estates himself.

Yet when William was aged just eleven, the first part of the prophecy came true. His older cousin, the prince of Orange, had no male heir. In 1544 he went off to war and named William as his heir before he went. No one thought much about it – until the prince was killed in battle. Messengers hastened to Dillenburg. Young William suddenly found himself one of the greatest landowners in the Low Countries.

Later that year he was taken by his father to Brussels and left there alone. He was allowed no friends, no companion, no servant. At first he was terribly homesick for his mother, brothers and sisters. Yet he soon adjusted: his good looks (blue eyes, brown hair, handsome features), a good sense of humour and native intelligence all helped him. He became fascinated by the sights and life of Brussels.

### Spanish rule of the Netherlands

At this time the Netherlands were part of the world-wide Spanish Empire. King Philip II ruled through his regent, the Duchess Margaret of Parma. She was supposed to consult the great nobles, including William, on the Council of State, but in practice she ruled with the help of Spanish advisers like Cardinal Granvelle.

In 1563 Margaret imposed a heavy new tax on the people. William and some friends threatened to resign as a protest, and there was rioting in the streets of Brussels. Granvelle decided to bring in Spanish troops. William went in person to see the duchess. He told her that he could not control the crowds unless Granvelle was expelled. Margaret sent word of this to King Philip, but at first he refused, fearing loss of face. Eventually he summoned Granvelle to return to Spain to see his 'dying mother'. Honour and the Dutch were satisfied. 'It is certain that the cardinal is leaving,' William wrote to his brother. 'God send him so far away that he never returns.' It had been a tough baptism for William. From now on he was to lead the opposition to Spain.

Two factors caused further unrest. Margaret of Parma tried to insist that all people should attend Catholic services, and ordered that no one was to become a Protestant. Secondly, these were years of high unemployment for the people. Many workers, like the Antwerp dockers, found work only at certain times of year. And the price of corn was rising. In August 1566, stirred up by Protestant preachers, people in the cities started to riot. In Antwerp, Delft, the Hague, Utrecht, they sacked churches, smashed windows, murdered Catholic priests.

King Philip was furious. A new regent was sent to replace Margaret. He was the duke of Alva, a soldier ready to use force on the people of the Netherlands. Immediately Alva set up his 'Council of Blood'. He arrested suspects and publicly hanged traitors and heretics. Two nobles, counts Egmont and Horn, were imprisoned as hostages for the good behaviour of the people. William wisely retreated to the security of Dillenburg.

In addition, Alva introduced a new 10 per cent tax on all sales. Traders and artisans were horrified. Further rioting took place. In 1568 Alva's army caught some Dutch troops in a skirmish and was defeated. But Dutch rejoicing was short-lived. In revenge, Alva brought Egmont and Horn from Ghent to Brussels and had them executed. In Dillenburg William was horrified at the news. He felt he had to do something.

*The Duke of Alva*

*Rioting at Antwerp, 1567*

*The harbour at Amsterdam*

## The Dutch secure their independence, 1572–9

As discontent spread, so many men took to robbery and violence. Gangs roamed the woods (Wild Beggars) and the Channel (Sea Beggars) attacking Philip's troops whenever they could. Their song rang through the land:

> O Netherlands, behold your choice,
> For death or life now give your voice.
> Or serve the tyrant king of Spain,
> Or follow now to break your chain
> The prince of Orange.

*Breughel's* The Massacre of the Innocents

Other propaganda was made by painters. Peter Breughel painted *The Massacre of the Innocents* which showed Dutch peasant women holding their babies, butchered by the armies of Spain.

Then in 1572 the Sea Beggars had a stroke of luck. After they had been refused permission to refuel and restock their ships in England, they sailed desperately to the port of Brill on the Dutch coast. They had just twenty-five ships and 200 men. But, by chance, the Spanish garrison of the port had been called away. The Beggars were cheered in by the local people and the Orange flag was flown above the town.

Heartened by this success, William's brother Louis of Nassau took the main Sea Beggar fleet up the Channel. They captured Flushing, then Rotterdam. Other towns overthrew their Spanish lords. Alva sent a messenger to Flushing to demand his rights. But the crowd laughed at the man and sent him back with a message: 'Let the duke come himself. We'll eat him alive.' William was now declared 'stadtholder of the Dutch Provinces'.

The next seven years saw an uncompromising struggle. In 1574 William captured Middleburg, but the following year he saw four of his brothers, including Louis, killed at the battle of Mook Heide. William, exhausted by effort and strain, was taken ill. The Spanish armies put on more pressure. The city of Leyden was besieged and seemed likely to fall. But the citizens bravely opened the dykes and flooded their homes rather than give in to the Spanish troops. William took heart from their courage. One writer said of him at this time, 'The prince is a rare man, of great authority, universally loved, very wise in all things. . . . He is not dismayed by any loss or defeat.' William continued to fight and in 1579 the seven Northern Provinces – Holland, Zeeland, Groningen, Gelderland, Overijssel, Friesland and Utrecht – joined together by the Union of Utrecht and broke away from Spanish rule.

Could they keep their freedom? William was murdered but his family carried on the fight. His son Maurice of Nassau became stadtholder and collected a powerful army together. Help arrived from England: Queen Elizabeth sent the earl of Leicester with 4000 infantry and 400 cavalry. Prince Maurice captured Breda in 1590 and ten years later won a great victory over the Spaniards at Nieuport. King Philip himself died in 1598 and in 1609 Spain sued for peace. William of Orange and his family had helped to create the Dutch Republic, the 'United Provinces'.

## The land and its people

The land of the United Provinces is nicknamed 'The Hard-Won Land'. Much of it lies below the level of the sea. Its three great rivers, the Rhine, Meuse and Scheldt, brought down sand and silt, and marshland or *hol-land* was built up. In the Middle Ages, the Dutch people saw that this could be good farming land, so they built dams as a wall against the sea and drainage to pump water away and the land began to be farmed. 'God created the world,' said one writer, 'but the Dutchmen made Holland.'

In the seventeenth century the work was continued. Between 1590 and 1615 nearly 40 000 hectares of marshland were drained and put under the plough. In 1616 the Beemster lake, 3600 hectares in area, was drained and polder dams were put around it. Families moved into the land and farming began. But, tragically, one of the polders broke and the land was flooded. Yet the determined Dutch people drained it a second time. Between 1615 and 1640 a further 44 000 hectares were added.

The people were hard-working, independent, proud. They used their new land well. They first planted rape-seed and cole-seed, useful cattle fodder which also drained the salt from the soil. Then they rotated crops scientifically: wheat, turnips or carrots, oats, clover. The turnips and clover helped to enrich the soil and provide fodder for cattle. The Friesian breed of cattle, the 'long-legged, short-horned, cow of the Dutch breed', became world-famous for the quality of its milk.

In the Province of Holland, many of the inhabitants lived in towns. There were 100 000 people in Amsterdam alone. Here industries grew up. Ships were built at the wharves along the great rivers. Sails and ropes were made, salt was treated, fish were loaded. Inland, fine textiles were made. Leyden became a world centre for cloth manufacture, Haarlem made linen and Utrecht magnificent velvet. The people of Amsterdam imported silk from China and Persia and wove it into

*De Hoche*, The Backyard Scene

beautiful fabric, for sale throughout the countries of the West.

Much of the wealth of the Netherlands came from the sea. It is estimated that the Provinces had 80 000 sailors, one in ten of the population. Every year, Dutch ships brought in an average of 568 000 tonnes of fish, more than the rest of Europe combined. The invention of the *fluit* or flyboat, an ocean-going ship with a huge hull for storage, then gave them the chance to trade. Dutch sailors carried corn, iron, timber and other products from the Baltic to southern Europe. On the return voyage they carried precious cargoes of salt from the Bay of Biscay. 'The riches and multitude of their shipping', said one London merchant, 'is the envy of the present and may be the wonder of all future generations.'

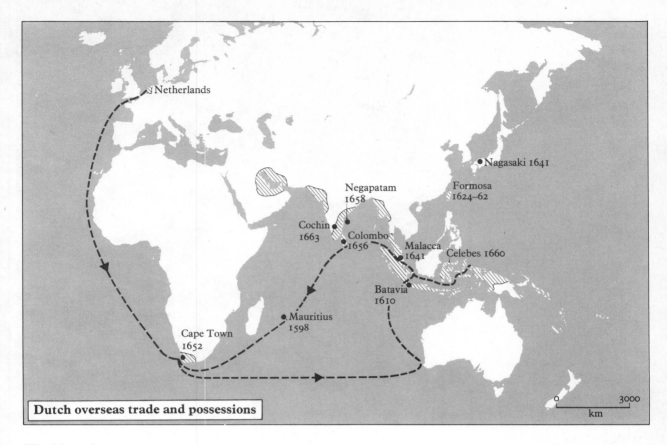

**Dutch overseas trade and possessions**

Map labels: Netherlands · Nagasaki 1641 · Formosa 1624–62 · Negapatam 1658 · Cochin 1663 · Colombo 1656 · Malacca 1641 · Celebes 1660 · Batavia 1610 · Mauritius 1598 · Cape Town 1652 · 3000 km

## World trade

Long before the end of the sixteenth century, Dutch traders had been exploring the islands and seas of the East. For two hundred years the ships of Portugal had patrolled these waters, carrying spices, pepper and luxury goods home to the West. Between 1598 and 1602, fifty-one Dutch ships sailed from the Netherlands to the East. They sailed from six different Dutch ports: Amsterdam, Middleburgh, Delft, Rotterdam, Hoorn and Enkhuizen. One fleet reached the Moluccas in 1599, loaded up with spices and returned home, all within a space of fourteen months. The sale of the goods brought huge profits.

A number of merchants now felt that it was time to organise such expeditions on a large scale. In 1602, therefore, they formed the Dutch East India Company. Seventeen directors (Heeren XVII) controlled the company from Amsterdam. They supplied ships, paid the captains, arranged protection and shared out the profits. In just over fifty years the company had over 100 ships, each of about 600 tonnes, carrying luxury goods back to the West.

The Heeren at Amsterdam were cautious, peaceful traders. But some of their sailors were more adventurous. One captain, Jan Pieterszoon Coen, hated the rival English and Portuguese sailors. He gave this advice to the Heeren in 1614:

*De Hoche,* Interior of a Dutch House

Your Honours should know that trade in Asia must be driven and protected by Your Honours' own weapons. The weapons must be paid for by the profits from trade. We cannot carry on trade without war.

Even if the Heeren objected to Coen's advice, they could do little. The spice islands were at least a nine-month sea voyage away from Amsterdam. So Coen and his followers used their own approach. The Company traded with many islands. Coen quickly realised that he needed one strong, well-fortified, central base. He chose Batavia, a small port on the island of Java. On 30 May 1619 he took it by force from the local sultan, although the Heeren had ordered him to negotiate peacefully.

Thereafter all Dutch ships sailed round the Cape and across the Indian Ocean direct to Batavia. All trade from the spice islands was taken there for collection and shipment. No rival could steal the goods or the profits. Moreover, the island served as a good base to conquer further trading posts all over the East. In 1641 Van Diemen captured Malacca and by 1658 a long war with the Portuguese in Ceylon ended with victory for the Dutch. In 1661 a war with the native peoples of Macassar gave the Dutch control of the town and in 1684 the pepper-rich sultanate of Bantam was captured. The warlike East India Company had removed all its rivals and now reigned supreme.

After 1619 a clear timetable of voyages was arranged. Three fleets left Amsterdam each year. One left in September, the others at Christmas and Easter. The first was the biggest, since it arrived in Batavia in April and goods could then be shipped to other islands before the next monsoon. Two annual return journeys were made, one in December, the other February. After 1652 all fleets called at the Cape for fresh water and food.

The wealth of the company was based on spices: pepper, nutmeg, cloves were all used in cooking throughout Europe. Such goods earned high profits. Ships also carried cottons and silks and later, from Ceylon, tea and coffee. Occasionally there was a cargo of slaves from Bali or elephants from Ceylon.

In the West, Dutch traders were much less successful. A Dutch fleet had sailed to the West Indies in 1590 in search of salt, but found stern opposition from the Spaniards. Many sailors were caught and sent by King Philip II to the galleys as slaves. The Dutch were outraged and determined to carry on the trade. In addition, Dutch trappers sailed to North America to seek beaver-skins. In 1609 Henryk Hudson sailed up the Hudson River and a small settlement, New Amsterdam, was started. In 1621 a West India Company was formed, but its ships spent more time in plundering Spanish merchantmen than they did in trade.

| 1579 | Union of Utrecht |
| 1584 | Assassination of William of Orange |
| 1602 | Formation of the East India Company |
| 1609 | Peace with Spain: the United Provinces recognised |

*Van Ruisdael*, The Mill

## Using the evidence: everyday life

*De Witte,* Interior with a Woman playing the Harpsichord

A town-house kitchen:

(1) In every house there was either a kitchen, a recess, or some kind of space where meals were prepared. In poor people's homes it was an alcove from which smoke, reeking with cooking odours, filled every corner of the house whenever the chimney was blocked.... Copper and pewter utensils shone all along the walls.... A glass-fronted cupboard contained the crockery, while another cupboard ... held provisions, the table linen in use at the time, sauceboats and trenchers. An enormous chimneypiece dominated one side of the room; the hearth, with its tarred rear-wall contained the fire-pot, a kind of primitive stove open at the top, and on it the stew pan. A small copper sink could be filled from a tap fed by a pump.... The walls of the room were whitewashed.

P. Zumthor, *Daily Life in Rembrandt's Holland*, Weidenfeld & Nicolson, 1962

*Vermeer,* The Maidservant pouring Milk

The house of a peasant:

(2) Peasant houses consisted of one large central room at ground level.... Furniture was more basic than in town.... A few chairs, a table, some chests and a spinning wheel would be considered sufficient furnishing.... The use of the chimney was unknown. Fires would be laid on the ground itself. Interior shutters of plain wood closed the few windows. The 'sleeping cupboards' were ranged around the central room, hidden during the day by doors or curtains. The walls remained bare, except perhaps in the case of prosperous peasants who would nail up small shelves on which they would display a few painted dishes.

P. Zumthor

*Vermeer*, The Little Street

*De Hoche*, A Mother's Duty

**Furniture:**

(3) As for domestic furniture, Holland is unsurpassed in neatness and elegance.

Erasmus, *Adages*, 1500

*A Dutch engraved table of the seventeenth century*

**The poor:**

(4) The dwellings of the poor were not so neat as the rooms we see in Vermeer's paintings, their clothing not so fine as that of the ladies and gentlemen portrayed by Rembrandt. Low pay was normal. Holidays were unknown. There was no respite on Sundays.... It was truly said that in Amsterdam, contagious diseases which took the lives of thousands of poor people, never afflicted 'burgomasters, aristocrats, ministers of the Church or town officials'.

It is only too true that the masses of the townspeople received a very small share in Dutch profits. Women and children were used as workers because they were 'cheaper'. Children of six years of age were forced to work as long as daylight permitted.

B. H. M. Vlekke, *Evolution of the Dutch Nation*, 1951

## *Questions and further work*

1 Look carefully at the illustrations and describe, in your own words, (a) the furniture, (b) the clothes people are wearing, (c) the household implements.
2 Make a list of the differences between the inside of a town house (Document 1) and that of a country house (Document 2). Which types of house do the pictures portray?
3 What opinions are expressed in Document 4? What other evidence supports these opinions?
4 What opinion does Erasmus express in Document 3? Which Documents support his view? Which do not?
5 Using the visuals and the Documents, describe one day in the life of the wife of a poor town artisan.

# Elizabeth I and the Stuarts

## 9 Queen Elizabeth (1558–1603)

### The young princess

In the evening of 7 September 1533, a beautiful dark-haired young lady lay in the agony of childbirth in a sumptuous bed in the royal palace at Greenwich. She was Anne Boleyn, queen of England and second wife of King Henry VIII. Soon her first child would be born. Her husband, now forty-two years of age, desperately wanted a son to succeed him on the throne. Doctors and soothsayers were confident that the child would be a boy. The name – Henry or Edward – had been picked. A tournament and other celebrations were prepared.

By nightfall, bells rang out, the waiting crowd cheered. But Anne did not produce the longed-for son; instead the crowds celebrated the birth of a daughter, Princess Elizabeth. Three years later Anne was executed as a traitor: Henry needed an heir and Anne had to be removed to allow him to remarry. So Elizabeth grew up under the care of governesses and tutors. She was a lively and intelligent girl, cared for by her father and particularly by his sixth wife Catherine Parr. She learned Latin and Greek as well as French and Italian and she also read widely in religion and the classics. She could ride and embroider, and by her father's death in 1547 she seemed an attractive and confident princess.

After 1547 she certainly needed all her qualities. She was third in line to the throne, after her sickly nine-year-old brother Edward, who became king, and her much older sister Mary. Two regents, the duke of Somerset and the earl of Warwick, plotted in turn to gain power over the young king, and Elizabeth figured in both schemes. Somerset planned to marry her himself and Warwick wanted her to marry his son. Then, when Edward was replaced by the Catholic Mary, Elizabeth was imprisoned in the Tower for refusing to worship in the Roman Catholic manner. She was interrogated but she was careful never to admit her real beliefs, and Mary would never allow her sister to be executed.

### The new queen

In 1558 Mary died, and a messenger from her husband, King Philip II of Spain, came to England to claim the throne for his master. Instead the messenger found a new queen and he wrote home, 'She seems to me incomparably more feared than her sister, and gives her orders and has her way as absolutely as her father did.'

Elizabeth was certainly the ruler of England: after her death it was said of her: 'When she smiled, it was pure sunshine that everyone did choose to bask in, if they could. But anon came a storm from a sudden gathering of clouds and the thunder fell in wondrous manner on all alike.' One foreign visitor to her court described her like this:

That day she was dressed in white silk, bordered with pearls the size of beans, and over it a mantle of black silk, shot with silver threads. . . . As she went along in all this state and magnificence, she spoke very graciously, first to one, then to another . . . in English, French and Italian. . . . Whoever speaks to her it is kneeling; now and then she raises some with her hand. While we were there, W. Slavata, a Bohemian baron, had letters to present to her; and she, after

*This picture of Queen Elizabeth is in the National Portrait Gallery, London. What is she standing on?*

pulling off her glove, gave him her right hand to kiss, sparkling with rings and jewels, a mark of particular favour. Wherever she turned her face as she went along, everybody fell down on their knees. . . . Petitions were presented to her, and she received them most graciously, which occasioned the acclamation of 'long live Queen Elizabeth!' She answered it with, 'I thank you, my good people'.

One of her greatest talents was the ability to choose good advisers. Her Chief Secretary was William Cecil, later Lord Burghley. She once

said to him, 'This judgement I have of you, that you will not be corrupted with any manner of gift and that you will be faithful to the state, and . . . give me that counsel that you think best.' Her judgement was proved correct. Cecil often disagreed with his queen, for instance over her refusal to marry, but he was always loyal and hard-working and his advice was good. In 1570 Cecil was made Treasurer and Sir Francis Walsingham became Chief Secretary. Walsingham was a withdrawn, severe Puritan, but he operated a secret service of spies and diplomats which uncovered every plot against Elizabeth's life.

## The religious settlement

When Elizabeth became queen in 1558, many Catholics and Protestants looked to her for support. Her father had broken the pope's control of the Church, but her sister Mary had returned to the old Catholic ways. What was she to do? Her own beliefs were probably Protestant, but, more important, she wanted to keep her country united and avoid the kind of civil war which was already beginning in France and elsewhere.

Her policy was to hold a middle path between Catholics and Protestants, to try to keep everyone loyal. In 1559 she persuaded Parliament to pass an Act of Supremacy and an Act of Uniformity:

*Act of Supremacy*   1 All Mary's religious laws were swept away
                  2 Elizabeth became Head of the Church of England

*A meeting of Convocation. These churchmen helped Elizabeth to steer her middle path in religion*

*John Whitgift, Archbishop of Canterbury from 1583. A moderate, he helped Elizabeth to set up the Church of England*

| | |
|---|---|
| *Act of Uniformity* | 1 The English Book of Common Prayer was to be used for all services |
| | 2 All Englishmen must attend services |
| | 3 Those who did not would be fined |

These and later religious policies were largely the work of three Archbishops of Canterbury: Matthew Parker, Edmund Grindal and John Whitgift.

## The Catholic problem

Catholics could not accept the two Acts of 1559, and so were always a potential threat to Elizabeth. Some obeyed the pope, the head of their church, in Rome, and plotted to murder Elizabeth. Others simply refused to worship in Elizabeth's churches. Wandering preachers, trained in France and Italy, came to spread their faith secretly in England. Two such men, Edmund Campion and Robert Parsons, set out on a preaching tour in 1580:

> We passed through most of the shires of England, preaching and administering the sacraments in almost every gentleman and nobleman's house that we passed by, whether he himself were a Catholic or no, if he had any Catholics in the house. . . . Sometimes when we are sitting at table, quite cheerfully conversing about matters of faith . . . if it happens that someone rings at the front door a little insistently, so that it can be put down as an official, immediately like deer that have heard the voice of hunters and prick their ears and look alert, all stop eating and commend themselves to God in the briefest of prayers. No word or sound is heard until the servants report what is the matter.

Can you imagine how their hosts felt at the prospect of being found out? Not all Catholics were disloyal to Elizabeth, but her spies closed in on such preachers. Campion was arrested, tried and executed in 1581;

*Robert Parsons and Edmund Campion on a preaching tour of England*

Parsons was forced to flee abroad.

Some Catholics were tortured. John Gerard was one of these. He was born in 1565, the son of a Catholic who later took part in revolts against the queen. He was educated at a Catholic school in France and in 1588 he returned to England as a preacher. He hid with a family in Norfolk and on one occasion stood for four hours, up to his knees in water, in the secret priest's hole of a manor house, while the house was being searched. Later he was betrayed and tortured:

Then they took me to a big upright pillar, one of the wooden posts which held the roof of this huge underground chamber. Driven into the top of it were iron staples for supporting heavy weights. Then they put my wrists into iron gauntlets and ordered me to climb two or three wicker steps.... Then, removing the wicker steps, one by one from under my feet, they left me hanging by my hands and arms fastened above my head....

Hanging like this I began to pray. The gentlemen standing around me now asked me whether I was willing to confess.

'I cannot and will not,' I answered.

But I could hardly utter the words, such a gripping pain came over me.... The pain was so intense that I thought I could not possibly endure it. Added to it I had an interior temptation. But with the temptation the Lord gave me relief. Seeing my agony and the struggle going on in my mind, He gave me this most merciful thought: the utmost and worst they can do is to kill you, and you have often wanted to give your life for your Lord God.... Some time after one o'clock, I think, I fainted.

Later Gerard was freed by some friends and he was still preaching in England when Elizabeth died. Few people were executed by Elizabeth. She preferred to punish by fine, imprisonment or exile.

*A Puritan family in Queen Elizabeth's time*

### The Puritans and Parliament

It was much more difficult for Elizabeth to deal with the Protestants called 'Puritans'. Many were wealthy and loyal to the crown, and some were members of Parliament. Parliament was an important body at this time. Most of the important laws were passed by the House of Commons and then the House of Lords before being sanctioned by the queen. In addition, Parliament had to approve any extra taxes which the queen wanted to raise for a particular purpose. The queen, therefore, needed Parliament's support. She could not afford to quarrel with it.

There were certain problems in Elizabeth's reign which the queen felt Parliament should not discuss:

|  | Elizabeth's view | Parliament's view |
|---|---|---|
| Queen's marriage | A private matter for Elizabeth to decide. | They should be consulted because a Protestant heir to the throne was needed. |
| Changes in religion | She should decide as 'Governor of the Church'. | They should be consulted since the people had to use the Prayer Book. |
| Free speech in Parliament | Parliament could discuss only those matters which she allowed. | They had to be free to discuss any matters which affected the people. |

Puritans believed that bishops were unnecessary, that there should be more preaching by ministers to their congregations and that the Prayer Book should be changed to allow them more freedom. Walter Strickland presented a bill to Parliament in 1571 to try to change things but he was hauled up before the Privy Council and banned from the Commons. In the same year Dr Thomas Cartwright published his *Admonition to Parliament* and the bishop of London wrote, 'The City will never be quiet until these authors of sedition, who are now esteemed as gods, be removed from the City.'

The chief spokesman of the Puritans was Peter Wentworth. He was a young, eloquent member of the Commons. In 1575 he made a forceful speech against the queen's policy, but Parliament stopped him before he could finish, and sent him to the Tower – perhaps for his own safety. Subsequently Wentworth raised the matter several times and each time was arrested by the Privy Council and imprisoned. Finally Elizabeth had to expressly forbid the Commons to discuss religious matters.

## Suitors for the queen

*The Earl of Essex*

The young Elizabeth certainly liked the company of men. She liked to be admired and she enjoyed the gaiety and laughter of the royal court. The men she admired were usually dashing, gallant and brave, men like Robert Dudley, the young earl of Leicester. When Elizabeth was ill with smallpox in 1562 and likely to die, she declared that she 'loved Lord Robert dearly, as God was her witness'. She might, in fact, have married him, but for the fact that two years earlier, his wife had been found lying dead at the foot of a staircase. No one knew how she died. Foul play was suspected but never proved. But Elizabeth was afraid that marriage to Leicester would set the gossips' tongues wagging.

Much later in the reign, after Leicester's death in 1584, Elizabeth became infatuated with the young earl of Essex. He was a brave and daring adventurer who seemed to sweep Elizabeth off her feet. He was forever disobeying her commands and going off on foreign expeditions, but she always forgave him.

In 1598, however, he disobeyed her once too often. In that year she made him Lord Deputy for Ireland and sent him to Dublin to quell an Irish revolt. He failed to do the job and on his return she had him arrested. He then formed a plot to capture the ageing queen. Elizabeth heard of it and summoned her favourite to explain himself. He failed to turn up, arrogantly believing he could not be condemned. But Elizabeth's patience had run out: Essex was declared a traitor and executed in the Tower in 1601.

In spite of her loves, however, Elizabeth would not marry. Many suitors wanted her hand. King Eric of Sweden was ready to embark for England in 1560 to woo her himself when a bad storm prevented his sailing. The queen mother of France was eager for Elizabeth to marry one of her sons to cement an Anglo-French alliance. But Elizabeth had to be careful. She saw herself as the bride and mother of England, and

*Robert Dudley, Earl of Leicester*

on one occasion she said to Leicester, 'God's death, my lord, I will have here but one mistress and no master.'

Her job was a full-time occupation: a husband would distract her. In addition, she and her country would have to take her husband's side in any quarrel – and that might not be in the country's best interests. Of course Parliament wanted Elizabeth to marry and have a son to succeed her, but she told them it was her private affair and none of their business.

## Mary, Queen of Scots

*The life of Mary Stuart, Queen of Scots, to 1569*

1542 Mary born, daughter of James V of Scotland; her father died; Mary became queen with her mother as regent

1558 Married Francis, dauphin of France. On the death of Mary Tudor, she claimed the English throne as a descendant of Henry VII

1561 Returned to Scotland after Francis' death

1566 Birth of her son, James

1568 Revolt of Scottish lords after the murder of Mary's husband Lord Darnley, and her sudden marriage to the earl of Bothwell; Mary abdicated and fled to England, leaving her baby son James VI as king of Scotland.

In 1568 Mary arrived in the north of England, just as rebellion was stirring. Many northerners preferred the traditional services and beliefs of the Catholic Church and distrusted any edict from London. The earls of Westmorland and Northumberland wanted to seize the queen, marry Mary to the earl of Norfolk and put them on the throne. Help would probably come from Spain: Mary told the Spanish ambassador, the meddlesome de Spes, 'If your master will help me, I shall be queen of England in three months, and mass shall be said all over the country.'

The situation was dangerous, but in 1569 Elizabeth got wind of the scheme. Norfolk was quickly arrested and imprisoned in the Tower. But still the plotting continued. Letters were sent to him concealed in bottles of wine and one of his servants got into the Tower as a guard.

At this point the northern earls met at Topcliffe in Yorkshire. Northumberland 'had no stomach for rebellion' but Westmorland 'threatened him with daggs' and they agreed to fight. On 15 November, their armies entered Durham, said mass in the cathedral and trampled on Elizabeth's Prayer Book. The earl of Sussex, the Lord President of the Council at York, was powerless against them, for he had only a small and badly equipped army. The rebels quickly marched south, heading for Tutbury where Mary was held prisoner.

In the nick of time Mary was removed to Coventry, and, perhaps because of the concentration of royal forces south of the Trent, the rebels hastily retreated into north Yorkshire. By 15 December the

*Part of a broadsheet which shows the main plots and conspiracies of Queen Elizabeth's reign*

plotters had dispersed and fled to Scotland without a fight. Their property was confiscated and their followers were treated harshly. Six hundred peasants were hanged. Norfolk remained in the Tower until Elizabeth forgave him and released him a year later.

Although the Northern Revolt was a disaster, English Catholics were encouraged. In 1570 the pope published a bull or decree excommunicating and deposing Elizabeth. This meant that any Catholic who assassinated the queen would be a hero. Philip II of Spain and his general in the Netherlands, the duke of Alva, were also anxious to stir up revolt.

As their agent they used an Italian banker called Roberto Ridolfi, who lived in London. It was to him that the pope sent copies of his bull for English publication. It was Ridolfi too who persuaded the weak-willed duke of Norfolk back into the plotting. After his release from the Tower, Norfolk took an oath to be loyal to Elizabeth. But Ridolfi promised him wealth and power, and Mary wrote loving letters to him and he agreed to join.

Their scheme was simple. Norfolk and other English Catholics were to rebel and release Mary from captivity; Alva was to send perhaps 10 000 men from the Netherlands; Elizabeth was to be deposed, and the Catholic faith restored. In March 1571 Ridolfi quietly left London for a European tour, to persuade Alva, the pope and Philip II to agree. Alva was a realistic soldier and knowing the dangers of the plan, he hesitated. But Rome and Madrid were more enthusiastic.

Unfortunately for the plot Ridolfi couldn't conceal his delight. He immediately sent a messenger to tell Norfolk the news, but the man was arrested at Dover. Cecil, the queen's secretary, knew something was afoot, but not all the messenger's letters were confiscated, and those that were were in code. At this point Cecil had a stroke of luck. Some servants of the duke of Norfolk were arrested on another matter in the north of England and under torture they revealed the whole plot. The conspirators were quickly rounded up. De Spes, the Spanish ambassador, was expelled in January 1572 and Norfolk was again imprisoned. Cecil, now Lord Burghley, wanted a speedy execution of Norfolk. The trial lasted a whole day (most unusual in the sixteenth century), and Norfolk was convicted of treason and sentenced to death.

Elizabeth, however, disliked the idea of execution. The date was fixed for 21 January, but she postponed it. Three further dates were fixed; all were countermanded. Burghley was exasperated: 'The Queen's Majesty,' he wrote, 'hath always been a merciful lady and by mercy hath taken more harm than by justice.' It was not until 2 June that Norfolk was finally beheaded. Parliament also wanted the execution of Mary, 'that monstrous and huge dragon'; one speaker suggested 'cut off her head and make no more ado about her'. But Elizabeth was unsympathetic and Mary remained a prisoner in Sheffield Castle under the supervision of the earl of Shrewsbury.

### The execution of Mary, Queen of Scots

In captivity, Mary's life was dull, but fairly free. She sewed and embroidered and sent Elizabeth presents of her work. Elizabeth treated her well: perhaps because they were related, both women and both queens. Walsingham had enough evidence to convict Mary of treason, but Elizabeth was unwilling to have her executed.

Between 1582 and 1586 a series of events, well-controlled by Walsingham and his network of spies, forced Elizabeth to give way. In 1582 Walsingham found that Mary had a regular and secret correspondence with the Spanish ambassador. She had suggested that the ambassador write his letters in alum soaked in a little clear water for twenty-four hours. The writing was then invisible unless soaked in water by the reader. Alternatively letters could be passed through her guards in the hollow high heels of shoes or slippers.

In the following year a Catholic gentleman called Sir Francis Throckmorton was shadowed by Walsingham's spies for six months before being arrested and tortured. On the rack he revealed Mary's relations with the Spanish ambassador and other plotters. All this information was communicated to Elizabeth.

The year 1584 was a time of Catholic unrest. Dr Parry, a member of Parliament, was executed for an attempt to kill the queen. In January 1585 Mary was moved to Chartley Manor and given a new jailer, a stern Puritan called Sir Amyas Paulet. Mary's secret post was completely stopped. By the end of the year her agents were desperate to reopen contact, so they sent a priest called Gilbert Gifford from France.

Walsingham was informed of the plan and he arrested Gifford at Dover and persuaded him to act as a double agent. A local brewer was then bribed by Walsingham to allow letters from Gifford to pass in sealed casks into Chartley and Mary's replies to come out in the empty casks. Of course, all letters which came from Mary's agents were intercepted, deciphered and copied by Walsingham before being passed in, and the same happened to Mary's replies as they came out. The trap was set and Mary knew nothing.

Soon afterwards several Catholic gentlemen led by one Anthony Babington plotted to kill the queen. Babington wrote to Mary to tell her she was to be released and Elizabeth murdered. Mary said that she fully supported the scheme. Both letters were copied by Walsingham. They served as incontrovertible proof of Mary's treason. The plotters were quickly rounded up and hung, drawn and quartered. Mary was arrested, found guilty by a special commission at Fotheringay Castle, and was executed in February 1587 after much delay.

*The trial of Mary, Queen of Scots*

*The execution of Mary, Queen of Scots, 1587*

At her execution Mary was brave and even humorous:

Her prayer being ended, the executioners, kneeling, desired her Grace to forgive them her death: who answered: 'I forgive you with all my heart, for now, I hope, you shall make an end of all my troubles.' Then they, with her two women, helping her up, began to disrobe her of her apparel; then she, laying her crucifix upon the stool, one of the executioners took from her neck the Agnus Dei, which she, laying hands off it, gave to one of her women, and told the executioner he should be answered money for it. Then she suffered them, with her two women, to disrobe her of her chain of pomander beads and all other her apparel most willingly, and with joy rather than sorrow, helped to make unready herself, putting on a pair of sleeves with her own hands which they had pulled off, and that with some haste, as if she had longed to be gone.

Then, groping for the block, she laid down her head, putting her chin over the block with both her hands, which, holding there still, had been cut off had they not been espied. Then lying upon the block most quietly, and stretching out her arms cried, *In manus tuas, Domine*, etc. three or four times. Then she, lying very still upon the block, one of the executioners holding her slightly with one of his hands, she endured two strokes of the other executioner with an axe, she making very small noise or none at all, and not stirring any part of her from the place where she lay....

### Elizabeth's last days

Wearied by all her responsibility, Elizabeth suffered much from the deaths of her closest advisers. Leicester died in 1588, Walsingham in 1590 and Lord Burghley in 1598. In 1600 she visited Sir Robert Sidney. 'Her Highness', he wrote, 'doth honour to my house by visiting me.... At going upstairs she called for a staff, and was much wearied in walking about the house.' By 1603 she suffered from loss of memory and 'a heavy dullness and a forwardness familiar to old age'. She sat alone for long periods in silence. On 24 March she died, and the reign of the Virgin Queen came to an end.

| | |
|---|---|
| 1558 | Elizabeth became Queen |
| 1559 | Acts of Supremacy and Uniformity |
| 1571 | Ridolfi Plot |
| 1587 | Execution of Mary, Queen of Scots |
| 1588 | Defeat of Spanish Armada |
| 1603 | Death of Elizabeth |

## *Using the evidence: the defeat of the Spanish Armada, 1588*

By 1588 King Philip II of Spain was still looking for revenge on England. Queen Elizabeth had succeeded his wife Mary to the throne, and her seamen, especially Sir Francis Drake, had been plundering the Spanish Main and the treasure ships that sailed to Spain. Elizabeth had also sent help to the Dutch rebels in the Spanish Netherlands, and Philip may have been anxious to convert England to Catholicism. There were many plots against Elizabeth, and Philip had become angry when in 1587 Mary, Queen of Scots had been executed.

On 9 May 1588 his mighty Armada was ready to sail from Lisbon. Heavy Atlantic gales and rain held them up. The pilots told the commander, the duke of Medina Sidonia, that the weather was more like December than May. Sidonia was a Spanish landowner with no experience of the sea. When invited by King Philip to lead the Armada, he replied:

(1) My health is bad and from my small experience of the water I know that I am always seasick. I have no money to spare. I am in debt by one million ducats and I have not a penny to spend on my clothes. This expedition is so great and its aims are so important that its leader ought to understand navigation and sea-fighting. I know nothing of either. Further I know none of the officers who are to serve under me and I know nothing of the state of England.

Philip wrote back to him, 'If you fail, you fail; but the cause being God's you cannot fail.' The fleet travelled only 250 kilometres in the first thirteen days and then off Corunna it was scattered by the worst storm of all. Many ships were forced out to sea by gales. It took valuable time to recover them. It was 29 July before the fleet reached the Lizard.

SHIPS

| | Spanish | | English |
|---|---|---|---|
| Galleons | 65 | Royal Navy galleys | 34 |
| | 65 | Storeships and smaller ships | 163 |
| | 130 | Total | 197 |

GUNS

| | Spanish | | English |
|---|---|---|---|
| | 124 | Gun-carrying ships | 172 |
| | 9 | Average guns per ship | 11.5 |
| | 163 | Cannons | 55 |
| | 326 | Periers (medium range) | 43 |
| | 635 | Culverines (short range) | 1874 |
| | 19 369 | Total shot thrown, in pounds | 14 677 |

MEN

| | Spanish | | English |
|---|---|---|---|
| | 18 973 | Soldiers | 1540 |
| | 8050 | Sailors | 14 385 |
| | 3633 | Others | – |
| | 30 656 | Total | 15 925 |

*Sir Francis Drake*

The commander of the English fleet was Lord Howard of Effingham. Second in command was Sir Francis Drake. This description of Drake was written by a Spanish captain after Drake had attacked his ship in 1579:

(2) On our part there was no resistance, nor had we more than six of our men awake on the whole boat, so they entered our ship with as little risk to themselves as though they were our friends. They did no personal harm to anyone, beyond seizing the swords and keys of the passengers. Having informed themselves as to who were on board ship, they ordered me to go in their boat to where their general was – a fact I was glad of, as it appeared to me that it gave me more time in which to recommend myself to God. But in a very short time we arrived where he was, on a very good galleon, as well-mounted with artillery as any I have seen in my life.

I found him promenading on deck, and on approaching him, I kissed his hands. He received me with a show of kindness, and took me to his cabin, where he bade me to be seated and said: 'I am a friend of those who tell me the truth, but with those who do not I get out of humour. Therefore you must tell me (for this is the best road to my favour) how much gold and silver does your ship carry?' I said to him, 'None.' He repeated the question. I answered, 'None, only some small plates that I use and some cups – that is all that is in her.'

He is called Francisco Drac, and is a man of about thirty-five years of age, low of stature, with a fair beard, and is one of the greatest mariners that sail the seas, both as a navigator and as a commander. His vessel is a galleon of nearly four hundred tons, and is a perfect sailer. She is manned with a hundred men, all of service, and of an age for warfare, and all are as practised therein as old soldiers from Italy could be. Each one takes particular pains to keep his arquebus clean. He treats them with affection, and they treat him with respect. He carries with him nine or ten cavaliers, cadets of English noblemen. These form a part of his council, which he calls together for even the most trivial matter, although he takes advice from no one. But he enjoys hearing what they say and afterwards issues his orders. He has no favourite.

There were many battles in the Channel. This woodcut shows how the English fireships sent in amongst the Spanish fleet at night forced them to cut their anchors and flee out of control before the wind.

the Inuincible Armada

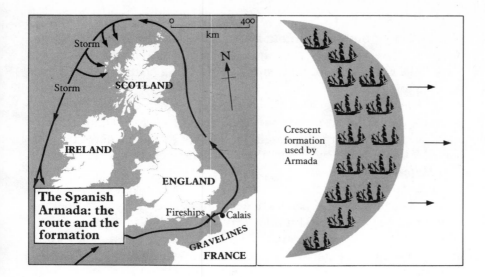

The Spanish Armada: the route and the formation

Crescent formation used by Armada

This letter, written soon after the Armada, gives one explanation of victory:

(3) From the 21st to the 26th they had skirmished and fired heavily at each other. But the Spaniards could not board, and the English, with their little ships, sailed so well and manoeuvred so skilfully, firing meanwhile, that the galleasses could not get at them.

This is Sir Walter Raleigh's explanation in his *History of the World*:

(4) Certainly he that will happily perform at sea must be skilful in making choice of weapons to fight in. . . . The Spaniards had an army aboard them and he (Hawkins) had none; they had more ships than he had and of a higher building and charging. So that, had he entangled himself with those great weapons, he had greatly endangered this kingdom.

But our admiral knew his advantage and held it . . . for a fleet of twenty ships, all good sailors and good ships, have the advantage on an open sea, of a hundred as good ships and of slower sailing.

*Sir Walter Raleigh*

## Questions and further work

1 The Duke of Medina-Sidonia gives several reasons for his unwillingness to lead the Armada (see Document 1). Which of these are genuine reasons, which are mere excuses? What can you learn from the Document about the duke?
2 Compare the two fleets. In what sort of fighting would the Spanish be successful? In what sort of battle would the English be likely to win?
3 Compare the qualities of leadership in the two commanders as revealed in Documents 1 and 2.
4 Documents 3 and 4 both try to explain why the Armada was defeated. On what points do they agree? Are they supported in the other Documents?

# 10 The court and city

London, the River Thames and London Bridge in the days of Queen Elizabeth

### An ambassador arrives, 1578

It was a bright but cold autumn afternoon in London. The tide of the River Thames was high, and the river drove powerfully against the bank. The water glinted in the sunlight as fishing boats and other craft plied to and fro.

On London Bridge a small crowd had gathered. One man was pointing down the river. There was a buzz of curious chatter. They could see the royal barge approaching. Perhaps the queen herself was on board! The crowd grew larger; there was some cheering. 'Hurrah for Her Majesty, the Queen!'

But as the barge passed quietly under London Bridge, it was clear that the queen was not aboard. On deck, alone, stood one man, looking with interest at all around him. He was tall, well-built, handsome. The crowd buzzed with excitement. 'Who is he?' some asked. They knew most of the queen's courtiers, but this man was new.

As the barge approached the royal palace of Whitehall the watermen,

dressed in scarlet, moved to their positions. The barge was moored carefully, and the man stepped on to the quay. He stopped and looked slowly around him. The air was cool and still as he climbed the stairway to the palace gate. The leaves from beech and oak trees lay over the dull green lawns of the palace gardens. Winter was coming. It was certainly colder in England than in France.

At the top of the stairway he was met by the queen's Lord Chancellor, Sir Christopher Hatton. 'Sir, you are welcome,' said Sir Christopher. He conducted the guest and his servants to the east wing of the royal palace. The servants carried trunks and packing cases. One of the trunks carried the initials 'J. de S.'

The man was Jean de Simier, ambassador from France. His master was the duke of Alençon, the king of France's brother. Simier had come to try and arrange a marriage between his master and Elizabeth, queen of England.

He was to stay in England for two weeks. What follows is a reconstruction of what Simier may have seen and heard during his visit.

Sir Christopher Hatton

### The queen's court

That evening, Simier was presented at court. He was led into the Privy Chamber for his first audience with the queen. This was a special honour for him, because the room was the queen's private sitting room. It was richly coloured. Around the walls were shelves of books, bound in red velvet with clasps of pearl or gold. Cushions and tapestries were also red and beautifully decorated. In one corner a pretty young girl of about fourteen was playing on a virginal, a small piano. Simier quickly surveyed the scene. But, as soon as he saw the queen, he relaxed.

Lord Burghley

She looked a marvellous figure. Now forty-six years old, she was still bright-eyed and alert. Her clothes were similar to those worn by the ladies at the French court, and there were pearls and jewels everywhere. Simier was struck by two ships, made out of pearls, which she wore in her hair. He noted the large stiff collar, the rich jewelled bodice, the wide puffed sleeves and the stiff hooped skirt.

The queen smiled and bade him welcome. He bowed low in respect. She asked after her 'little frog'. Everyone laughed. What did she mean? The queen observed Simier's confusion and explained that when his master Alençon had last been in England, that had been her nickname for him. Simier smiled.

He gave the queen a brooch of gold and rubies, a present from his master. She, in turn, gave him a purple garter. Simier thought that the chances of a marriage would be good.

At that point, Lord Burghley walked into the chamber. He was Lord High Treasurer and the queen's most trusted adviser. Simier knew that Burghley strongly favoured the marriage and they greeted each other warmly. Burghley invited Simier to stay for a few days with his family at Theobalds, his large country house in Hertfordshire. It would give Simier a chance to see the English countryside.

*A painting of the queen's court by
Marcus Gheerhaerts the Elder*

*The Great Hall of Hampton Court.
Banquets were often held here*

Simier happily accepted the invitation, and then left to dress for a banquet prepared in his honour that evening.

## A royal banquet

At the banquet, Simier found he was sitting on the queen's right with Burghley on her left. He was the guest of honour. Altogether there were about sixty guests, including some of Simier's friends from France. The meal was to begin.

First came a countess dressed in white silk who, after she had bowed three times in a most graceful manner, approached the table and rubbed the plates with bread and salt. Then the Yeomen of the Guard entered, bare-headed, clothed in scarlet with the design of a golden rose upon their backs, bringing in a course of dishes, served on gilt plates. These were placed on the table; then a lady taster gave each of the guards a mouthful of the particular dish he had brought, for fear of any poison. During the time that the guards (the tallest and stoutest men to be found in all England) were bringing dinner, twelve trumpets and two kettle-drums made the hall ring for half an hour.

As they were eating, Simier noticed much about the queen:

Her hands were small, her fingers long, and her stature neither tall nor low; her air was stately, her manner of speaking mild and obliging. Her bosom was uncovered, as all the English ladies have it, till they marry; and she had on a necklace of exceeding fine jewels. She was dressed in white silk, bordered with pearls the size of beans, and over it a mantle of black silk, shot with silver threads.

As they talked, the marriage was mentioned once or twice. But the queen said nothing definite about it.

Simier enjoyed the meal. But he was required to eat far too much. They started with 'tansies' (scrambled eggs made with cream and the juice of strawberry leaves and walnut buds). Then there followed several main courses, boiled, stewed, roast, and several fowls – Simier particularly enjoyed the mallard duck, but disliked the peacock. Burghley, laughing, told him that a peacock was only useful 'for keeping the yard clear of toads and newts'. The meal ended with Florentines (kidneys, herbs, eggs and cream baked in a pastry and served in a deep pewter dish). At the end Simier had to loosen his belt. Perhaps the best part of the meal was the wines: her Majesty told him with evident pleasure that all were from Bordeaux. This made him feel very proud.

After the meal, all the guests sat and watched a short play, performed by a company of actors. Lord Burghley introduced him to his son, Sir Thomas Cecil, who offered to show Simier around London next day. 'I know a tailor in Cornhill. No one knows London better than Master John Stow,' said Sir Thomas.

## The city of London

'We must start at the river Thames, the centre of our marvellous city,'

A cover for a copy of the New Testament. Elizabeth worked the embroidery herself

Queen Elizabeth I

said Master John Stow, when they met him next morning. 'London is the fairest, largest, richest and best-inhabited city in the world. And do you know what one Italian visitor told me recently?' Simier shook his head. 'He thought the Thames quite charming, full of swans white as snow.'

Simier remembered the smell and dirt of the river he had come up the day before. He wondered whether John Stow would show them the real London. But he did not have time to think about it for long, because they were off, heading towards the river.

By London Bridge they dismounted and climbed aboard a wherry, one of the many small boats which ferried passengers up, down and across the river.

In the autumn sunshine the river looked beautiful. Fishermen were drawing in their nets filled with salmon. On the south bank they could see the green fields and trees of Southwark while on the north side the large houses of the Strand with their long gardens, lawns and flower beds down to the river looked wealthy and magnificent. 'Perhaps that Italian was right after all,' said Simier.

Master Stow seemed to be reading his mind. 'Ah,' he said, 'not all London is so beautiful.' They passed under one of the twenty arches of London Bridge and Master Stow pointed to Barkingside and Limehouse. Simier thought he'd misjudged the man:

'There', he said, 'is where the sailors live. We have some desperate cutters who always carry two rapiers or two daggers, and in every drunken fray they are known to work much mischief with them. No man travels without his sword or some such weapon.'

Such thoughts made Master Stow unhappy. 'Why don't we climb the Tower,' said Sir Thomas, to cheer them up. 'From the top you can see the whole of London.'

As they approached the Tower, John Stow told them about it.

'This tower is a citadel, to defend or command the city, a royal place for assemblies and treaties, a prison for the most dangerous offenders, the only place of coinage for all England at this time, the armoury, and the treasury of the ornaments and jewels of the crown. And as well as all that the records of the king's courts of justice are kept here.'

As they climbed a circular staircase in the Tower, Master Stow remarked that they were fortunate to have such a clear day. 'We have such thick fog sometimes in autumn that you can see very little,' he added. From the top they could see the city laid out below, with its narrow streets and high houses and shops, Westminster away to the west, and the fields and bear pits of Southwark across the river. To the north, fields and woods surrounded the parishes of St Pancras, Paddington and St Giles. Stow pointed out the tavern at St Giles where convicted criminals on their way to be hung at Tyburn were given their last drink. And there was St Paul's, and there the newly opened Royal Exchange where merchants from all over the world met to discuss trade and business.

*This picture of the Tower of London was drawn by a Dutch visitor in 1615*

'Come on,' said Stow at last, 'I want to show you the real London. The houses of the citizens are very narrow at the front, but are built five or six roofs high, commonly of timber and clay with plaster. . . . The whole room towards the streets may be reserved for the shops of tradesmen.' They wandered round the narrow streets looking at the shops: the goldsmiths in Cheapside, the butchers of East Cheap and John Stow's own tailor's shop in Cornhill.

At last they came to St Paul's. The church was full of people – gentlemen and lawyers as well as beggars, ruffians, and cut-throats. The central nave of the church was filled with such people arguing, fighting, doing business.

Simier asked Master Stow if this always happened in the churches of London. The tailor sighed.

'There's a lot I don't like about London these days,' he said. 'The number of drays, carts and coaches is dangerous, as is proved every day. The coachman rides behind the horse's tails, lashing them and not looking behind him. The drayman sits and sleeps on his dray and lets his horse lead him home. I know that by the good laws and customs of this city, carts are forbidden to enter, but in recent years they have become very common.'

Like many old people, Master Stow did not like new things. 'Ah dear, the place gets bigger and noisier every year,' lamented the old tailor. When he saw the rubbish in the streets he was ashamed of his city. And there had been so much building in recent years: citizens kept leather buckets in case of fires but many houses burned down each year.

'You must not upset yourself,' said Sir Thomas. 'Let's take a wherry across to see the bear-baiting in Southwark; that'll cheer you up.' As they were rowed across the Thames, Stow told them about London Bridge and its drapery shops and houses:

'The bridge is among the miracles of the world. The building and foundations are laid upon twenty-one piles of stone, with twenty arches under which barges may pass. The houses built upon the bridge are as great and high as those built upon the land, so really you don't know you're on a bridge. You would judge yourself to be in the street.'

Master Stow seemed to have recovered his enthusiasm for London. Simier was glad, for he had come to like his guide. Certainly his eyes brightened when they approached the bear pit. 'The queen herself often comes here,' said Sir Thomas proudly, 'sometimes with visitors and ambassadors from overseas.'

*Cock-fighting and gambling*

Like all people in the sixteenth century Simier was used to cruelty and violence, but what he saw in the bear pit sickened him. A bear was chained to a stake in the centre, and a bulldog was yapping at him, trying to snap his leg with his teeth. The bear was muzzled so he could not bite back, but he suddenly swung his huge paw and ripped the dog's back. Blood poured out as the dog yelped out of the pit. A second dog now tried his luck. The poor bear looked helpless as the dog's teeth sank into his leg but again his paw tore the dog's flesh. The crowd roared.

This dog was a favourite and much money was wagered on him. The bear went wild with pain as a third dog attacked him. Simier could stand no more. He pushed his way through the cheering crowd and the others were forced to follow him. As they headed back to the river a great roar indicated that the bear was dead.

On their way back to the wherry they passed Bank Side. A small theatre built here two years before would, in fifteen years' time, be the home of William Shakespeare's company.

On the other side of the river they bade farewell to John Stow. 'You should write down your knowledge of the city to help other foreign visitors,' said Simier. The old man smiled his appreciation. Perhaps he would. As they returned to Whitehall for dinner Simier thanked Sir Thomas. 'A place of infinite variety, London.'

'Yes,' replied Sir Thomas proudly. 'There are nearly 200 000 people here at certain times of the year. We have other great cities in England: York, Bristol, Norwich, all with over 20 000 people. But London is our joy. Let me tell you, one poet recently wrote of London, "Thou hast all things to make thee fairest, and all things in thee to make thee foulest".'

'I can see what he meant,' said Simier appreciatively.

### A foreigner's view of London

Just before he left France, Simier had seen a letter which a German duke had sent to his master. It was about London.

London is a large, excellent and mighty city of business.... Most of the inhabitants are employed in buying and selling merchandise, and trading in every corner of the world, since the river is most useful for this purpose....

It is a very populous city, so that one can scarcely pass along the streets, on account of the throng.

The inhabitants are magnificently apparelled and are extremely proud and overbearing.... They care little for foreigners but scoff and laugh at them.

### How do we know?

This chapter and the next are closely based on primary sources of evidence. One of the most important of these is the *Survey of London* written by John Stow, who actually lived in the reign of Elizabeth I.

John Stow was born in 1525 and died at the age of eighty in 1605. The *Survey* was first published in 1598, but London would have changed little in the twenty years before that date. Stow tells us a great deal about life in London, the buildings and the people. When he died, a friend wrote:

He was tall, lean of body and face, of a pleasant cheerful countenance, his sight and memory very good; very sober, mild and courteous to any that required his instructions ... he always protested never to have written anything either for malice, fear or favour; and that his only pain and care was to write truth.

As a result we know a great deal about sixteenth-century London. We can form for ourselves a clear idea of the impression which its sights are likely to have made on visitors such as Jean de Simier.

*A plan of London. Which features can you identify?*

*The Swan Theatre in London. The audience sat in the balconies around the sides. The stage was raised up in the centre*

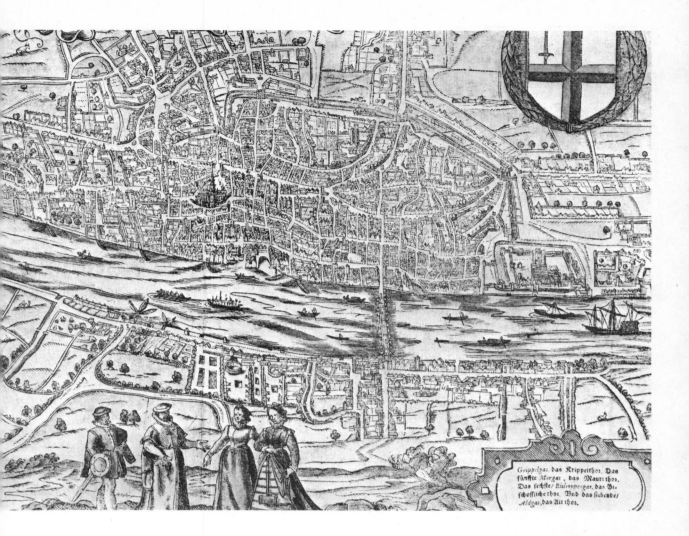

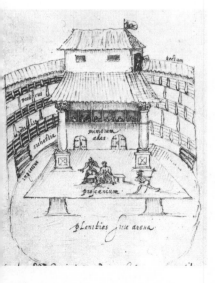

## Questions and further work

1 Imagine you are Simier on the morning after the banquet. Write a report to your master to tell him of your experiences so far. Bear in mind the purpose of your visit.

2 Make a list of the opinions which the German duke expressed about London. Which do you think Simier would not agree with?

3 Many of the quotations in the chapter are taken from John Stow's description. What aspects of London made him proud? What did he not like about the city?

4 Write a short play for three characters: Stow, Simier and Sir Thomas. Describe three scenes: near the Thames; the top of the Tower; the bear pit in Southwark. Then write what the three men said to each other in each scene. Try to include the words of this chapter as far as possible. Then, in groups of three, act out some of the scenes before your class.

## 11 Life in the country

### The road to Theobalds

After two more days in London, Simier and Sir Thomas set off one morning for Theobalds, Lord Burghley's country house in Hertfordshire. Riding at a steady canter, they were quickly in open country. It was a grey, misty autumn morning and the pair were soon lost. The land was deserted.

They rode aimlessly until at last they came to a village. They walked their horses slowly through until they saw a peasant on the road.

*Sir Thomas*: I pray you, set us a little in our right way out of the village.
*Ploughman*: Keep still to the right hand until you come to a corner of a wood. Then turn at the left hand.
*Sir Thomas*: Have we no thieves in that forest?
*Ploughman*: No, sir. For the provost-marshal hung the other day half a dozen at the gallows which you see before you at the top of that hill.
*Sir Thomas*: Truly, I fear lest we here be robbed. We shall spur a little harder.

'Our highwaymen,' said Sir Thomas to Simier as they rode on, 'are of the best. Coming over Shooter's Hill in Kent one day, there came a fellow to me, like a sailor, and asked me for money. While I kept my horse still to draw my purse, he took advantage of a little bank and leapt behind me, whipped my purse away and with a sudden jerk I know not how, threw me at least three yards out of my saddle. I never was so robbed in all my life.'

*Queen Elizabeth in procession to Nonsuch Palace in 1582. Notice the methods of transport*

*The courtyard of a large inn in Tudor times*

After they had safely cleared the woods, conversation turned to the roads. Most men who travelled rode on horseback. Only great lords could afford a carriage and six horses. But even for them travel was uncomfortable. Carriages had no springs and roads were pitted with holes; dry and dusty in summer, full of water and mud in winter. Parishes were responsible for keeping roads in good repair but few did so.

Sir Thomas told Simier that Parliament had decreed that all men should work on the roads for six days in summer. 'Yet the rich', he added, 'make so little of their responsibilities, and the poor are so reluctant to work that of all the six scarcely two days' work are well performed. Besides this, those whose land runs to the roads utterly neglect to ditch and scour their drains: if they would, the roads wouldn't be so difficult in winter.'

Clearly travel was a difficult and dangerous business. But at last they came to an inn and decided to halt for food. As they ate, Sir Thomas boasted:

As soon as a passenger comes to an inn, the servants run to him and one takes his horse and walks him till he be cold, then rubs him and gives him meat. Another servant gives the passenger his private chamber and kindles his fire; the third pulls off his boots and makes them clean. If he will eat with the host or the other guests his meal will cost him six pence, but if he eats in his room he can ask for as much as he wants.

Each comer-in is sure to lie in clean sheets, wherein no man hath been lodged since they came from the laundress. If the traveller hath a horse, his bed doth cost him nothing. But if he be on foot, he is sure to pay a penny for the same. . . .

In all our inns we have plenty of ale, beer and sundry kinds of wine. Such is the capacity of some of them that they are able to lodge two hundred or three hundred persons and their horses at ease.

After another hour on the road they finally ended their journey.

## Theobalds

Lord Burghley's house was very impressive. It was still not finished, but already Simier's breath was taken away. That night he wrote to the duke of Alençon, his master:

The handsome and delightful hall . . . which is so ornamental and artistic that its equal is not to be met with. For, besides other embellishments, there is a very high rock of all colours made with real stones, out of which gushes a splendid fountain. . . . The ceiling is very artistically constructed. It contains the twelve signs of the zodiac, so that at night you can see the stars proper to each. . . . On each side of the hall are six trees, having the natural bark so artfully joined, with birds' nests and leaves as well as fruit upon them, so that you could not distinguish the natural from the artificial. . . .

In another hall is depicted the kingdom of England, with all its cities, towns and villages, mountains and rivers. And also the armorial bearings of every esquire, knight, lord and noble who possess lands and retainers.

The gardens too impressed Simier:

The garden is encompassed with a moat full of water, large enough for me to have the pleasure of going in a boat and rowing between the shrubs. Here are a great variety of trees and plants, a fountain with a basin of white marble and columns of wood and other material up and down the garden. After seeing these we were led by the gardener into the summer house, in the lower part of which are the twelve Roman emperors in white marble.

As Simier and Sir Thomas walked with the gardener, Simier showed great interest in country life. He told them about peasants he had seen in some parts of France: they lived in hovels, dressed in rags and often starved.

'Things are hard in England too,' replied Sir Thomas, with obvious feeling. He told Simier of a survey conducted in 1569; 13 000 beggars had been discovered in England. 'It's the poor who cannot help themselves that I feel sorry for,' he continued, 'the aged, the sick, those who cannot find work. But I've no sympathy for sturdy beggars.'

He then explained how a beggar was whipped the first time he was caught, branded in the ear the second time, and hung the third time. But for the needy poor, 'houses of correction' were set up in every parish and citizens paid so much a year to feed and clothe them. Sir Thomas felt it should be better organised, though. He argued that poor people and their children should be 'set on work', and 'overseers' should be paid to see that they did it.

By now Simier knew Sir Thomas quite well. He was an Englishman through and through. He was certainly proud of attempts to improve

the land and the life of the people. They sat down in the evening sunshine.

*Hatfield House in Hertfordshire. Burghley's house at Theobalds probably looked similar to this*

Sir Thomas talked about schools. Many children all over the country were being taught to read and write Latin grammar. Many could now read the Bible in English. The schools might only be a small room with one teacher and a few pupils, but it was a start. 'There are not many towns now, under the queen's domain, that have not one grammar school at least, with a sufficient living for a master, and an usher appointed.'

Englishmen also enjoyed their sport. Hunting the hare and deer were popular. Sometimes crossbowmen waited in ambush in a thicket and they shot the deer driven into their path. Sometimes a pack of hounds was used to chase the deer into the ground. Sir Thomas told Simier of an occasion when the queen had to cancel her engagements for three days because of the aches and pains she had after a long day's hunting.

Even the less wealthy had their sports. On Sunday afternoons many gambled on their favourites in cock-fights – cocks were cheered by large crowds to fight to the death – while the more energetic played pallowe or village football: 'a strong and moving sport in the open fields with a great ball of double leather filled with wind and driven to and fro'. Children had their games too: hide and seek, leapfrog, blind man's buff, and tournaments with knights riding pig-a-back at each other.

England seemed a happy place to Simier. And life in France at that

*Three witches were hanged in Chelmsford, Essex, in 1589. Notice their 'familiars', cats and toads*

time was not so happy. Back home he had left his family in Paris in the middle of a civil war. There was constant worry about the plague, and constant fear of witches.

'We've had both in England,' commented Sir Thomas, 'but not so much in recent years.' The gardener, who had remained quiet throughout their conversation, now spoke up:

There be two or three women in our town which I like not, but especially one old woman. I have been as careful to please her as ever I was to please my own mother and to give her ever anon one thing or another. And yet methinks she frowns at me now and then. And I had a hog which ate his meat with his fellows and was very well to our thinking over night. And in the morning he was stark dead. Some of my neighbours wish me to burn something alive, as a hen or a dog. Others will me to seek help from a cunning man before I have any further harm. I should be glad to do for the best.

Simier told them of torture used against witches in France – the rack, the thumbscrew and others – to make witches confess. Sir Thomas asked if it was the torture rather than their crimes which made them witches. He added proudly that torture was never used in such cases in England. Instead, witches were bound up hand and foot and hurled into a pond or river. If they floated, the water rejected them and they were guilty – water was sacred and used in baptism. If they sank, they were innocent. Sir Thomas thought this not always a fair system, but it was better than torture.

Certainly people everywhere feared witches. The gardener could hardly stop talking about them.

### A country estate

The next morning they took horses and rode to Enfield, one of Lord Burghley's tenant farms. As they approached the farm the whole place was buzzing with activity. In the field to their left, where the harvest had been gathered the previous month, a pair of oxen were pulling a heavy wooden plough through the soil and the stubble. On their right, the field had already been ploughed and sown with rye. Four or five small children, armed with slings and sticks and stones, were scaring off pigeons, rooks and crows from the newly sown seed.

As they approached the house, there was a curious banging noise from the two large barns. 'That', explained Sir Thomas, 'is the noise of the flails. Women will be threshing the corn to remove the grain and make bread. Then they have to clean it and let the wind blow away the chaff. It's a long process.'

At the farmhouse they dismounted. A groom met them and took their sweating horses for a rub-down and feed. John Wilson, the tenant farmer, came out, his face creased by a huge grin. He paid rent to Lord Burghley for his land. He and Sir Thomas had always got on well. Simier felt his hand crushed in John's grip. The farmer was a huge man, weatherbeaten and strong.

He offered to show them round to stretch their legs before dinner.

*This witch, Mary Sutton, was put to the ordeal of 'swimming' in 1612*

The farmhouse was built of brick with a tiled roof. So were the large brew-house and bake-house and dairy at the back. But the barns, stables, sheds and cottages were built of wood and all had thatched roofs. Only the farmhouse and bake-house had a chimney.

They strolled slowly across the yard to a row of labourers' cottages. The window of the first cottage was open. There was a smell of cooking. The three men looked inside. There was just one large room with a fire and a hearth at the far end. A woman was cooking something on a large pot over the fire. There was no chimney, so the smoke came out through the open window. Simier thought it was a good job it wasn't raining. Three or four hens were scratching around inside the cottage, others outside in the cottage garden.

Just then the woman's husband and son approached. It was time for their midday dinner. They told John Wilson that they had just started putting up a fence behind the barn. The man's face suddenly darkened. He said he was worried by all the talk of enclosure. Many men had been put out of work in the west because enclosed land needed just one shepherd to look after the sheep. Sir Thomas tried to calm his fears. 'My father does not want to enclose your land,' he said. 'You grow good grain here. There are many people in London. John here can sell his produce at a good price in the markets there. As long as he pays his rent, my father is happy.'

'Ah, but my lease runs out next year.' Now John looked worried.

'How much more will I have to pay in rent to renew it?' As they walked back to the farmhouse, Sir Thomas tried to reassure John. After all, John had been a tenant of the Cecils since Sir Thomas was a boy, and his father before him. But John was not to be put off. These were times of change and many were suffering.

Inside, the farmhouse consisted of one large room with the fireplace at one end. The smoke from the fire curled upwards into a chimney. The room was very bare, much different from the palace at Whitehall and Theobalds. There was a long trestle table with eight or nine chairs around it, a long bench down the far wall and a wooden dresser in the corner with pewter dishes and cups on it.

They sat down at the table. John's wife complained that they had not told her of their coming; they were simple people and the food was plain. There was chicken broth and dumplings and various vegetables and bread. Simier tried some English ale and said that he preferred wine, particularly French wine. John laughed at that.

Over dinner John told them about his farm. It wasn't large but he had over twenty cottagers and labourers working for him and it had been a good summer. The field newly sown with winter corn had been left fallow during the summer to recover its goodness. Simier thought this was wasteful and John agreed. The other field had produced a good harvest of wheat and all the peasants held strips in it and they had all helped to gather it in together. A third field had produced barley and again they had had a good year. Three weeks ago they had a harvest supper to celebrate, everyone out in the yard eating and drinking all through the night. There was plenty of hay gathered in and the grass in the meadow was still lush. They would not have to kill any cattle this year, as they could feed them through the winter. That meant more manure for the fields and gardens in the spring, and fresh meat all through the winter. At the moment times were good.

At this point in their conversation Simier surprised them. He told

them of a visit he had recently paid to the Low Countries. 'There,' he said, 'instead of leaving the land fallow they grow turnips. These vegetables can be used to feed the cattle and at the same time they seem to enrich the soil for wheat. The Dutch don't have strips for each peasant as you do. They have a small field each with hedges around it. No cattle strays from the common on to the crops and the wind on the flat land doesn't ruin the crops.' John Wilson said that he had heard of turnips. But enclosure frightened him. 'The whole time-honoured method of ploughing and harvesting will be changed,' he said. 'And what about the common land? My tenants keep animals on it and cut fuel in the woodland for their fires.'

Everyone seemed uncertain. This was a time of change all right. It was hard to understand.

## Questions and further work

1 What aspects of English country life is Sir Thomas fond of? What aspects is he critical of? What is he ashamed of?
2 What changes were occurring in English town and country during Simier's visit? Why were some people unhappy about these changes?
3 Imagine you are Simier near the end of your visit to England. Write a letter to your wife in France. Tell her of the things that have most impressed you and the things that have horrified you during your stay.
4 Make a list of the ways in which the lives of John Stow and John Wilson differed.
5 Many social problems existed in Elizabethan England. Make a list of the main ones mentioned in this chapter and the previous one. What steps would you take to solve them?

### King James I

On the evening of 27 March 1603, King James VI of Scotland was sitting quietly in the antechamber of the royal palace in Edinburgh. Suddenly there was noise and excitement. Sir Robert Carey, an envoy from England, entered the room. He was breathless, 'beblooded after a long ride, with great falls and bruises'. James' aunt, he gasped, Queen Elizabeth of England, had died three days before. James was to be the new king.

Preparations were quickly made for the march south. By 6 April he and his court reached Berwick. The loud crash of cannon greeted and applauded the new king. For the next month, he journeyed slowly towards London. At Durham,

Upon Sunday, being 10 April, His Majesty went to Church and the bishop of Durham preached. And that day ... being spent in devotion, he rested till Monday, which he bestowed in viewing the town, the manner and beauty of the bridge and quay....

Besides he released all prisoners from the jail, except those that lay for treason, murder or papistry: giving great sums of money for the release of many that were imprisoned for debt; who heartily praised God for their unexpected liberty.

Why do you think James did these things? What would the people of Durham think?

The 21st day of April, being Thursday, His Highness took his way towards Newark-upon-Trent; where, that night, he lodged in the castle, being his own house....

In this town was taken a cutpurse (pick-pocket) doing the deed; and, being a base, pilfering thief, yet was all gentleman-like on the outside. This fellow had a good store of coin found about him: and upon his examination, confessed that he had, from Berwick to that place, played the cutpurse in the court.... For this, His Majesty directed a warrant to the recorder of Newark to have him hanged: which was accordingly executed.

(a) What evidence does the author give against this thief?
(b) Why does he stress it?
(c) What would the people of Newark feel about the king's action?

In London James was crowned king of England. This description of him was written by the Venetian ambassador:

He is sufficiently tall, of a noble presence, his physical constitution robust, and he is at pains to preserve it by taking much exercise at the chase, which he passionately loves.... He is a prince of intelligence and culture above the common, thanks to his pleasure in study when young.... He is by nature placid, averse from cruelty, a lover of justice.... He loves quiet and repose, has no inclination to war, nay is opposed to it, a fact that little pleases many of his subjects....

He does not love the people nor make them that good cheer that the late Queen did. The English adore their sovereigns ... but this king shows no taste for them but contempt and dislike. The result is that he is despised and almost hated.

## Early problems

*King James I in progress to Parliament*

In his first year as king, James came to understand many of his future difficulties. He was very short of money. Here are some of his expenses in 1603:

| | |
|---|---|
| £10 000 | Journey south and entertainment |
| £14 000 | Gifts to favourites |
| £17 000 | Queen Elizabeth's funeral |
| £400 000 | Debts from Queen Elizabeth's wars in Ireland 1602–3 |
| £100 000 | Costs of the royal court |

How could he pay these expenses? Parliament would have to be called to grant taxes.

In addition James realised that many Englishmen had strongly held religious beliefs. Catholics were looking to him for support. At first, he allowed them to worship in peace as long as they did so secretly and did not try to convert others.

But some Catholics, led by the Jesuits from Douai, were not content. One mad priest, Father Watson, plotted to capture James, force him to tolerate Catholics and then release him. But Watson was such a scatterbrain that other Catholics betrayed him to the king.

In the same year, some members of the king's court plotted to murder

James. Led by Sir Gervase Markham and Lord Grey of Wilton, they persuaded Sir Walter Raleigh, the much loved Elizabethan sea-dog, to join them. But again the plan was betrayed and the plotters tried and sentenced to death for treason.

Yet James' actions at this point were strange. Markham and Grey were brought to the scaffold. They bade farewell to their friends, then on a trivial excuse they were told to wait. In pouring rain, they shivered while all their crimes were read aloud to them. Only after that were they told that the king had decided to pardon them. The people of England were very confused by this.

They were even more confused by James' treatment of Raleigh. The popular hero was stripped of all his lands, given an unfair trial, convicted on very flimsy evidence, then put in the Tower for life. Even James' son, Prince Henry, was critical: 'None but my father would have found such a cage for such a bird.' Raleigh was looked on as a martyr, James as something of a villain.

### Religion, money, Parliament

Since Catholics and Puritans were all looking to him for support, James decided to call a meeting of clergymen to discuss religion. They met at Hampton Court Palace in 1604. At one point in the debate, one member mentioned the word 'presbytery'. In Scotland the presbytery was a group of important people who chose the priests. It had been very powerful, advising priests and ministers and even the king. James was horrified. He wanted no presbytery where 'Tom and Dick shall meet and at their pleasure censure me and my council. When I mean to live under a presbytery I shall go into Scotland again, but while I am in England I will have bishops to govern the Church.' Puritans would have to accept his bishops or 'I will harry them out of the land, or else do worse.'

All clergymen were expected to accept *The Book of Common Prayer*. About ninety refused and were dismissed. Some sailed overseas to find more freedom, in Holland or America. There was another result of the conference: it ordered a group of churchmen to prepare a new translation of the Bible, and this, the famous Authorised Version, came out in 1611.

Later, James determined that he alone should rule the country. 'It is treason', he wrote, 'to dispute what a king may do.' He tried to raise taxes himself, without asking Parliament's approval. In 1608, for instance, he tried to increase customs duties on articles coming into the country. He also increased the number of monopolies sold to wealthy merchants and noblemen: one man would pay the king a sum of money to have sole right to sell a particular article; he then sold it at a high price and kept the profit. But prices were much higher as a result, and Parliament objected. In 1610, for example, they refused the king's request for more money.

*The Duke of Buckingham in 1626*

Der Staat Madrill Obrigkeit so den himmel dragen.

*The entry of Prince Charles to Madrid in 1623. The Prinz van Gales is the Prince of Wales*

### The marriage of Prince Charles

King James also quarrelled with Parliament over his son's marriage. In 1621 Parliament wanted war against Spain. James, however, had other ideas. He wanted his son to marry the Spanish Infanta, Donna Maria, sister of King Philip IV.

At this point a daring plan was conceived. It came from Prince Charles' most trusted friend, George Villiers, duke of Buckingham. He and Charles should ride in secret to Madrid dressed as two brothers, Thomas and John Smith. They would woo the Infanta, and she would agree to elope with Charles to England.

In February 1623 they left for France. Charles was seasick but they arrived in Paris safely. There they entered the public gallery of the Louvre, still in disguise. They saw the young king of France and his mother before setting off for Madrid. At first their secret was kept but soon all Madrid knew of the two royal visitors. On 7 April Charles and the Infanta finally met. He was overcome. He blurted out his love for her, but she turned away cold and aloof. In addition, King Philip made conditions for their marriage: all Catholics in England must be allowed to worship freely.

Buckingham decided they might as well leave. Marriage was out of the question. The expedition had been a fiasco. And it had been expensive: a large fleet had waited for months to bring the Infanta to England in great style. Parliament was angry.

*A Puritan view of bishops and priests. Above is the careful Puritan minister who shoulders the burden of his church. On the opposite page the careless priest who holds three churches at the same time is shown*

King James received his son with welcoming tears of joy. The king had been ill and within two years he died. Prince Charles was king.

## King Charles I

The first three years of the reign were dominated by Buckingham. He 'lay for the first night of the reign in the king's bedchamber and the three nights after in the next lodging'. He was Charles' constant companion and adviser.

Buckingham was anxious for victory over Spain. In 1625 an English troop was sent to attack Cadiz harbour. One diarist recorded that most of the army were vagabonds, dressed in rags, were hungry and often drunk. Their leader, Lord Wimbledon, had never before been to sea. They landed and marched in blazing sun towards Cadiz. They could get little food but plenty of Spanish wine. They were easily defeated and chased to their ships. They returned to England with scurvy, ridden with lice and were billeted on the people of Southampton and Plymouth. Charles and Buckingham became even more unpopular.

Meanwhile Charles was finding life with his new French wife, Henrietta Maria, difficult. She did not like England and was slow to learn its language and its ways. She hated Buckingham, who called her friends 'monsers'. After one quarrel, Charles locked her in a room and she tried to escape by breaking the glass and tearing the flesh on both her hands. Their marriage seemed in ruins.

But a visit from a French diplomat, de Bassompierre, saved it. They agreed that the 'monsers' should go home to France, but Henrietta Maria was allowed a few close friends. Within a year she had borne Charles' first child and written to her father that she was the 'happiest queen in the world'.

The following year, Buckingham led another disastrous overseas expedition, this time to France. Despite his own bravery, it returned 'with no little dishonour to our nation, excessive charge to our treasury and a great slaughter of our men'. Parliament demanded an inquiry. They accused Buckingham of treason and presented a petition, the Petition of Right, to Charles. Posters in London said, 'Who rules the kingdom? The king. Who rules the king? The duke. Who rules the duke? The Devil.'

On 17 August 1628 Buckingham and his wife left London for Portsmouth. Two days later, one of his ex-officers went to a cutler's shop on Tower Hill. He bought a dagger with 10d he had borrowed from his mother. His name was John Felton, a lonely, bitter man.

Felton then set off to walk to Portsmouth. He arrived on the morning of 22 August and went straight to Buckingham's house. He entered and hid behind a curtain. The duke was having breakfast. When he finished he stood up and walked out of the room into the corridor. Felton stepped out from behind the curtain and stabbed him in the chest. The duke fell, his last words being, 'The villain hath killed me.'

Felton was immediately overpowered and taken to London to the

Tower. Few mourned as Charles buried Buckingham at Westminster Abbey, but many wept as Felton was executed at Tyburn.

## Rule without Parliament, 1629–49

After Buckingham's death Charles decided to rule without Parliament. But he still needed to raise money. He tried various ways of doing this. He revived an old law by which men of wealth had to become knights and pay a fee for the privilege. He also laid claim to all forest land belonging to the crown which had been stolen or taken over since the Middle Ages. Many families had held this land for two or three hundred years. Now they had to pay for it. It is not surprising that many began to object to King Charles' rule.

Many people objected to the Church of England. Charles was advised by William Laud, Archbishop of Canterbury from 1633 and called by his enemies 'a little, low, red-faced man'. Laud thought the Church must be controlled by bishops and priests, but many people found fault with this. One Cambridge Doctor of Theology, John Bastwick, wrote:

I pray, compare Christ and His apostles and the prelates and priests of our own age together. Christ was humble and meek; they are proud and arrogant.... Christ went abroad preaching and teaching; they neither preach, nor teach, nor cure; neither will they suffer others to do.

And those men who dared to criticise were severely punished. Henry Sherfield, from Salisbury in Wiltshire, objected to some pictures of God on a stained-glass window in a Salisbury church. He 'got himself into the church, made the doors fast to him, and then with his staff brake divers holes in the said window'. Sherfield was brought before the Court of Star Chamber, committed to the Fleet and fined the huge sum of £500.

The punishment of three other critics in 1637 was also severe.

Friday last, Doctor Bastwick, Mr Burton and Mr Prynne stood in the pillory in the palace of Westminster. As Doctor Bastwick came from the gatehouse towards the palace the light common people strowed herbs and flowers before him; Prynne and he stood upon one scaffold and Mr Burton upon another by himself. They all three talked to the people.... Mr Burton said it was the happiest pulpit he had ever preached in.

After two hours the hangman began to cut off their ears; he began with Mr Burton's. There were very many people; they wept and grieved much for Mr Burton, and at the cutting of each ear there was such a roaring as if every one of them had at the same instant lost an ear. Bastwick gave the hangman a knife, and taught him to cut off his ears quickly and very close, that he might come there no more. The hangman burnt Prynne in both cheeks (with the letters S L – Seditious Libeller), and as I hear, because he burnt one cheek with a letter the wrong way, he burnt that again; presently a surgeon clapt on a plaster to take out the fire. The hangman hewed off Prynne's ears very scurvily, which put him to much pain, and after he stood long in the pillory before his head could be got out....

Bastwick, Burton and Prynne were known as Puritans, men who criticised Laud's church. What evidence is there in the passage that the onlookers supported them? Another Puritan, John Lilburne, was put in the pillory. Even with his hands and feet bound, he cried out against Laud:

whereupon the Court of Star Chamber (then sitting, being informed) immediately ordered Lilburne to be gagged during the residue of the time he was to stand in the pillory, which was done accordingly; and when he could not speak, he stamped with his feet, thereby intimating to the beholders, he would still speak were his mouth at liberty. . . .

It was no wonder that men came to oppose the Church of Laud and Charles. Even in the country, away from London, there were critics, as this story shows. It was told by the Puritan, Richard Baxter, in his autobiography:

My father's name also was Richard Baxter: his habitation and estate at a village called Eaton Constantine, five miles [eight kilometres] from Shrewsbury in Shropshire, a village most pleasantly and healthfully situate. My mother's name was Beatrice, of High Ercoll in the same county. There I was born AD 1615 on 12 November, being the Lord's Day, in the morning at the time of Divine worship. . . .

*A Puritan drawing showing Archbishop Laud eating Prynne's ears for dinner*

We lived in a country that had but little preaching at all. In the village where I was born there were four readers successively in six years. Ignorant men and two of them immoral in their lives, who were all my schoolmasters. In the village where my father lived, there was a reader of about eighty years of age that never preached, and had two churches about twenty miles distant. His eyesight failing him, he said Common Prayer without book; and for the readings of the psalms and chapters he got a common day-labourer one year and a tailor another year (for the clerk could not read well); and then at last he had a kinsman of his own (the excellentest stage player in all the country and a good gamester and a good fellow) that got orders and filled one of his places. . . . Only three or four competent constant preachers lived near us and any who had gone to hear them was made the derision of the vulgar rabble under the odious name of a Puritan.

In the village where I lived the reader read the Common Prayer briefly and the rest of the Lord's day, even till dark night almost, except eating time was spent in dancing under a maypole and a great tree not far from my father's door; where all the town did meet together. And though one of my father's own tenants was the piper he could not restrain him or break the sport. So that we could not read the scriptures in my family without the great disturbances of the tabor and pipe and noise in the street. Many times my mind was inclined to be among them and sometimes I broke loose from conscience and joined with them; and the more I did it the more I was inclined to it. But when I heard them call my father Puritan it did much to cure me and alienate me from them; for I considered that my father's exercise of reading the scriptures was better than theirs. . . .

What reasons encouraged Baxter to criticise the Church?

## Opposition grows, 1635–40

During this period of 'personal rule', Charles I had to raise money. Previously Parliament had to be asked for new taxes: now Charles was determined to go it alone. In 1636, for instance, he issued a writ that ship money should be levied all over England. This was a tax paid by

The riot in St Giles's Church,
Edinburgh, in 1637. A young girl
called Jenny Geddes threw a stool at
the bishop when he tried to introduce
Laud's Prayer Book

ports towards the expenses of running the navy. Charles wanted inland
counties to pay it as well.

But some people refused to pay. John Hampden, a rich landowner
from Buckinghamshire, would not pay the £1 11s 6d due from him. He
argued that he received no benefits from the navy, and anyway the tax
had not been approved by Parliament.

In 1637 Hampden was brought to court and the case was tried. The
king's lawyers showed that money was needed to build ships. Pirates
were attacking trading ships in the Channel and valuable cargoes had to
be defended. Everyone in the land would benefit from this.

Eventually the twelve judges gave their verdict. Seven decided for the
king, five for Hampden. The king had won the case, but his enemies
gained much publicity from the trial.

## Rebellion in Scotland

In the same year as the judges' verdict, rioting broke out in Scotland.
Charles had long wanted his Scottish subjects to use a form of religious
service similar to that used in England. In July, a new prayer book was
given out to the congregation at St Giles' Cathedral, Edinburgh. As the
bishop tried to read the service, rioting began. Women threw their
stools at the clergy; it was said that some were apprentices dressed in
skirts. Order was restored and the offenders were put outside. But then
they smashed the cathedral windows.

ONCILIVM SEPTEM NOBILIVM ANGLORVMCONIVRANTIVM IN NECEM IACOBI·
MAGNÆ BRITANNIÆ REGIS TOTIVSQ· ANGLICI CONVOCATI PARLEMENTI·

Robert Winter · Christopher Wright · Iohn Wright · Thomas Percy · Guido Fawkes · Robert Catesby · Thomas Winter

*The Gunpowder Plotters*

This revolt was bound to happen. Many Scots were Presbyterian: they disliked bishops ruling the church and issuing prayer books. They were also hostile to anything that came from London. Quickly an army was formed under Alexander Leslie. The king would have to march against them if he wanted to get his way.

But when Charles tried to raise an army, he found that many of his enemies in England sympathised with the Scots. Every week the Scottish army grew stronger. Charles was getting desperate. The earl of Strafford advised him to summon Parliament to get support and money. In April 1640 Charles did just this. But members spent the first two weeks complaining of Charles' bad government. In vain Charles sent requests to the Commons for money to fight the Scots. After another week, in disgust, he dissolved Parliament.

Now he tried other means to raise an army; his wife even wrote to ask the pope. Little was forthcoming. Meanwhile there were riots in London: one mob tried to lynch Archbishop Laud. The army mutinied and the Scots invaded Northumberland and captured Newcastle. For the second time Charles was desperate. His attempt to rule without Parliament had failed. In November it was summoned again. This famous 'Long Parliament' was to last thirteen years and bring about the death of King Charles.

## Using the evidence: the mystery of the Gunpowder Plot

### The story of the Plot (1605)

Most books tell the following story of the Gunpowder Plot:

When James I became king he promised certain freedoms for Roman Catholics. But his chief adviser, Sir Robert Cecil, Lord Treasurer, persuaded him to outlaw all practising Catholics. In 1604, therefore, a small group of Catholic noblemen, led by Robert Catesby, Thomas Percy, Thomas Winter and Francis Tresham, decided to blow up the king and his lords when Parliament next assembled.

They rented a house near Westminster Palace and tried to tunnel through under the House of Lords. The going was hard and slow. Then they found that the house next door had a cellar to let which ran under the House of Lords. By March 1605 they had heaped thirty-six barrels of gunpowder into the cellar and covered them up. They then scattered to wait till the State Opening of Parliament in November.

In October, Francis Tresham, a cowardly, weak-willed man, panicked. He wrote a note to his cousin, Lord Mounteagle, a man close to Cecil but also popular among the Catholics, to warn him not to attend the opening. The note was clearly written, but Mounteagle asked his manservant to read it aloud to him. He then dashed post-haste to London to warn Cecil. It was 24 October. There were still twelve days before the opening of Parliament.

Cecil told the king of the contents of the letter, but it was not until midnight of the night of 4 November that guards swept into the cellar to find a bewildered Guy Fawkes looking after the gunpowder.

The plotters were then traced. Catesby and Percy were killed by the same bullet at Holbeach House in Worcestershire. Most of the other lesser conspirators were tried and sentenced to be hung, drawn and quartered. This was done in January 1606.

*Part of the letter Lord Mounteagle received*

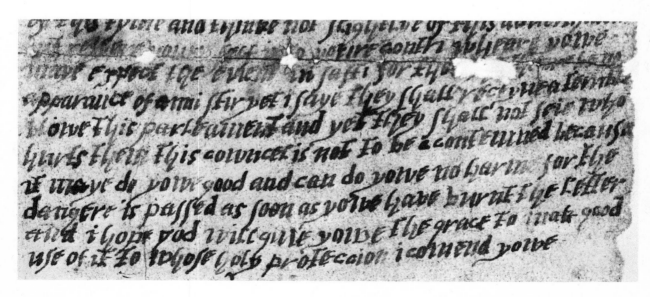

### Some clues to the story

1 Gunpowder at this time was a government monopoly. All supplies were kept in the Tower of London. Under torture, Guy Fawkes said, 'The powder was bought from the common purse of the confederates.' But the gunpowder was not mentioned at the trial. There is a further mystery: the ordnance account for the Tower stores for 1604 is missing, presumably lost or destroyed.

2 The man who rented the cellar to the plotters was John Whynniard, keeper of the King's Wardrobe, an acquaintance of Sir Robert Cecil. He died very suddenly on the morning of 5 November. The cause of death is unknown.

3 When the main conspirators were surrounded at Holbeach House, they had few weapons and made little resistance. Yet most were shot. At the trial Cecil was said to have told the guards, 'Let me never see them alive.'

4 Lord Mounteagle received the letter from Tresham on 24 October. He asked his manservant to read it aloud to him. Then he interrupted his dinner to dash urgently to tell Cecil.

5 All the plotters were killed or captured quickly, except one, Francis Tresham. He was left free until 12 December, after the trial. He was imprisoned in the Tower and he died of a sudden mysterious illness on 23 December.

6 At the trial, the evidence against the plotters came from two sources:

(a) a confession by Guy Fawkes, taken under torture

(b) a confession by Thomas Winter, the only chief plotter to be

*A Dutch drawing of the execution of the plotters in January 1605*

captured. The handwriting of this confession is certainly like Winter's.

But Winter was badly wounded by a crossbow bolt in his right shoulder when he was captured on 8 November. On 12 November he could not sign his own statement.

The original confession was kept by Cecil. He never showed it to anyone. A copy was used at the trial.

Take each of the above six points in turn and ask yourself the following questions:

1 In what way does it question the original story?
2 What further information do we require to decide the matter?

*Two opinions about the Plot*

(1) Those that have practical experience of the way in which things are done hold it as certain that there has been foul play and that some of the Council secretly spun a web to entangle these poor gentlemen.

An Italian visitor in 1605

(2) Because Cecil would show his service to the state he would first plan, then discover, a treason. And the more odious the treason, the service would be the greater.

Godfrey Goodman, *Court of King James I*, 1879

3 What opinions are expressed in these two Documents?
4 What evidence supports each of the opinions?
5 What evidence challenges each of the opinions?
6 Can you suggest, in class discussion:
   (a) why Lord Mounteagle may have had the letter from Tresham read aloud by his manservant?
   (b) why he dashed off to tell Cecil that same night?
   (c) why Tresham was not arrested until after the trial?

*The 'confession' by Thomas Winter*

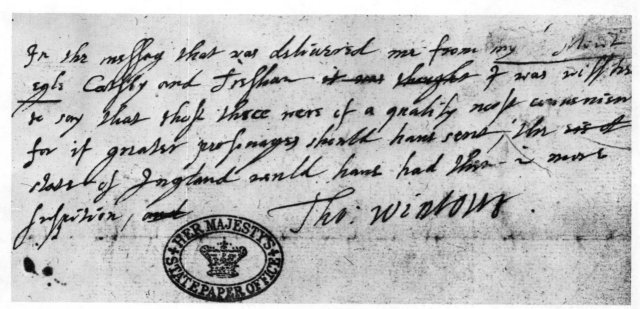

# The English Civil War

## The five MPs

In January 1642 John Rushworth was a young assistant clerk in the House of Commons. He recorded daily events and speeches 'in cypher' (shorthand) using a quill pen and ink. On Tuesday 4 January, King Charles I visited the House on a vitally important matter. Rushworth recorded what happened. Later he was taken before the king. There he had to use his shorthand notes to write a full report. The account of the king's visit below comes from that report.

King Charles knew that many of his enemies were in the House. He also knew that he had supporters there. He conceived a bold plan to arrest the five ringleaders, hoping that that would leave him supreme. On 3 January he sent a message to the House, asking them to surrender the five – Pym, Hampden, Holles, Strode and Haselrig. The House refused. Charles was furious and his wife, Henrietta Maria, was rumoured to have said, 'Go pull those rogues out by the ears, or never see my face again.'

The next day Charles set out to do just that. Rushworth takes up the story:

The House was no sooner in their places, but they were informed by one Captain Langrish . . . that His Majesty was coming with a guard of military men, commanders and soldiers. . . . Whereupon a certain member of the House having also private information from the countess of Carlisle . . . that endeavours would be used this day to apprehend the five members, the House

*A painting of King Charles I attempting to arrest the five members. The Speaker kneels before the king to emphasise their rights*

required the five to depart forthwith, to the end to avoid combustion in the House if the soldiers should use violence to pull any of them out. To which command four of the said members yielded ready obedience, but Mr Strode was obdurate till Sir Walter Earl (an old friend) pulled him out by force, the king being already at New Palace Yard at Westminster.

The king's halberdiers formed a guard of honour as he entered the House. He looked quickly round for the five members but could not see them.

Then His Majesty made this speech.
'Gentlemen,
I am sorry for this occasion of coming unto you. Yesterday I sent a sergeant-at-arms upon a very important occasion, to apprehend some that by my command were accused of high treason; whereunto I did expect obedience and not a message.

'And I must declare unto you here, that . . . no king that ever was in England shall be more careful of your privileges . . . than I shall be; yet you must know that in cases of treason no person hath a privilege. And therefore I am come to know if any of those persons that were accused are here. [Amid complete silence he looked round] . . . Well, since I see all the birds are flown, I do expect from you that you shall send them unto me as soon as they return hither. . . .'

When the king was looking about the House, the Speaker standing below by the Chair, His Majesty asked him whether any of these persons were in the House. . . . To which the Speaker, falling on his knee, thus answered, 'May it please Your Majesty, I have neither eyes to see nor tongue to speak in this place, but as the House is pleased to direct me, whose servant I am here; and I humbly beg Your Majesty's pardon that I cannot give any other answer than this. . . .'

The king . . . went out of the House, which was in great disorder, and many members cried out aloud, so as he might hear them, 'Privilege, privilege.'

*Archbishop Laud*

1  Rushworth had to give Charles a detailed but truthful account. Make a list of the difficulties he would have in doing this.
2  Obviously the king would be angry about the proceedings. How does Rushworth try to prevent Charles being angry with him?
3  The Commons urged the five to flee. Why does Rushworth say they did this? Are there any other possible reasons? Why does Rushworth give this one?

## The road to war

Charles I had long been at odds with the House of Commons. After their Petition of Right in 1628, Charles had tried to rule without summoning Parliament for eleven years. During that time he had relied on unpopular ministers like William Laud and 'Black Tom Tyrant', the earl of Strafford. He had raised unpopular taxes like ship money and he had ordered severe punishments for popular Puritans like William Prynne.

Then in April 1640 Charles had summoned Parliament. He had to raise money to crush the Scots' revolt against the new Prayer Book. But Parliament provided none and was dismissed. In November another Parliament was called. Again they refused money, but they passed a Bill of Attainder against 'Black Tom', imprisoned Laud, abolished illegal

*The Earl of Strafford*

A. Doctor Vſher Lord Pri[...]
te of Ireland.
B the Sherifes of London.
C the Earle of Strafford.
D. his kindred and Friends

*The execution of 'Black Tom' Strafford, outside the Tower of London, 1641*

*John Pym was the leader of Charles's enemies in the House of Commons. He was one of the five members Charles wished to arrest, largely because he had prepared the Grand Remonstrance*

taxes and passed a Triennial Act which gave them the right to meet regularly without Charles' approval.

Charles' problems were now increasing. The rebellion in Scotland was followed by a fierce uprising in Ireland. And in the autumn of 1641 the House of Commons prepared a Grand Remonstrance. In this they stated all their grievances against the king and asked for reform. There was much debate in the House: argument was heated and tempers were fierce; one member even took out his sword. At last the Remonstrance was approved by 159 votes to 148.

Charles now knew he had some friends in the House. But his attempt in January 1642 to arrest five of the enemy ringleaders made many hate him. He seemed to threaten their privileges, and he had failed and looked ridiculous. There was rioting in London that night. Men barricaded the streets and set up cannon. Catholics were attacked and several murdered. On 10 January Charles left London and moved north.

The two sides now began to collect their armies. In Leicestershire, in July,

The Lord Ruthven and Sir Arthur Haselrig (who are Deputy Lieutenants) did train a good part of the trained bands two days last week; and hearing that the king was coming with a good force ... they departed towards London for avoiding blood-shedding.

On 22 August King Charles raised his standard in a wet, muddy field near Nottingham. It took twenty men to raise the heavy flagpole. After a short ceremony everyone fled for cover from the rain. Two days later the flagpole fell down in a storm.

## The two sides

The war divided the country. The south-east, including London, and the eastern counties were for Parliament. The west, Wales, and the north-west supported Charles, who set up his headquarters at Oxford. Yet some parts of the west country and counties like Lancashire were split. Local rivals placed themselves on either side and fought for power. In some places even families were divided.

This chart shows some of the main differences, although it is not entirely accurate. For example, not all of the king's opponents were Puritans.

|  | *Royalist* | *Parliamentarian* |
|---|---|---|
| Nicknames | 'Cavaliers' | 'Roundheads' |
| Age | Some younger men | Some older or middle-aged men |
| Background | Largely rural | Cities, towns, seaports |
| Social status | Peers, nobles, gentry and supporters | Middle-class merchants traders, yeomen |
| Religious beliefs | Anglican, some Catholic | Puritan |

The king made the first move of the war by marching towards London. His army was led by his twenty-three-year-old nephew, Prince Rupert of the Rhine, a young man with a brilliant career in foreign wars

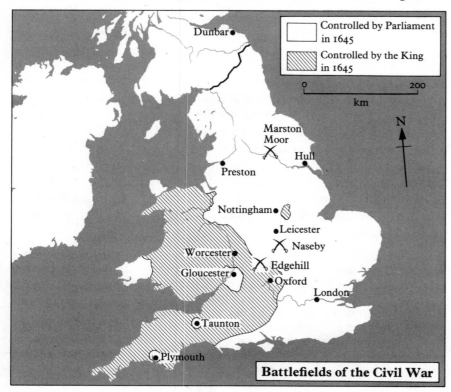

Battlefields of the Civil War

already behind him. Men said he had made a pact with the Devil: that alone could explain his success. Even his great dog, Boy, who always ran beside his master's horse, was said to be the Devil's agent.

On 23 October, north of Oxford, the royalist army came face to face with the earl of Essex's roundheads. At Edgehill the first major battle of the war was fought. Rupert's first charge scattered the roundheads, but his cavalry then broke up in pursuing the enemy. Meanwhile, Essex's troops reformed, and defeated the remaining royalists. Charles lost more men, but Essex retreated to London. The first battle was a draw.

Charles' army continued its march. Parliament fought for time by sending agents to treat with Charles for peace. Meanwhile, men, women and children frantically repaired defences around the city. Cannon were placed in strategic positions, soldiers manned the gates and walls. Essex managed to rouse the city apprentices to join the remains of his army.

On 13 November Essex led 24 000 men to bar the king's approach at Turnham Green near Brentford. They formed into battle formations and one old Puritan soldier went round encouraging them: 'Come, my boys, my brave boys, let us pray heartily and fight heartily. I will run the same fortunes and hazards with you. Remember the cause is for God, and for the defence of your selves, your wives and your children.' Most important, Essex had cannon and musketeers surrounding the whole battlefield.

Rupert's army drew up less than a kilometre away. But no battle was fought. Rupert had fewer men and his cavalry feared the enemy cannon. Charles' army retreated to Oxford for the winter.

## The king's chance, 1643

In the spring and summer of 1643 Charles came near to winning the war. He planned a three-pronged attack on London. One attack would come from Devon and Somerset via the southern counties, one from Yorkshire in the north and his own army from Oxford. But after many initial successes the plan failed.

In Yorkshire, Hull was still loyal to Parliament. When the king's armies under the duke of Newcastle moved south the garrison came out and raided the Yorkshire towns. The duke had to return to Yorkshire. One battle, at Seacroft Moor, was described by the Parliamentary general, Lord Fairfax:

I made an attempt on Tadcaster.... Here we stayed three or four hours destroying the works. Newcastle sent back twenty troops of horse and dragoons to relieve Tadcaster; I had not above three troops.

I marched my foot in two divisions and the horse in the rear. The enemy followed, about two musket-shot from us, in three good bodies, and thus we got over the open country. But having gotten to some little enclosures, our men, thinking themselves more secure, were more careless in keeping good order; and while their officers were getting them out of houses, where they sought for drink, it being an exceedingly hot day, the enemy (got past us) another way.

*Cavaliers*

They, seeing us in some disorder, charged us both in flank and rear. The countrymen (local farmers and labourers) cast down their arms and fled; the foot soon after, which, for want of pikes were not able to withstand their horse. Few of our horse stood the charge.

Elsewhere the royalists came to grief. A short siege of Gloucester ended with the city, holding for Parliament, down to its last three barrels of gunpowder. But Essex arrived in time with an army to chase the royalists away. At Newbury, Prince Rupert's cavalry was scattered by well-aimed musket-fire and the king's march to London was again halted. And, in the north, Lord Fairfax linked up with the new young Colonel of the Eastern Association, Oliver Cromwell, to smash the royalist hopes in Lincolnshire and Leicestershire.

## Using the evidence: the battle of Marston Moor, 1644

By the middle of June 1644 the royalist armies in the Civil War were being hard pressed. The king had been forced to flee from his base at Oxford, and was pursued north to Evesham by the soldiers of Parliament under Essex. Charles was given a short breathing-space when Essex failed to follow up his advantage. Nonetheless, the king was desperate for help.

Meanwhile, in the north Prince Rupert was holding much of Lancashire, but in Yorkshire things were going badly for the king. The

*Roundheads. How do their weapons and dress differ from those of the Cavaliers on page 151?*

duke of Newcastle was surrounded in York by the armies of Parliament: siege engines were in place, artillery was firing and mines and explosives were placed under the walls. The position of Newcastle and his adviser, Lord Eythin, was desperate. They were rationing their armies, but at most they could hold out for no more than two weeks. Their only hope was probably Prince Rupert. On 14 June Charles wrote to him, 'If York be lost, I shall esteem my crown little less than lost . . . but if York be relieved and you beat the rebel armies which are before it – then, but not otherwise, I may make a shift.'

On 23 June Rupert left Preston to march east. Within a week his incredible march took him to Knaresborough, just twenty-nine kilometres from York. The Parliamentary generals decided to leave their siege and intercept him. After all, they could not afford to let Rupert link up with Newcastle and Eythin. So they marched west to Marston Moor to block the roads from Knaresborough.

Rupert's next move was remarkable. In the space of one day, 1 July, his army marched thirty-five kilometres, crossed the rivers Ouse and Swale, then turned south and defeated a 'regiment of dragooners' at Popleton. By nightfall he was just outside York. That night his cavalry had little rest: by 4 a.m. they were on the move again, towards Marston Moor.

At 9 a.m. Rupert, now established in a good position on the moor, was joined by Newcastle from York. Sometime in mid-afternoon they were further joined by Eythin with the bulk of the royalist infantry from

York. At about 4 p.m. the three men held a council of war: were they to
fight? If so, when? Or was there some other action they could take?

The following evidence would undoubtedly affect their discussion.
(1) The size of the two armies:

|  | Royalists | Parliament |
| --- | --- | --- |
| Horse | 6000 | 8000 |
| Dragoons | — | 1000 |
| Foot | 12 000 | 19 000 |
| Total | 18 000 | 28 000 |

In addition, within two or three days Parliament could be reinforced
by a sizeable army under the earl of Denbigh from the west Midlands,
while Rupert could count on another 3000 men from Cumberland
under Colonel Clavering.

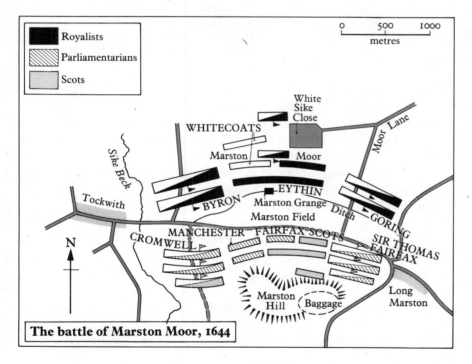

The battle of Marston Moor, 1644

(2) (a) Marston Moor was flat with few trees or obstacles. Marston
    Field was ploughed and enclosed to grow rye.
    (b) A long ditch divided the armies. This was quite wide in the east..
    (c) The ground was clay and very marshy on the eastern side.
    (d) The ground sloped gently downwards from south to north.
(3) Newcastle's discussions with Rupert (this account is by Newcastle's
wife):

After some conferences, he declared his mind to the prince, desiring His
Highness not to attempt anything as yet upon the enemy; for he had intel-

*Prince Rupert*

ligence that there was some discontent between them, and that they were resolved to divide themselves, and so to raise the siege without fighting: besides my lord expected within two days Colonel Cleavering (Sir Robert Clavering), with above three thousand men out of the north, and two thousand drawn out of several garrisons (who also came at the same time, though it was then too late). But His Highness answered my lord, that he had a letter from His Majesty (then at Oxford), with a positive and absolute command to fight the enemy; which in obedience and according to his duty he was bound to perform. Thereupon my lord replied that he was ready and willing, for his part, to obey His Highness in all things, no otherwise than if His Majesty was there in person himself; and though several of my lord's friends advised him not to engage in battle, because the command (as they said) was taken from him: yet my lord answered them, that happen what would, he would not shun to fight, for he had no other ambition, but to live and die a loyal subject to His Majesty.

(4) The meeting of Eythin and Rupert (the following is a contemporary account):

The prince demanded of Eythin how he liked the marshalling of his army, who replied he did not approve of it being drawn too near the enemy, and in place of disadvantage, then said the prince, 'they may be drawn to a further distance'. 'No, sir,' said Eythin, 'it is too late.' Eythin dissuaded the prince from fighting, saying, 'Sir, your forwardness lost us the day in Germany (at Lemgo), where yourself was taken prisoner.'

(5) Some other considerations.
(a) When they had hurriedly left the siege of York, the Parliamentary armies had left much of their ammunition and supply. Rupert would know that a quick victory for Parliament would enable them to recover their losses. A royalist victory would enable him to capture them.
(b) Most of the royalist infantry in York had spent the night plundering the supplies. They had also quarrelled with Eythin over their pay. They did not arrive on the moor until mid-afternoon.
(c) It would not be dusk until about 9 p.m.
(d) Rupert had acted rashly in one or two previous battles. He could not afford a humiliating defeat.
(e) The battle would probably produce a decisive result for one side or the other.
(f) The victorious army would control the north of England and increase the morale of its side.
(g) The king desperately needed Rupert's help in the south.

Prince Rupert had to make a decision as the two armies faced each other on the field of battle. There are several stages in making a judgement:
(a) considering all the available evidence
(b) drawing up a list of all possible courses of action
(c) considering the possible outcomes, the advantages and disadvantages, of each course of action
(d) deciding which is the best course of action.
Go through each of these stages as if you were Prince Rupert.
(a) Consider the evidence. Evidence consists of fact and opinion. Which pieces of evidence here are fact, which opinion? What was the opinion of

Newcastle? What facts did he give to support his opinion? What questions would Rupert ask to verify the facts? What was the opinion of Eythin? Would Rupert be likely to respect that opinion?

(b) Draw up a list of all possible courses of action.

(c) Consider the possible outcomes of each. Which possible outcomes are not clear? What questions would Rupert need to ask to make them clearer? To whom would he address those questions?

(d) Decide which is the best course of action.

### The battle itself

From 4 p.m. until about 7 p.m. Rupert hesitated and watched. At first the two armies faced each other in silence, then the ranks of Parliament began the singing of psalms. The sky darkened and a sudden hailstorm broke. Rupert decided there would be no fighting that day. 'We will charge them tomorrow morning,' he told Newcastle. Both men retired to eat supper. The troopers sat down and relaxed to eat theirs.

Cromwell saw this happen. He took this golden opportunity. He ordered his cavalry forward, swept down the hill and across the ditch and arrived with hailstones in the enemy ranks. Byron's cavalry turned to flee, but Rupert, quickly recovering, forced them to fight. The fiercest hand-to-hand combat followed. 'Such a noise, with shot and clamour of shouts that we lost our ears. The smoke of powder was so thick that we saw no light but what proceeded from the mouths of guns.'

The battle went on long after dark. At last the arrival of David Leslie's Scots and the Eastern Association's infantry swung it to Parliament. After midnight, Sir Thomas Fairfax, his face covered in blood, rode among the troops crying, 'Put up your swords, spare your countrymen.' The battle was over. From a farmhouse on the field, Cromwell wrote to his sister's husband:

Truly England and the Church of God hath had a great favour from the Lord, in this great victory given to us. . . . Sir , God hath taken away your eldest son by a cannon shot. It brake his leg. We were necessitated to have it cut off, whereof he died. . . . He was a gallant young man, exceeding gracious. God give you His comfort.

*A Roundhead cavalry helmet*

## The New Model Army

Surprisingly, that summer the Parliamentary armies under Essex were less successful in the south. So by 1645 there was still deadlock. In one letter Prince Rupert wrote:

The English nation is in danger of destroying one another or of degenerating into such cruelty that all elements of charity, compassion and brotherly affection shall be extinguished.

The deadlock was broken that year by two main events, the establishment of the New Model Army and Parliament's victory at Naseby. The New Model Ordinance set up a national army of 22 000 men, organised in 11 regiments of horse, 12 regiments of foot and 10

*Oliver Cromwell in about 1649*

companies of dragoons. Its commander-in-chief was Sir Thomas Fairfax, a professional soldier, brave, determined, and experienced.

The eleven cavalry regiments, under the command of Oliver Cromwell, were quickly recruited. Each had 600 troopers, paid 2s a day. Most provided their own horse and armour, 'back and breast', as well as sword and a pair of pistols. Cromwell always kept full control in battle and rarely charged at full pace. They went at 'a pretty round trot' and used sword and pistol to gain the advantage.

Each infantry regiment consisted of 1200 men, half musketeers, half pikemen. All wore the redcoat uniform of the Eastern Association. Pikemen carried a 16-foot or 18-foot [5 or 6 metres] pike with a heavy iron head as well as sword and pack. They wore little armour. Musketeers carried a matchlock musket and a lighted length of match or cord boiled in vinegar. The match always had to be kept alight when battle threatened, a very difficult job in wet weather. The musket was heavy and difficult to load in wet weather. In battle the troops stood six men deep, the front row firing a salvo, then moving to the back, and so on. The musket could kill at 400 metres, but was not accurate beyond 150 metres.

Dragoons, artillery and others supported cavalry and infantry. Dragoons were mounted but rarely fought on horseback. They carried swords and short muskets and were often used as a police force on the edge of a battle. The artillery was just becoming important in war. The New Model Army had fifty field guns, requiring over 1000 horses to pull them and their ammunition. They were useful to attack town walls but inaccurate in battle. They were supported by no specialist engineers or sappers and few doctors or surgeons.

### The battle of Naseby and the end of the war, 1645–6

In the early summer of 1645 the new army under Fairfax was full of enthusiasm. They marched towards Oxford but the king, hearing of their advance, moved away to Leicester. Rupert now decided on a once-for-all battle, a battle to end the war. He ordered all royalist forces to meet him at Market Harborough.

Langdale and his northern horsemen arrived quickly, but the Welsh and Goring's crack horsemen from the west did not turn up. In contrast Fairfax had all his men and Cromwell's horsemen at the ready. Fairfax, like Rupert, wanted battle, especially when his scouts captured messengers coming from Goring to tell the king that his cavalry would not be coming. Fairfax knew this was his chance.

At dawn the two armies moved cautiously into position. They faced each other 1.2 kilometres apart. Each controlled a ridge of high ground with a marshy hollow in between. A strong wind faced Parliament's troops but otherwise neither side had an advantage.

The two armies took up their positions as shown in a contemporary print (see page 157). In the centre, infantry pikemen were protected by their 18-foot (6 metre) pikes. On the right was Cromwell's cavalry, on the left that of the stubborn and determined General Ireton. Beyond Ireton a troop of dragoons under Colonel Okey provided crossfire from behind Sully Hedges. The king's army had a similar layout with Rupert on the right and Langdale on the left.

At Naseby the royalists attacked first. Their infantry came down the hill and locked with Parliament's pikemen in hand-to-hand combat. At this point Rupert's cavalry thundered down the hill, passed the infantry and smashed Ireton's troops and forced them to flee. The royalists chased them into Naseby village and Rupert was away from the battlefield for nearly an hour.

In this time the battle was lost. Langdale followed Rupert down the hill, but Cromwell watched and waited. His men charged full-tilt just as the royalists were slowed down by the marsh and the hill. Langdale's troop was routed and all the remaining Parliamentarians, including the dragoons, closed in on the infantry.

Charles saw that his army desperately needed reinforcement. He spurred his horse forward, but one of his lords took hold of his bridle. 'Will you go upon your death, my lord?' The battle was lost. Charles retreated to Leicester, his cause in ruins. The next year he gave himself up to the Scots who handed him over to Parliament. The Civil War was over.

| 1642 | The Grand Remonstrance passed |
| 1644 | The battle of Marston Moor |
| 1645 | The battle of Naseby |
| 1646 | The end of the Civil War |

*The battlefield at Naseby*

# 14 Oliver Cromwell

### The trial of the king, 1649

Friday 19 January. Outside Windsor Castle. A cold day. Men clapped and rubbed their hands for warmth. Their breath hung on the air.

A coach, drawn by six horses, drove in through the gates of the castle and stopped. All the horses were restless. But on the walls of the castle, lines of musketeers and pikemen stood still.

Quickly and quietly a hooded figure was led from the castle by guards. The coachman cracked his whip. They were on the move. Now to right and left, front and rear rode a troop of horse. Over the hard, frostbound roads to St James's Palace, London.

The lone figure in the coach was King Charles I. Since the summer of 1647 he had been a prisoner at Carisbrooke Castle on the Isle of Wight. His armies had lost the Civil War. He had tried to come to terms with his enemies, first with the army and the Commons, then behind their backs with the Scots. A Scottish army had invaded England in 1648 but was defeated at Preston.

The real leader of the Parliamentary forces was now Oliver Cromwell. He argued that Charles' tyranny had caused the Civil War; he must pay with his life. Many more moderate members of Parliament were horrified. They wanted to negotiate with the king, not kill him. So Cromwell sent Colonel Pride with some troops to the Commons: they 'purged' the House and cleared out forty-one Presbyterian members and another ninety-six moderates. That left just sixty members loyal to the army and hostile to the king.

That January night, as Charles sat lonely and cold at his supper at St James's, he knew nothing of all this. He had been told only that he would be brought to trial next morning.

The night was frosty and the morning made the king shiver. He was marched in a closed sedan chair, surrounded by close-packed foot-soldiers, to Whitehall. Then, as ice cracked on the Thames he sailed upstream in a sealed barge to the house of Sir Robert Cotton. Here he was to stay during his trial.

Meanwhile, at noon, seventy or so commissioners had met in the Painted Chamber of Westminster Palace for a preliminary meeting before the trial. They knew that they were about to kill a king. Several lost their nerve and slipped away quietly, not to return. What, asked others, if Charles said they were not a legal court? 'In the name of the Commons in Parliament Assembled and all the good people of England,' voiced another. That brought relief. Now the remainder were resolute.

Yet all knew the danger. The President of the Court, the lawyer John Bradshaw, wore a hat lined with steel in case any of the king's supporters tried to shoot him. And when, at 2 p.m., the sixty-eight commissioners took their seats on tiered benches covered in red baize, they were surrounded by guards. Oliver Cromwell summed up their feelings, 'This is a more prodigious matter than any that hath been before.'

The prisoner entered, guarded by twelve halberdiers. Charles was

Every plant which my heavenly Father hath not planted shall be rooted out, Matt 13

Singing men    Deanes    Bishop

*A detail from the Solemn League and Covenant signed between Parliament and the Scots. This is a plea to remove bishops and deans on the ground that there is no mention of them in the Bible*

*The trial of King Charles I. What steps did Parliament take to ensure that they would be protected? Notice the large numbers in the public galleries. Why did they need so many judges to decide the King's fate?*

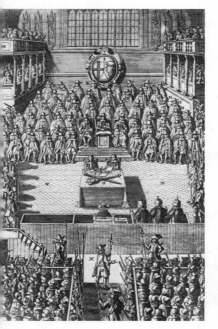

dressed dramatically all in black, with the large silver star of the Garter on his cloak. There was complete silence. He sat down in the red velvet chair and faced the court with great dignity.

Bradshaw stood up:

'Charles Stuart, King of England, the Commons assembled in Parliament, being sensible of the great calamities that have been brought upon this nation and of the innocent blood that hath been shed, which are referred to you, as the author of it. . . .'

Then John Cook, the prosecuting lawyer, read the charge:

'My Lord, on behalf of the Commons of England and of all the people thereof, I do accuse Charles Stuart, here present, of high treason.'

The main charges were two: Charles had a 'wicked design to overthrow the rights and liberties of the people' and he had 'maliciously levied war against the Parliament and the people'. Cook called the king a 'tyrant, traitor, and murderer'.

At this Charles, who so far had sat unmoved, 'laughed in the face of the court'. He spoke out strong and clear to answer the charge:

'I would know by what power I am called hither. I would know by what authority, I mean *lawful*. . . . Remember I am your king, your lawful king. . . . I have a trust committed to me by God, by old and lawful descent. I will not betray it.'

Charles simply refused to take part in the trial: it was illegal. Bradshaw was speechless. He declared the case adjourned until Monday. As Charles left the court cries of 'God save the king' were heard from the public gallery.

The trial lasted a week. Throughout Charles refused to defend himself. At last, on Saturday 27 January, without a proper trial, the Commissioners had to decide. They declared him guilty and Bradshaw prepared to read out the sentence. He began by listing Charles' crimes

against 'the people'. Suddenly two masked ladies cried from the gallery, 'Not a half, nor even a quarter of the people of England. Oliver Cromwell is the traitor.' Guards quickly removed them.

Now Charles asked permission to speak. But he too was removed. There was uproar in the gallery. As he left, his guards chanted 'Execute, justice, execute,' to drown the noise. But one of the king's servants standing near by commented, 'Poor creatures, for sixpence they will say as much of their own commanders.'

Three days later, the king was executed. One eye-witness wrote this in his diary:

Tuesday, 30 Jan. I stood amongst the crowd in the street before Whitehall gate, where the scaffold was erected, and saw what was done, but was not so near as to hear anything. The blow I saw given and can truly say with a sad heart; at the instant whereof, I remember well, there was such a groan by the thousand then present as I never heard before. (Two troops of cavalry were then used) to scatter and disperse the people, so that I had much ado amongst the rest to escape home without hurt.

### Oliver Cromwell's early life

'I was by birth a gentleman, living neither in any considerable height nor yet in obscurity.' Oliver Cromwell was born in Huntingdon on 25 April 1599. He was the son of Robert, a descendant of King Henry VIII's chief adviser, Thomas Cromwell. His parents had ten children, but Oliver was the only one to survive infancy. He went to the local grammar school, where the master was a local preacher, and then in

1616 to Sidney Sussex College, Cambridge. He stayed for just one year, spending more time at football, cudgels or other 'boisterous sport or game' than at his books.

In June 1617 his father died. Oliver returned home to farm the family estates. There he stayed until 1628 when he was elected MP for Huntingdon and his long political career began. In 1620 he married Elizabeth Bourchier, the daughter of a wealthy London merchant.

Thereafter his life became more concerned with politics. He was a relative of Sir John Hampden and supported him over Ship Money. He sat in the Long Parliament that produced the Grand Remonstrance. When the Civil War started, Oliver formed a troop of horse, and his skill as a soldier was quickly recognised. He was made commander of the cavalry in the New Model Army. When the war finished, he and his 'Independents' in the army determined that the king must die. Thus in January 1649 the Commonwealth was established.

*The steel-lined helmet of lawyer Bradshaw*

## The Commonwealth 1640–53

It was not just the king who died in 1649. His law courts and Parliament, purged by Colonel Pride, were dead too. How was England to be ruled without them? Oliver Cromwell provided the answer.

*The title page of a pamphlet published in 1660 at the Restoration of King Charles II. Why do you think it was written? Why was it published in 1660?*

| *The bodies* | *Their jobs* |
| --- | --- |
| The Rump Parliament | To make laws. |
| The Council of State (41 members at Whitehall) | Controlled taxes, the army and navy; gave orders to carry out laws. |
| High Court of Justice (New JPs) | Tried royalists and criminals. |

Cromwell himself led the new system. He was a prominent member of Parliament, and at first Chairman of the Council of State and Commander of the army. But the new regime was not popular.

Abroad, the Scots harboured the dead king's son; the Irish plotted with the Stuart agent, the earl of Ormonde; French pirates helped Prince Rupert to raid English merchantmen and the Russian tsar dismissed the English ambassador from his court. When Parliament's ambassador in the Netherlands was murdered, the Dutch did nothing to punish the assassins.

There were problems for Cromwell at home too. The royalists were no threat: 'When we meet', said one, 'it is but to consult to what foreign plantation we shall fly.' But others were more determined. John Lilburne wrote a book called *The Agreement of the People*: the Council of State, he argued, was just like another king; people in England were not really free.

Some soldiers in the New Model Army took up Lilburne's call. One Captain William Thomson led a mutiny in Banbury. Cromwell marched west from London to face the rebels. He took money, confiscated from the Admiralty, to pay off the troops, and then marched

Cromwell's
*Bloody Slaughter-house;*
OR,
His Damnable Designes
laid and practised by him and his *Negro's*, in Contriving the Murther of his Sacred Majesty KING
CHARLES I.
DISCOVERED.

*By a Person of Honor.*

LONDON:
Printed for *James Davis*, and are to be sold at the *Grey-hound* in St. Pauls Church-yard. 1660.

by night to catch up with Thomson and the ringleaders at Burford. He surprised them just after midnight. A few were killed but most were locked up in Burford church for over a week. One soldier, Antony Sedley, was so bored that he carved his name on a wooden pillar in the church. It can still be seen today. Eventually the rebels were released and dispersed, though one or two of the leaders were hanged. Later Parliament passed a Treason Act: in future it would be treason to stir up revolt against the Commonwealth.

### The Irish rebellion, 1649

In August, Cromwell sailed with 10 000 troops to Dublin. Catholic nobles had rebelled and taken the city of Drogheda. Cromwell besieged it and at length the garrison surrendered.

Being in the heat of action I forbade them to spare any that were in arms in the town; and I think that night they put to the sword about 2000 men.

Eighty climbed the steeple of St Peter's church:

'Whereon I ordered the church steeple to be fired.'

All eighty perished in the flames.

Then Cromwell's army marched to Wexford. Again they took the city, again they massacred the inhabitants. He described the event himself:

And when they were come into the market place, the enemy making stiff resistance, our forces brake them and then put all to the sword that came their way. Two boatfuls of the enemy attempting to escape, being overprest with numbers sank, whereby were drowned nearly three hundred of them. I believe in all there was lost of the enemy not many less than two thousand; and I believe not twenty of ours killed from first to last.

*This satire on the English soldier in Ireland lays great emphasis on his appetite for plunder*

Cromwell has been severely criticised for this needless slaughter. One historian called the Drogheda massacre 'an incident of unhappy fame'. Afterwards Cromwell tried to explain his reasons. He said he gave the order 'in the heat of action'; he also condemned the Irish for murdering Protestants in 1641:

I am persuaded that this is a righteous judgement of God upon those barbarous wretches who have spilt so much innocent blood. And that it will tend to prevent the effusion of blood in the future.

Ludlow, one of Cromwell's friends, excused the massacre: it was 'to discourage others from making opposition'.

### Dunbar and Worcester, 1650-51

Meanwhile, trouble was brewing in Scotland. There, the Presbyterians, in addition to protecting the young Charles Stuart, refused to allow freedom of worship. On his return from Ireland in 1650, Cromwell marched north. But on their way to Edinburgh his army could find no food: the Scots had burned the crops as far south as Berwick. 'Poor, shattered, hungry and discouraged' Cromwell's army had to retreat to

*Oliver Cromwell attacks Drogheda*

Dunbar. Leslie followed them and trapped them, with an army twice their size.

Leslie was a patient man; he could afford to wait to starve Cromwell out. But his Presbyterian ministers saw an opportunity to do God's work: let the enemy be crushed, they said. On a wet and stormy night, Leslie's troops were forced down the hills towards Dunbar. Cromwell seized his chance: at dawn his horse swept up at the ragged Scottish left; his artillery pounded the Scottish right and the Scots fled in panic.

Exactly one year later, 3 September 1651, Cromwell faced the Scots again. They had marched south to Worcester under the young Charles Stuart. They hoped that English royalists would join them but few did.

There is a story that the night before the battle, Cromwell and a Colonel Lindsay went into a nearby wood. They met a 'grave, elderly man with a roll of parchment in his hand'. Lindsay felt a cold shiver go down his back. The man, the agent of Satan, promised Cromwell 'to have his will then, and in all else, for seven years'; then the Devil would take his soul to Hell. At this Lindsay ran in terror from the wood and fled home to Norfolk. There he told the story to a local minister who wrote it down. Such legends and stories are common in history. Who do you think would spread this one, and why?

On the next day, the battle was bravely fought for five hours before Charles was defeated. After many adventures he escaped to France, while Cromwell rode in great triumph to London. Parliament gave him an extra £4000 a year and Hampton Court Palace as his home. Crowds turned out in their thousands to acclaim him with cheering and the firing of muskets.

## Oliver Cromwell the man

Cromwell was a man of medium height, 'rather well set', 'strong and robust', 'a face like a piece of wood'. He had a powerful masculine face with a ruddy complexion, chestnut brown hair, large green-grey piercing eyes and a very prominent nose. Indeed 'Nose' was his nickname: a 'glow-worm glistening', so red that some of his enemies said he was a heavy drinker.

He was affectionate, often lively and good-humoured; but above all, he was forceful and decisive, conscious of his duty to God, his family and his country. One night he and Ireton were out walking. They were stopped by their guards and asked their names. But the guards refused to believe them. Cromwell commended them and gave them a pound. The guards later said they knew who he was, but they had to be strict to follow his example.

Yet Cromwell was a family man and a good friend. He enjoyed a friendly chat over a pipe of tobacco: 'He would sometimes be very cheerful with us', wrote one friend, 'and exceeding familiar.' He was also a keen practical joker: at the wedding of one of his daughters he put some sticky substance on the seats of important lady guests.

His love for his wife, Elizabeth, was constant. Round-faced, plump,

*A Dutch engraving of Cromwell dissolving the Long Parliament. 'This House to let', says the notice. 'Begone you rogues,' says Cromwell*

kindly, she was content to remain at home while he travelled. Even after thirty years of marriage he wrote from Dunbar in 1650:

I have not leisure to write much. . . . Thou art dearer to me than any creature, let that suffice.

She replied:

My dearest, truly my life is but a half-life in your absence.

Then he wrote:

Pray for me. Truly I do daily for thee and the dear family. . . . My love to the dear little ones, I pray for grace for them. I thank them for their letters; let me have them often.

A loving father, Oliver suffered much from the deaths of his two eldest sons. On his own deathbed he clutched his Bible and said, 'This Scripture once did save my life, when my eldest son died, which went as a dagger to my heart, indeed it did.' He also grieved much over the long and painful cancer which finally killed his beloved daughter 'Betty'.

## The Lord Protector, 1653–58

After his victories at Dunbar and Worcester, Oliver Cromwell was the hero of the Commonwealth. Yet he quickly began to feel that the Rump Parliament and the Council of State were not doing a good job. 'Five or six men', he commented, 'would do God's work better in one day than this Parliament has done in a hundred.' It was the army, he believed, who had fought against the king; the army should now govern the country.

On 20 April 1653 Cromwell discussed this with other army leaders. Then he went to take his seat in the Commons. A debate was in progress. But 'in a furious manner' he rose to his feet. He spoke, according to one account, 'with so much passion and discomposure of mind as if he had been distracted'. He pointed to certain members, called them 'drunkards', 'whoremasters', corrupt and unjust men. 'Come, come, I will put an end to your prating.'

Then walking up and down the House like a madman, and kicking the ground with his feet, he cried out, 'You are no Parliament; I will put an end to your sitting. Call them in.'

Whereupon the sergeant attending the Parliament opened the doors and two files of musketeers entered the House.

The Speaker was pulled from his chair. Cromwell took his seat and his mace: 'What shall we do with this bauble?' he asked. 'Here, take it away.' The House was emptied and locked. Someone later wrote on the locked door 'This house to let, now unfurnished'.

That afternoon, Cromwell visited the Council of State where the same happened. The Commonwealth was over.

Now Cromwell had to govern the country. At first he decided that another Parliament should be formed. 'One hundred and thirty-nine God-fearing men,' throughout the country, should be nominated by

The Rump Parliament. What makes you think that the author of this set of playing cards was opposed to Oliver Cromwell?

The Rump and dregs of the house of Com remaining after the good members were purged out.

The Lord Protector, Oliver
Cromwell

local church congregations. Cromwell and other army officers were also
members of this 'Parliament of the Saints'. His enemies called it
'Barebones Parliament' after one of its members, Praise-God Barbon.

This Assembly did much good work: it improved prisons, took better
care of the mentally ill and registered all births and deaths. But its
members had little experience of politics and law. Gradually they
resigned their powers to Cromwell. He was now at a loss. Stories
circulated that he wished to be king, that a crown and sceptre were
being made for him at Cheapside, that men were asked to raise their hats
to him as they had done to Charles Stuart. But these stories were untrue.

Cromwell did live in the Palace of Whitehall. But he was called 'Lord
Protector' and he divided England into eleven districts, each ruled by a
major-general. These men acted like policemen: preventing riots,
watching Catholics, capturing criminals. They also watched the morals
of the people: there was to be no cockfighting, gambling, bear-baiting
or drunkenness.

Yet plotting against the Protector continued. When some of the
major-generals asked him a second time to become king, he again
refused. But his enemies were very suspicious. A pamphlet published in

*Praise-God Barbon*

*King Charles II*

1657 called *Killing No Murder* argued that Cromwell was a tyrant who should be killed.

However, the plots were not necessary. On 3 September 1658, the anniversary of Dunbar and Worcester, Cromwell died after a short sudden illness, possibly malaria. Two years later Charles Stuart was crowned king and the monarchy was restored.

## Using the evidence: Cromwell's master spy

The following letter was written by an Englishman in January 1655. It was addressed to Charles Stuart, the son of the executed Charles I and later (in 1660) to be King Charles II.

(1) Most Gracious Majesty
Having business with Secretary of State Thurloe, I was admitted into his Chamber. He, being busy with some others, I cast my eyes upon a bundle of papers. Seeing some of them signed Charles Gerard and dated from Paris, I looked nearer unto them. I found that the Lord Gerard hath treated with Mr Thurloe for the poisoning Your Majesty.

I beseech God bless you from his malice, and grant that this letter may come safe into Your Majesty's hands. In his letters Lord Gerard complains much of Your Majesty's slighting of him, and shows reasons why the Protector ought to have no bad opinion of him. . . . For payment he desires only to retire home into England and to have a regiment of horse. This is all I could learn, for I had no more time. . . .

    Your Majesty's Humble and Devoted Servant
    And Faithful Subject
    F. Coniers

1 What is F. Coniers writing to tell Charles?
2 What can we learn from the letter about Mr Thurloe's job as Secretary of State? (This letter probably never reached Charles. It was found among the many documents collected in Mr Thurloe's papers.)
3 Can you suggest who Mr Thurloe may be working for?

Under the same month and year, January 1655, and in the same batch, the following papers were found in Mr Thurloe's collection:
(2) A letter of intelligence from Mr Thurloe's special agent in Amsterdam, Holland. The letter stated that Charles' supporters in Amsterdam were preparing to invade England. They were offering £4 to every horseman who joined them, £1.50 to every footsoldier.
(3) The following verse, written in the handwriting of Colonel Overton. Overton was a leader of Parliament's army in Scotland. Overton pleaded that someone else had written the verse:

> A Protector, what's that? 'Tis a stately thing
> That confesseth itself but the ape of a king.
> A tragical Caesar, acted by a clown,
> Or a brass farthing stamped with a kind of crown. . . .
> In short, he is one, we may protector call,
> From whom the king of kings protect us all.

(4) Papers recording the examination of porters and servants. They were asked where they had received a number of heavy trunks which they then delivered all over the country. The trunks contained arms and ammunition. All those questioned replied that they thought the guns were for the colonists in Virginia.

(5) The statement of a gunsmith called Oliver Williams. This tells that a man called Fryer, a ships' chandler, had filled three barges at Botolph's Wharf with arms and ammunition. Williams had followed Fryer and three servants one night. He had pretended to be drunk, reeling over the road, to avoid suspicion. When he saw the barges, he went to tell a captain of a troop of cavalry and Fryer had been arrested.

(6) The statement of Ann Cunliffe, aged nineteen. She was a maid in the house of a Lime Street merchant. On Christmas Day a coach had come to the door but she had no idea who was in it.

(7) The record of the examination of a bookseller called Jones. He had been imprisoned for selling a book called *The Protector Unveiled*.

4 What can we learn from this batch of papers about Mr Thurloe and his job?

5 What, from this evidence, can we say *for certain* is happening in England in January 1655?

6 Can you suggest why these things may be happening? What evidence do you have for your suggestion? Is this evidence fact or opinion?

The following documents are also found among Thurloe's papers:
A letter, dated 18 July 1653, from the Dutch ambassador in London to a friend in Holland:

(8) Sir, I dare not write much news. All our actions are spied. We have spies set to watch us in our houses. We cannot be certain of anything that we do.

A letter, dated December 1653, from the French ambassador in The Hague to the ambassador in London. He had expected a letter from him inside an official packet:

(9) but I find none for me. Now it may be that the packet hath been opened, and that, finding therein yours to me they have taken it out to translate at their leisure.... I shall desire you in future that you will send your letters to me under a merchant's cover, and I shall do the like.

A note, added to a letter from Charles II, written by Thurloe:

(10) Charles Stuart's letter to Sir Henry Slingsby, brought by J. Cooper and delivered to John Walters to be carried to Slingsby. It was delivered to me by Walters.... Having taken a copy thereof I gave it to Walters to be carried as he had direction.

7 What do you think the word 'translate' may mean in Document 9?

8 What do these three Documents tell you of Thurloe's methods?

9 Thurloe was said to have £70 000 a year to spend on his job. Study all the extracts and make a list of the payments you think he may have had to make.

# The
# Seventeenth
# Century

# 15 A century of war

In the seventeenth century, the states of Europe were constantly involved in wars. Between 1618 and 1648, the Holy Roman Empire, Spain, France, the princes of Germany and the countries around the Baltic Sea were involved in the Thirty Years War. Many contemporary writers thought the war had destroyed the lands of Germany: the following passage, taken from a book called *The Tears of Germany*, was written in 1638, just after the worst years of the war.

Soldiers, violent, desperate, have broken into our colleges and schools, our monasteries and churches.... Our priests are forced to flee into other countries. Many hundreds have miserably perished with their wives and children. Many of our famous schools and colleges are burned to the ground. Libraries are consumed by flames.... Torture and torment are brought to men of all ages and conditions.... There has been murder and killing on every acre of ground in Germany.

The writer of this passage was obviously very upset. Here are some other statements made about the Thirty Years War in Germany:
1 Officers and men saw the war as a way to get rich quick.
2 Armies were small. Gustavus Adolphus, king of Sweden, had about 15 000 men. His opponent, Wallenstein, had perhaps 20 000.
3 The fighting season was short, from May to October. Armies went home for the long winter.
4 6009 people were buried in the city of Nijmegen in 1636. The population of the city was about 15 000 in 1635.
5 More people were killed by plague than by war.
6 Some places did well from the war. The town of Essen sold weapons and ammunition to both sides at great profit.

1 Which of these facts and opinions support the argument in *The Tears of Germany*?
2 Which disagree with its argument?
3 How do you think the author would have formed his opinion?

## The army of Louis XIV

The Thirty Years War ended, for most of Europe, with the Peace of Westphalia in 1648. In the next decade many European rulers faced rebellions in their own lands, just as Charles I had fought a civil war with Parliament in England. So they were too busy to go to war. Yet the long reign (1660–1715) of Louis XIV of France saw almost continuous war again.

Louis XIV gloried in his army. In 1679 it consisted of 280 000 men, and was easily the largest in Europe. All were volunteers: they joined because they were paid regularly and well. Discipline was very strict, but conditions – food, supplies, uniforms, weapons – were excellent. On 5 January 1679 John Locke, an English writer who travelled in France, was a spectator in Paris:

This day was the review of the infantry of the 'Maison du Roy', for so the horse and foot guards are called. There were thirty companies, if one may reckon by their colours, all new-habited, both officers and men. The officers of the

French wear gold or (for the most part) silver embroidery, or lace in blue.

The French common soldiers all in new clothes, the coats and breeches of cloth almost white, red vests laced with silver . . . shoulder belt of buff leather . . . red stockings and new shoes. A new hat laced, adorned with a great white woollen feather. A new pair of white gloves and a new sword, copper gilt hilt. All of which . . . cost forty-four livres which is deducted out of their pay. . . .

As the king passed at the head of the line . . . the officers at the heads of their companies and regiments in armour with pikes in their hands saluted him with their pikes and then with their hats. He very courteously put off his hat to them.

The king loved to show off his army. On this occasion he rode along the lines of troops followed by the queen and other royal ladies in an open carriage. Ladies were often invited to watch the last stages of the capture of a foreign town.

But officers were not wise to spend too much time at court, as a diarist recorded:

M. de Louvois spoke very haughtily to M. de Nogaret the other day. 'Sir, your company is in very poor shape.'

'Sir,' said he, 'I did not know it was.'

'You should know,' said M. de Louvois. 'Have you looked at it?'

'No,' said M. de Nogaret.

'Well, you should have done! You must make up your mind whether to be a courtier or do your duty as an officer.'

Louis always wanted to ensure that his army was well-supplied and well-armed. Louvois, one of his Secretaries of State for War, was nicknamed the 'great victualler'. He built up supply stations, ammunition dumps and an excellent transport system. Soldiers were armed

*The Defenestration of Prague, 1618. Bohemian patriots threw two Hapsburg councillors through the windows of the royal palace at Prague. The emperor's reply was to send an army to Prague. In 1621 forty-five Bohemian noblemen were executed by the Hapsburgs in Prague*

with the new flintlock musket and their battle tactics were properly organised. And in his minister, Vauban, Louis had a master of sieges. 'A town besieged by Vauban', so the saying went, 'was a town captured – but a town defended by him was impregnable.' Vauban surrounded the fortress with lines of troops, launched mortar bombs and mined under the walls. He could usually say when the town would surrender.

In all his efforts, Louis was aided by the many French ambassadors, agents and spies abroad. Soldiers, priests and lawyers all served in these roles. They sent information back to Paris, to the Secretary of State for Foreign Affairs, but often in secret directly to Louis himself. They were not regularly paid but their messages flooded in. Often they were in code, and several intelligence men acted as decoders at Versailles.

*European wars 1667–1714*

During Louis' reign, France saw many wars. The major ones were:

The wars of Louis XIV

| | |
|---|---|
| War of Devolution 1667–8 | Against Spain in the Netherlands and Burgundy. |
| The Dutch War 1672–9 | Against the Netherlands. After 1674 also against Spain, the Hapsburg Emperor, and many German princes. |
| The War of the League of Augsburg 1688–97 | Against Spain, Sweden, the Emperor and German princes. |
| The War of the Spanish Succession 1702–14 | Against Spain, England, Brandenburg and many German princes. |

Louis ruled France for fifty-five years, from 1661 until 1715. How many of these saw France at war? For how many years was she at peace?

## The Baltic states

There were wars elsewhere in Europe. In the lands surrounding the Baltic Sea, the great powers in the seventeenth century were Sweden, Brandenburg–Prussia and Russia.

Sweden's rise in the early seventeenth century had been swift. She gained much land by conquest in war, and always confirmed her possessions in treaties. Most important, she defeated Denmark and gained freedom from tolls on all her ships using the Sound, the narrow entrance to the Baltic Sea. The man responsible for this success was King Gustavus Adolphus (1611–32).

Gustavus inherited from his father a country riddled with problems: a war with King Christian IV of Denmark, an inefficient navy, a badly organised army, a government that was unpopular with the people, and very little money. But Gustavus was an unusual man: intelligent, brave and very much a leader who could inspire others. He had a good education and he seems to have mastered several languages quickly. His

King Louis XIV's army was well disciplined and regularly paid

Loading a musket. (*1*) Bite off the cartridge (*2*) Ram down the ball (*3*) Fire

Europe at the Peace of Westphalia, 1648

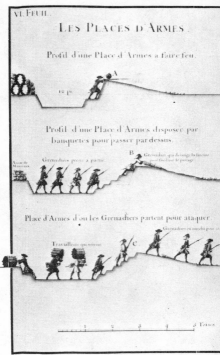

*Military tactics described by King Louis XIV's engineer Vauban in his book on sieges*

particular interests, however, were history, and the study of war: he talked long and often to soldiers who visited Stockholm about their experiences in foreign wars.

It took all of Gustavus' qualities to ensure Sweden's survival in the first ten years of his reign. He and his chancellor, Axel Oxenstierna, reformed the government, the army and the tax system at home. The monarchy became more popular. And abroad, lands were gained from Russia by the Treaty of Stolbora in 1617, Denmark was held at bay, and the claims of Poland to the Swedish crown were thwarted. Finally in 1620 Gustavus secured a favourable marriage, to Maria Eleonora, the daughter of the Elector of Brandenburg. Because her mother opposed the match, he had to go to Berlin in disguise to meet her. Once there, however, the couple fell madly in love, and Eleonora persuaded her mother to allow the marriage.

The next ten years of Gustavus' reign saw Sweden gain control of the Baltic Sea. The Thirty Years War had started in 1618, but at first Gustavus did not want to be involved. He refused to join an alliance

*Artillery in the French army*

with Denmark and England against the Holy Roman Empire. But in 1624 Denmark was defeated and by 1628 the emperor's troops controlled the whole of north Germany. Gustavus had to act to save Sweden. In 1628 he sent troops to save Stralsund, the last garrison to hold out, and in 1630 he himself led an army of 13000 men to Pomerania to fight the might of the Empire.

He had no allies at first. He persuaded the duke of Pomerania to support him and then France, realising his value against the emperor, gave him enough money to finance 36000 troops. Forcefully Gustavus marched south. When Brandenburg refused to help him, he sacked and burned its capital Magdeburg. At last he came face to face with the emperor's troops at Breitenfeld.

Five hours of desperate fighting saw the emperor's infantry force the Swedes back. But Swedish cavalry counter-attacked down both wings, routed their opponents, captured their artillery and then turned inwards and butchered the infantry. Only nightfall saved the enemy: 15000 were killed or captured. One Swedish soldier wrote home:

Ragged, tattered and dirty were our men after their long march. The enemy were glittering, gilded and plume-decked. Our Swedish nags looked underfed next to their German chargers. Our peasant lads looked nothing on the field next to the veterans of Tilly. . . . But they fell to and basted the enemy's hide so briskly that he had to yield.

Further success followed, but in 1632 Gustavus died on the battlefield at Lutzen and his only child, a six-year-old girl Christina, became queen of Sweden. In her reign and that of her two successors, Charles X

*The grenadier. Throwing such a grenade was a risky business.*

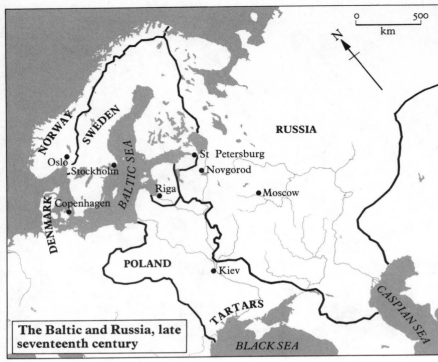

**The Baltic and Russia, late seventeenth century**

and the boy Charles XI, Sweden's old problems returned. Warring nobles prevented unity at home and the gains of Gustavus were frittered away. However, at the peace of Nijmegen in 1679 her ally France insisted that Sweden should lose no territory.

### Peter the Great of Russia (1682–1725)

In the sixteenth and early seventeenth centuries there was little contact between Russia and the West. Some Europeans had gone to Russia to live there and there had long been trading between Moscow and England. Yet Russians were suspicious of Western ideas: in 1547 the tsar could not import Western engineers and mechanics, to help his industry and army, because the Livonians, with whom Russia was at war, barred the way. Later, when new ideas were being discussed in the Russian church, many cried out against 'abominable German customs'.

But this situation was changed by Tsar Peter the Great. Peter became tsar at the age of ten and he was protected by his mother Sophia for the first twelve years. He had to grow up to be hard. He lived in constant fear of assassination, and he watched helplessly when one day in 1682 the palace guards hacked his beloved teacher Matvéev to pieces with their swords. There is a record kept of the toys he played with as a boy: pistols, drums, cannon, bows and arrows. He was given his first sabre at the age of three.

Peter had little education. He heard stories of Russian history, looked at pictures of foreign capitals and ships in the royal palaces, and

*Peter the Great*

*Peter the Great with his scissors*

discussed the fighting of battles. He learned various crafts and trades from Dutch and German visitors, yet at sixteen he could still barely write.

In 1689 after his mother Sophia had plotted to kill him, Peter turned the tables on her and she was assassinated. He thus took over the government himself. He was a tall man, and powerfully built with great square shoulders. He was hard-working, hugely energetic, but often cruel and bloodthirsty. Perhaps he had to be, to survive.

When he became tsar one of his first acts was to visit Holland and England. They were Russia's allies and Russia traded with them. They also had the great navies of the world and Peter was fascinated by the sea and ships. In Holland he called himself 'Master Peter' and told no one his real identity. He stayed at the home of an ironsmith and worked in the shipyards, on the canals and in a sawmill.

After four months in the shipyards of Amsterdam he moved to England. He haunted the arsenal at Woolwich and the ships at Deptford. He even lived as an apprentice and said later, 'If I had not come here, I should always have been a fine carpenter.' He went to sea with an English squadron and when the water became stormy he joked with the sailors, 'Have you ever heard of a tsar who was drowned?' Later he went on a tour of England: the places he visited tell us much about him: the armoury at the Tower of London, Greenwich Observatory, the Royal Mint, Oxford University (where he invited several young mathematicians to join his service). Some writers tried to make scandal out of his visit: they said he dressed in bearskins, that he was often drunk and that he smashed up an inn in Deptford. Yet even one of the pope's advisers commented that 'he was courteous and discreet, with the manners of a well-bred man'.

Back home in Russia Peter immediately set about changing things and introducing Western ideas. He set up schools for navigation, mathematics, artillery and engineering, both in Moscow and in the provinces. He started newspapers and even reformed the alphabet. In 1702 he passed a decree allowing foreigners freely into the country. Many Russians were horrified at their 'outlandish' dress and manners. He allowed religious toleration, changed the calendar so that the year began on 1 January as in the West, and introduced the first hospital in 1706. He stopped the selling of serfs like slaves and allowed women for the first time the right to object to a marriage. In 1704 he founded a new capital, St Petersburg, on the Baltic Sea, nearer the West than Moscow was, and a useful base for the navy he began to develop.

Peter's changes were often unpopular, not least when he himself took a pair of scissors to the long beards of some of his nobles. ('In the West they wear their beards short!' Peter said.) Many plotted and rebelled against him, but such rebellions were quelled. The Scot Patrick Gordon helped Peter. 'The whole month of October', he wrote, 'was spent in lacerating the backs of rebels with the knout and with flames . . . or else they were broken on the wheel or driven to the gibbet or slain with the axe.' Indeed, such was Peter's cruelty that he butchered his own son Alexis because he disagreed with his father's policies.

### The Great Northern War, 1700–1721

At the end of the seventeenth century the two great states of the Baltic fought a long war to decide who should control the Baltic Sea and the trade that went on it. The new Swedish king, Charles XII, was a restless man and one who loved a challenge. In 1699 he had attacked Copenhagen and forced the king of Denmark to surrender to him. Now he faced war against Russia. He marched in haste with just 8000 picked men. They found the Russian army, 32 000 strong, besieging the fortress of Narva. In a heavy snowstorm Charles decided to attack. His men drove Peter's army from the field and captured their artillery. Peter realised that his organisation, his supplies and his men were just not good enough.

Fortunately for him, Charles XII did not follow up his advantage. It was another eight years before he invaded Russia. Meanwhile Peter had been preparing. His army retreated before the Swedes, burning their crops and hiding deeper and deeper in Russian territory. Charles, with his 44 000 men, could never catch up with the Russians to fight them. In a very bad winter two-thirds of his men died and the rest, tired and dispirited, hungry and with little ammunition, were annihilated by the Russians at Poltava (1709). In 1718 Charles was shot dead in Norway in mysterious circumstances and in 1721 the war was ended. Russia's freedom and power in the Baltic were secure.

*Gustavus Adolphus*

*The battle of Lutzen, 1632*

## Using the evidence: the battle of Lutzen, 1632

Read through the story of the battle of Lutzen and imagine that you have to make certain decisions. Remember that generals in battle only have seconds to make decisions: cavalry are charging, artillery is firing, men are yelling, screaming. There is noise, smoke, confusion.

### Stage 1

The date is 5 November 1632. Gustavus Adolphus, king of Sweden, had the previous year defeated the armies of the Holy Roman Empire at Brietenfeld. Now, with the famous Count Wallenstein back in command of the imperial armies, he faced them again.

Wallenstein had all his troops concentrated on Saxony. He wanted to smash the alliance between its duke and Gustavus. One of his generals held Leipzig and he himself was at Lutzen. Since winter was near, he thought Gustavus would start no further war until spring; therefore he sent 8000 cavalry under Pappenheim to Halle. On 5 November they were half a day's ride away from Lutzen.

Gustavus knew that on 4 November he had slightly more men than Wallenstein. He had also sent to John George of Saxony to ask for reinforcements. He knew that John George would try to come but that

*Foreign troops in the Swedish army*

he would find it difficult. So on 5 November Gustavus' army marched towards Lutzen. On the way they were surprised by a cavalry troop from Wallenstein's army. The cavalry resisted the Swedish attack, delayed them and sent word back to Wallenstein that Gustavus was coming. It was late on the night of 5 November when the Swedish army finally reached Lutzen.

1 If you were Gustavus on the night of 5 November, would you:
   (a) organise your battle lines to fight first thing next morning;
   (b) retreat into winter quarters without fighting;
   (c) send out urgent requests to John George of Saxony and wait until he arrived?
Give reasons for your decision.

### Stage 2

Look at the plan of the battlefield on page 180. Wallenstein's army was on slightly higher ground, with a hill on their right. Their artillery were on the right on the higher ground, looking down towards the Swedes.

Gustavus' problem was simple. He had to attack because Wallenstein was in such a good defensive position. Moreover he had to attack quickly, because he knew that Pappenheim's 8000 cavalry could be on the field by mid-afternoon.

Just before 8 a.m. Gustavus moved his army into battle stations. But he was unlucky because the morning was dark: a heavy mist hung over

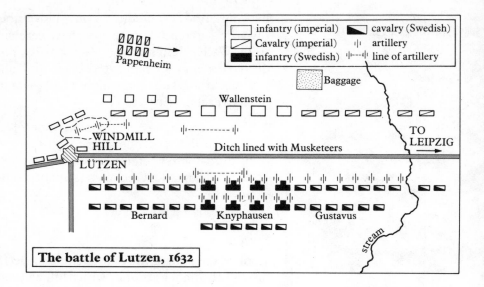

The battle of Lutzen, 1632

the plain. By 10 a.m. the army was ready in position but there was too much mist. Just before 11 a.m. the sun began to break through, the mist began slowly to disappear.

2 Imagine you were Gustavus at this time. Would you
  (a) order the whole army to attack at once;
  (b) order the centre infantry to march forward and also set your own right wing of cavalry forward;
  (c) wait for the fog to clear completely before attacking;
  (d) retire from the battlefield to wait for John George to arrive?
Give reasons for your decisions.

### Stage 3

Gustavus in fact ordered his infantry forward and his own right wing charged. They dispersed the enemy musketeers on the ditch, smashed the enemy left and began to bore in from the flank on the enemy centre.

At this point Pappenheim arrived behind Wallenstein's army. In a gap in the fog he saw the left in danger and charged. He himself was the first man to engage the Swedes. But suddenly when on the point of breaking Gustavus' troops, he was thrown from his horse, mortally wounded by a cannon ball.

His second in command, von Hofkirchen, saw his commander fall. His troops were shaken. In addition, Hofkirchen was a Protestant like the Swedes (the Emperor's army was largely Catholic) and he had a brother in the Swedish army.

3 Imagine you were Hofkirchen. Would you
  (a) try to rally your men and continue the attack,
  (b) lead your men out of the battle,
  (c) just take flight yourself?
If your answer to the question is 1 (a), how would you try to do it?

## Stage 4

In fact Hofkirchen took his men to the rear of the army and Gustavus continued his brutal attack on Wallenstein's infantry. The Swedes seemed to have won once more. But then the fog came down thicker than ever.

This turned to Wallenstein's advantage. His own army could not see Gustavus' success. And Gustavus himself could not see the field. Moreover, 'the king was shot through the arm and his horse's neck'. Meanwhile on the Swedish left, the cavalry of Bernard of Saxe-Weimar were under pressure. Wallenstein's artillery and cavalry had blasted them. Gustavus heard a rumour that Bernard's cavalry was in retreat.

4 Imagine you were Gustavus. Would you
   (a) order the retreat for the whole army;
   (b) continue to attack the enemy infantry and hope that the fog would soon clear to give you a view of the field;
   (c) retreat yourself to the rear to have your wound attended to;
   (d) take a regiment or two of cavalry to help Bernard's cavalry on the left;
   (e) take any other course of action?
5 In fact Gustavus took one regiment of cavalry to help Bernard. What were the possible dangers of this?

## Stage 5

As Gustavus' cavalry were riding to the aid of the left, he himself got separated from his troop in the fog. He was caught up in a mêlée. An enemy horseman fired a pistol at his back. He slumped in the saddle, fell, but caught one foot in the stirrup. He was dragged through the mud before he could loosen himself. Then another trooper fired a ball through his head. Plunderers took his ring, watch and chain, and spurs.

'The king is dead,' went up the cry. The army seemed to freeze. Bernard was now the commander. He consulted Knyphausen, the infantry commander: Knyphausen advised retreat. They were a long way from home and there was no hope of victory, he argued.

6 Draw a plan of the battlefield as it now appears to you.
7 Bernard was very loyal to Gustavus. He wanted to avenge his death. Was there any way he could still win the battle?

## Postscript

Bernard rallied his own and Gustavus' cavalry. His Protestant chaplain started a group of over a hundred infantry singing Protestant hymns. This singing became a rallying cry. All were anxious to avenge Gustavus' death.

Bernard's cavalry charged and after heavy losses captured the enemy guns on Windmill Hill. They turned the guns on the enemy. This in turn rallied the Swedish infantry. At dusk Wallenstein conceded defeat.

It seems that about 6000 Swedes and even more of their enemy died in the battle.

## 16 The France of Louis XIV

### The people of France

Between 1675 and 1679 an Englishman journeyed throughout France. He visited many people, talked to the poor peasants and townsmen, and wrote about them in his diary. His name was John Locke, and this is what he wrote about the life of peasants in Bordeaux:

Talking in this country with a poor peasant's wife, she told us she had three children; that her husband got usually seven sous per day, which was to maintain their family, five in number. She herself got three sous per day when she could get work, which was but seldom. . . . Out of his seven sous, they were five to be maintained, house-rent paid, taxes and Sundays and holy days to be provided for.

For their house . . . which was a poor one room and one storey open to the tiles, without window . . . they paid twelve écus per annum rent and for *taille* four livres, for which, not long since, the collector had taken their frying pan and dishes, money not being ready. . . . Their ordinary food rye bread and water. Meat is a thing seldom seasons their pots . . . . And yet they say that in Saintouge and several other parts of France, the peasants are much more miserable than these.

In the late seventeenth century there were about twenty million people in France, as opposed to six or seven million in England. Of these, perhaps nine out of every ten were peasants like those described by John Locke. The other tenth of the population was made up of large-scale landowners, like the nobility and the church, and townsmen, ranging from rich merchants to humble artisans. Paris was the

*A French peasant family*

only French town of any real size – her suburbs teemed with over half a million people – but no other town could boast 100 000.

These, then, were the people of France, the subjects of King Louis XIV.

### Louis' early life

Louis XIV was born on 5 September 1638, the child of King Louis XIII and Anne of Austria. His parents despised each other; his father was shy and religious, a man who liked to be alone, while his mother was beautiful, vivacious, lazy and fond of company.

Because his father died in 1643, Louis became king at the tender age of four. His mother, however, was determined to retain power for herself, and she was helped by her closest ally, Cardinal Mazarin – a subtle and clever Italian diplomat with whom Anne probably fell in love. Together they schemed to control France until the young Louis came of age.

They certainly steered France successfully through the closing stages of the Thirty Years War and the peace negotiations which followed. At home, however, they faced insoluble problems, including a civil war involving nobles, lawyers and peasants. These disturbances were known as the '*Frondes*', after a children's game which involved throwing stones with a catapult. On two occasions the rioting in Paris was so bad that Mazarin had to flee into temporary exile.

It was against this background that Louis XIV grew up. He was spoiled by his mother who always gave him his own way. His education was often neglected. The Venetian ambassador wrote in 1652, when Louis was fourteen, that 'games, hunting, dances and fun are the king's whole life'. Every evening, however, Mazarin taught Louis about French history and explained how France was governed.

Louis was taught to write by spelling over and over again the words, 'Homage is due to kings. They do what they please.' And he was introduced by Mazarin into the various ceremonial occasions of the court, wearing a coat 'so covered with gold embroidery that neither the stuff nor its colour could be seen'. When Mazarin died in 1661 there was no doubt that Louis was ready to take personal control of the government. Under him, France became, in the words of one contemporary, 'the most beautiful country, the most powerful kingdom, and the most glorious monarchy of Europe. I could, perhaps, justly say, "of the whole world", but I don't want to appear too biased.'

### The Sun King (1661–1715)

Look at the picture of Louis XIV on page 188. What sort of man, what sort of king, does it show him to be?

The following descriptions were both written by women of the court who admired him:

His body is tall, ample, robust; his chest and shoulders broad, his legs big,

*Peasant poverty in the reign of King Louis XIV*

well-proportioned and sweet. Even should he disguise himself, one would know that he is the master, for he has the air by which we recognise the gods.

His manner is often cold; he speaks little except to people with whom he is familiar, and then he speaks well and effectively and to the point. He jokes agreeably and always in good taste. He has natural goodness, is charitable, liberal and a true king.

For fifty-four years Louis lived in the public eye at the centre of a magnificent court. Most of his time was spent in the great palace at Versailles. This had been the setting of one of his father's palaces, but Louis liked it so much that he extended the gardens, glades, stables, fountains and sculptures. In 1661 a zoo was included in the estates and in 1668 Louis decided to rebuild the whole estate completely as a new and permanent home for the royal court. The magnificence of the palace is clear from photographs. However, many thousands of workmen, digging canals to carry water for the fountains, died of marsh fever and were buried at night, 'so as not to frighten the other workers or reveal the bad air around Versailles'.

Louis' daily life at Versailles followed a very regular routine. Our information about this comes from the diaries and letters of a number of courtiers, and especially the Duke of Saint-Simon, who was never really very successful at court and hence remained bitter and somewhat critical of palace-life.

Even in his bedroom the king followed a regular routine and had little privacy: his servants rose at 7 a.m. and lit fires and opened shutters; at 7.30 a.m. the first valet woke the king with the ritual words, 'Sire, it is time'; his attendants then rubbed him down and changed his nightshirt.

Then came the *grandes entrées*:

Those who had entry and might see the king while he was in bed were Monseigneur [Louis' son, the Dauphin]; the dukes of Burgundy, Berry, Orleans and Bourbon; the Duke of Maine and the Count of Toulouse. Similarly privileged were the grand Chamberlain, the first four gentlemen of the chamber ... the first physician and the first surgeon.

The Grand Chamberlain then drew aside the curtains around the four-poster bed and Louis met his audience. The rest of the proceedings – his prayers, his choosing of his wigs, his breakfast and toilette – were similarly public and regulated, as were the evening entertainments, the balls, the ballet, the comedies of playwrights, and the gambling. One courtier describes a professional gambler, Dangeau, who made a profitable living at court:

He profits by every mistake; he never throws a chance away. The queen and the ladies of court talk incessantly: 'How many hearts have you?' 'I have one,' 'I have two.' He is delighted with their chatter. He thinks of nothing but the game. He wins where others lose.

By day, however, Louis worked conscientiously and with tremendous energy at the job of governing France: he summoned various advisers and councils, he made decisions and policies, he wrote letters

*The bustle of Paris. The Pont-Neuf over the River Seine*

*The Palace of Versailles from a painting in 1668. More buildings were added later by King Louis XIV*

*Cardinal Mazarin*

*A royal hunting party in 1679*

to diplomats abroad and royal officials in the provinces. He controlled the affairs not only of his own twenty million subjects, but also of many of the people of western Europe.

Above all else, he wanted glory, both for himself and for his kingdom. He wanted a unified powerful state, obedient to his will and respected by all the other powers of Europe. By his death in 1715 he had succeeded, but many thousands of ordinary people died and millions suffered in the process of achieving these aims.

### The administration of France

Louis XIV was an absolute king. 'Kings are absolute lords,' he told his son, the Dauphin. 'They naturally have completely free disposal of all the belongings of their subjects.' At Versailles, Louis made all the major decisions himself: 'The king must know everything, he must be vigorous, vigilant and hard-working.' He allowed his mother, his brother and other members of the royal family no say in the government at all. He had a council to advise him, but he summoned it when he needed it – and no one had a right to attend. Louis also made laws for the French people himself, and he could legally arrest or imprison or accuse any man in France, bring him to trial and punish him in his own council meetings. There were law courts called *'Parlements'* all over France – but he could cancel their decisions or remove any of their cases to the royal court.

*Jean-Baptiste Colbert (see page 188)*

Perhaps the greatest difficulty Louis had to overcome was that of governing the provinces, many of them distant from Versailles and used to their own ways. The people of Brittany had always objected to the king's officials and tax collectors, while the Huguenots (or Protestants) of Languedoc had many times opposed Catholic priests and bishops.

Louis solved this problem by sending his own special representatives, called intendants, into the provinces. Many of these were young men, full of drive and energy, perhaps ambitious lawyers or politicians; most important, they were men who were loyal to the king. By 1715 the intendant of Brittany had so organised the province that he had eighty-six assistants and other important officials like the Lieutenant-General of Police and the Inspector of Mines and Manufacturers working for him.

*The king visits the famous Gobelins tapestry factory*

Typical of Louis' intendants was Lamoignon de Baville, the intendant of Languedoc. Born in 1648, the son of a prominent Paris lawyer, he qualified as a lawyer himself at the age of eighteen and became one of Louis' chief officials while in his early thirties. He remained intendant of the Huguenot province of Languedoc for thirty-three years.

In his post he was responsible for converting the Huguenots to Catholicism and punishing those who refused. To do this, he built roads through the whole region covered by the Cevennes mountains, wide enough for cannon to pass through and for his dragoons to ride quickly to the scene of any riot. In addition, he recruited twelve new regiments of Catholic troops and arranged for them to be clothed, paid and supplied. He also arranged for three large new forts to be built at Nîmes, Alais and St Hippolyte, and he tried to educate more Catholic priests who could go to the people to teach men about Catholicism. All in all, Baville's efficiency showed how Louis could govern even his most distance provinces.

### The prosperity of France

Perhaps Louis' most loyal and able adviser was Jean-Baptiste Colbert. Colbert was a born civil servant: like others, he secured a great private fortune, he married his daughters to noblemen, and he promoted his brothers and sons. Yet his great love was planning and organising the collection of taxes and the improvement of industry and agriculture.

The most productive tax in France was the land-tax or *taille*. 'Less than half the land of the kingdom is liable to *taille*,' wrote one intendant; 'the nobles who own most of it pay nothing; only the miserable peasant has to pay.' In addition, officials who collected the tax were corrupt and inefficient: some falsified their accounts and put money into their own pockets. Colbert reckoned that of the eighty-five million livres collected in 1661, only thirty-two million livres actually reached the crown. He never managed to defeat this problem completely, though by keeping more accurate records and checking carefully on certain collectors he was able to reduce the amount lost.

*Improvements in river transport in seventeenth-century France. Notice the opening bridge in the centre*

In other areas, however, he was more successful. He recruited skilled craftsmen from all over France to help stimulate industries like silk-making, paper-making and glass-blowing; he imported engineers, iron-founders, and naval experts from England and Holland; he improved roads, bridges and canals to carry the new industrial produce, and he encouraged trading companies to sell French goods overseas and secure new raw materials for his industries. All this helped to make France a more prosperous country with more employment for Louis XIV's subjects.

*Threshing. This drawing comes from the famous French Encyclopaedia of the eighteenth century*

## Religion in France

Seventeenth-century France was a Roman Catholic country. But one million of its people were Huguenots, or Protestants. An earlier king, Henry IV, had given them important rights and privileges in his Edict of Nantes in 1595. As a result, most remained loyal to the Crown; some served in the army and navy, and others became prominent and wealthy in industry, trade, and professions like medicine.

For the first part of his reign, Louis XIV was prepared to allow Huguenots their rights, though he hoped that many would become Catholics. But, very suddenly, after 1677, his policy changed. He

*The Revocation of the Edict of Nantes at Fontainebleau, 1685*

determined to stamp out their religion. Madame de Maintenon, one of the Catholic ladies at court, wrote:

In twenty years there will be not one Huguenot left in France.

In 1685, at Fontainebleau, Louis cancelled or revoked the Edict of Nantes.

## Using the evidence: what happened to the Huguenots?

In his memoirs of Louis XIV's reign, the sharp-tongued diarist, Saint-Simon, presents a lively view of Louis' treatment of Huguenots:

(1) The revocation of the Edict of Nantes . . . depopulated one quarter of the kingdom, destroyed its commerce, caused widespread pillage, restarted the dragonnades, allowed torture which killed many thousands of innocent people . . . and caused industrious people to move abroad where they flourished and brought wealth to other states.

In expressing these opinions Saint-Simon would be well aware of many of the following pieces of evidence. The Edict of Fontainebleau itself said:

(2) Clause 4. We command all ministers and priests of the Huguenots, who do not wish to become Catholics, to leave our kingdom within fifteen days, without during that time preaching to their people, upon pain of being sent to the galleys.

Clause 7. We forbid private schools for the instruction of the children of the said Huguenots.

Clause 8. All children who may be born to Huguenots are to be baptised by Catholic priests ... and thereafter to be brought up in the Catholic faith.

Clause 10. We emphasise that none of our Huguenot subjects are to leave our kingdom or send their goods abroad, upon pain of being sent to the galleys.

'The galleys' was a particularly frightening punishment. John Evelyn describes how he saw them:

(3) It was strange to see so many hundreds of miserably naked persons, having their heads shaven close, a pair of rough canvas drawers, their whole backs and legs naked, chained about their middle and their legs. . . . They are ruled and punished by strokes of the whip on their backs and soles of their feet on the least disorder and without the least humanity.

In face of such punishments, many Huguenots fled abroad. Some went as far as the Cape of Good Hope, a Dutch colony in South Africa.

*The Revocation Edict of Fontainebleau*

(4) Numbers of Huguenots arriving at the city of Magdeburg in Prussia

| Year | 1685 | 1686 | 1687 | 1688 | 1689 | 1690 | 1692 | 1695 | 1698 | 1699 |
|------|------|------|------|------|------|------|------|------|------|------|
| Number | 18 | 84 | 118 | 109 | 43 | 31 | 119 | 22 | 109 | 155 |

(5) Occupations of Huguenots in Bristol in 1705

Weavers 50    Sailors 47    Merchants 15

Tailors 7    Doctors 4    Hatters and pastors 3

Goldsmiths, shoemakers, coopers 2 each

Tiler, joiner, labourer, locksmith, landowner, farm labourer, clockmaker, student, wig-maker, halberdier 1 each

Yet Louis did not drive all the Huguenots from France. In 1702 Abraham Mazel and other 'Camisard' rebels used violence themselves!

(6) At dusk (early 1702) we set out for Saint-André to put to death the parish priest, to burn his house and set fire to the church. The next morning we entered the priest's house but found no one, for the priest had fled to the top of the belltower with provisions and weapons. After having burned his house, we broke down the door of the church and destroyed the altar and the images. . . . Then the priest revealed himself to us by throwing stones at us. Immediately four of our men placed a ladder by the church wall and climbed on the roof armed with pistols and halberts. The priest tried to fire at them, but his weapons failed to work, so, seeing that he was irretrievably lost, he jumped from the tower and killed himself. . . . I can also say that we took his weapons which would not fire, and in our hands they never misfired.

## Questions and further work

1 What punishments were given to the Huguenots in France?

2 What opinions are expressed by Saint-Simon in Document 1?

3 What point is the writer trying to make in the last sentence of Document 6?

4 For what reasons did so many Huguenots leave France after 1685?

5 Which Documents would support Saint-Simon's opinions?

6 Which of his opinions are not supported in the Documents?

# 17

# Europe and the New World

## Using the evidence: the Indians of North America

(1) Look at the drawing of a village in 1562. It was built by a tribe of Indians in Florida, on the eastern coast of America. The chief's house stands in the centre.

1 What makes you think this may be a newly built village?
2 Notice the entrance at the bottom of the picture, and the two huts with holes in. Why do you think they were built like this?
3 Do you find anything in the picture surprising?

The drawing was done by a Frenchman, Jacques le Moyne. He was a member of two expeditions to Florida, in 1562 and 1564. Underneath his drawing he wrote:

(2) The Indians are accustomed to build their fortified towns as follows: a position is selected near the channel of some swift stream. They level it as even as possible, and then dig a ditch in a circle around the site, in which they set thick round pales, close together, to twice the height of a man; and they carry this paling some ways past the beginning of it, spiral-wise, to make a narrow entrance admitting not more than two persons abreast. The course of the stream is also diverted to this entrance; and at each end of it they are accustomed to erect a small round building, each full of cracks and holes, and built, considering their means, with much elegance. In these they station as sentinels men who can smell traces of an enemy at a great distance, and who, as soon as they perceive such traces, set off to discover them. As soon as they find them, they set up a cry which summons those within the town to the defence, armed with bows and arrows and clubs.

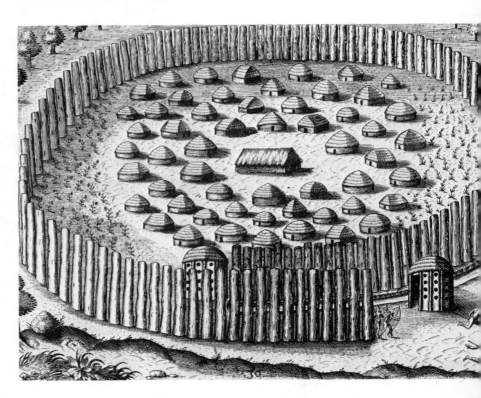

Another man who saw and described the Indians at this time was an English scientist, Thomas Harriott. He sailed with Sir Walter Raleigh in 1586 to Virginia. He wrote about a tribe of Indians who lived farther north:

(3) Their towns are but small and near the sea coast but few, some containing but ten or twelve houses, some twenty. . . . If they be walled it is only done with barks of trees made fast to stakes.

Their houses are made of small poles made fast at the tops . . . covered with barks or with artificial mats made of long rushes.

## Indian methods of farming

(4) The Indians were farmers and hunters. Le Moyne drew them working in the fields in Florida.

Their hoes were made of fish bones on long wooden handles. First they cleared away weeds and stones; then they made holes in the ground and placed grains of maize in the holes.

Harriott also wrote about farming in Virginia:

(5) The ground they never fatten with muck, dung or any other thing, neither plough nor dig it, as we in England. A few days before they sow or set, the men, with wooden instruments, made almost in form of mattocks or hoes with long handles, . . . do only break the upper part of the ground to raise up the weeds. The which, after a day or two drying in the sun, being scraped up into many small heaps, they burn to ashes. . . . This is all the husbanding of the ground that they use.

Then their sowing is after this manner. Beginning in one corner of the plot they make a hole, wherein they put four grains, with the care that they touch not one another, and cover them with the soil again. And so throughout the whole plot; with this regard, that the holes be made in ranks, half a yard apart.

(6) As hunters, too, they were skilled.

Thomas Harriott:

(7) Squirrels, which are of grey colour, we have taken or eaten. Bears are all of black colour. The bears of this country are good meat. The inhabitants in time of winter do take and eat many, so also sometimes did we. They are taken in this way: in some places where they are being hunted for, as soon as they spy a man, they presently run away. Being chased they climb up the next tree they can. From whence with arrows they are shot down stark dead, or with those wounds that they may after easily be killed.

4 Draw an outline plan from above of the Florida village. Make a list of its defensive strengths.
5 How did the Virginia village differ from the Florida one?
6 Look carefully at Documents 4 and 6. Do you think they actually happened as le Moyne has drawn them?
7 What can we learn from the written accounts that we cannot tell from the drawings? What can we learn from the drawings that we cannot tell from the writing?

## The Indians at war

(8) Many Indian tribes were peace-loving. But some chiefs were fond of battle. In one picture the Florida chief, Ontina, marches to war.

Le Moyne wrote, 'He used to march with regular ranks like an organised army. . . . After sunset they halt and are never wont to give battle.'

8 How can you tell the chiefs in the picture?
9 What weapons and armour do the Indians carry?
10 What do you think the men with spears are running off to do?

(9) The young men trained for war by their sports.

Le Moyne wrote:

(10) Their youth are trained in running, and a prize is offered for him who can run longest without stopping. They frequently practise with the bow. They also play a game of ball as follows: in the middle of an open space is set up a tree some eight or nine fathoms [16–18 metres] high with a square frame woven of twigs on the top. This is to be hit with a ball. He who strikes it first gets a prize. They are also fond of hunting and fishing.

## Indian religion

Harriott wrote about the Indians in Virginia:

(11) They believe there are many gods. One only Chief and great God who made the sun, moon and stars as lesser gods. They think that all gods are of human shape and therefore they represent them by images.

11 Describe what is happening in the picture above. Notice the faces and hands of the Indians.

12 Give one piece of evidence which suggests that Indians were:
(a) helpful to their neighbours
(b) cunning
(c) well-organised.

13 Imagine you were a young Indian. Describe one day in your life from morning till night. Record the things you did and how you felt about them.

14 From the evidence, make a list of
(a) aspects of Indian life which Europeans may find threatening or puzzling
(b) aspects of Indian life which may encourage Europeans to sail to America.

## Pioneers from Europe

In Europe stories were quickly circulated about the Indians and their land. Le Moyne's drawings, for instance, were made into a book in 1591 and widely circulated. Men of adventure wanted to visit this new world.

They had many reasons for going. Some wanted wealth. Vast areas of unfarmed land, good fishing in the seas, huge pine and fir trees which would fuel the shipyards of Europe. And there were stories of gold, silver and precious jewels. English and Dutch adventurers hoped to find gold just as the Spaniards had done in South America.

Governments, too, had an interest in colonies. England and Holland and France would welcome war-bases to keep an eye on Spanish bases in the Caribbean. In addition, they hoped to find a route to the wealth of the East, which the Spanish and Portuguese did not control. Hence the famous search for the North-West Passage.

Yet, for many, adventure was the main motive. In the reign of Elizabeth, Sir Richard Grenville wrote:

> Who seeks the way to win renown
> Or flies with wings of high desire;
> Who seeks to wear the laurel crown,
> Or hath the mind that would aspire;
> Tell him his native soil eschew,
> Tell him go range and seek anew.
> To pass the seas some think a toil,
> Some think it strange abroad to roam,
> Some think it grief to leave their soil,
> Their parents, kinsfolk, and their home;
> Think so who list, I like it not,
> I must abroad to try my lot.

*The* Mayflower *leaves Plymouth in 1620.*

### The Pilgrim Fathers

One or two small groups of people had yet another reason for moving to the New World. The charter of the first colonists in Virginia stated that 'the true word of God is to be preached to the colonists and the savages'. Some religious people tried to find land where they would be free to worship as they wished. Among these were the Pilgrim Fathers.

They had left England in 1608, no longer able to worship in the Anglican churches of King James I. They had settled in Amsterdam, working and living happily with the Dutch. But in 1620 a group of them, who were unhappy that their children were growing up with Dutch speech and manners, decided to venture to the New World, to America.

They sailed to England, and from Plymouth they took ship on 5 August 1620 in two vessels, the *Speedwell* and the *Mayflower*. After some days at sea the *Speedwell* sprung a leak and both ships returned to Dartmouth for repairs. Finally the hundred or so pilgrims all packed into the *Mayflower* and on 6 September they set sail again.

Look carefully at the picture of the *Mayflower* on the right. She was

*The landing at Cape Cod*

an ordinary merchant ship of about 180 tonnes, perhaps twenty-seven metres long and 7.5 metres wide. She had two decks; between them was stored a rowing boat or shallop. The beak or prow at the front would help the ship to break over high waves; the high castle at the back would give a clear view out to sea and a defence against pirates or other attackers. The ship had a large, round hull used for storing cargo. Here the stench of stagnant water and the ever-present rats would be a great problem.

What was it like to make a long voyage aboard such a ship? Clearly, she was overcrowded, the living space was cramped. Food consisted of salted pork and herrings and ship's biscuit. Occasionally there might be cheese, onion or dried peas. Fresh water was carried in casks but it quickly became foul, so casks of wine were also carried. There was no fresh fruit or vegetables: diseases like scurvy were common. Sailors didn't help themselves much over this: most ships were filthy, with no system of sanitation at all.

The pilgrims started the voyage in good heart. Then a strong wind blew up. Many were seasick. One young crewman laughed at them and told them that:

he hoped to cast half of them overboard before they came to their journey's end, and to make merry with what property they had. And if he were by any gently reproved, he would curse and swear most bitterly.

But it pleased God, before they came half the seas over, to smite this young man with a grievous disease; of which he died in a desperate manner. And so he himself was the first that was thrown overboard.

Then the ship met even stormier weather:

And met with many fierce storms; with which the ship was shrewdly shaken and her upper works made very leaky. In sundry of these storms, the winds were so fierce and the seas so high as they could not bear a knot of sail. . . . And in one of them, as they lay hull in a highty storm, a lusty young man called John Howland, coming upon some occasion above the grating, was thrown into the sea. But it pleased God that he caught hold of the sail halyards, which hung overboard and ran out at length. Yet he held this hold, though he was sundry fathoms under water, till he was hauled up, by the same rope, to the brim of the water. And then with a boathook and other means, was got into the ship again, and his life saved. And though he was something ill with it, yet he lived many years after.

Again God seemed to be on the pilgrims' side. In fact, John Howland lived until 1673 and had ten children.

Finally on 9 November, near to Cape Cod Bay, they sighted land. It was a cold, grey day and they had been at sea for over two months. Small wonder that 'they fell upon their knees and blessed the God of Heaven, who had brought them over the vast and furious ocean'.

*A modern painting of the First Thanksgiving for safe arrival and delivery in America*

## The growth of colonies

The first Englishman to try to set up a colony in North America was Sir Humphrey Gilbert. He found men of many countries in Newfoundland but claimed it for the queen in 1583. Unfortunately he was drowned when returning to England the following year and Newfoundland finally became a British colony in 1621.

It was Gilbert's brother-in-law, Sir Walter Raleigh, who really explored the North American coast. In 1584 he sent two small ships on a reconnaissance. On their return the captain told him of the fine land in Virginia: 'many and goodly woods full of deer, hares and fowl, in the midst of summer, in incredible abundance'. Even the natives were friendly. The first Indian they saw came aboard their ship and then proceeded to sit in his boat and fish.

Raleigh was delighted. The following year he sent seven ships, and 107 settlers, to Virginia, but they found it difficult to grow crops and the Indians would not supply any. So the next year they came home. Further attempts were later made but it was not until the Virginia Company was founded in 1606 that real colonisation started. In 1610 many colonists died of starvation in a severe winter. In 1622 Indians massacred over 350 of them. Even when tobacco began to be grown in Virginia times remained hard.

*Above left: The inside of a New England settler's home, early seventeenth century*

*Above right: A New England settlement in 1623. Notice how the houses are built*

*An advertisement of 1609. What is it advertising? Is it a good advertisement?*

Farther north, other English colonies flourished. Over 1000 members of the Massachusetts Bay Company settled in Boston in 1630. Rhode Island, Long Island, New Haven and Maine all became prosperous trading centres. Maryland in 1632 and Carolina in 1663, were also founded in this period.

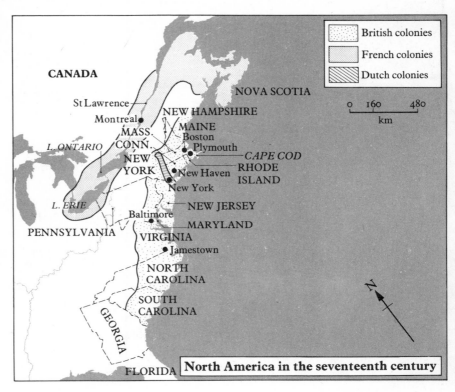

North America in the seventeenth century

### Dutch and French colonies

Dutch and French adventurers were also active. The main French trading post was established at Quebec in 1608. In 1627 the Company of New France was set up in what is now Canada. It was later supported by armies from Louis XIV and may have had a population of nearly 10 000 by the end of the seventeenth century. In 1642 Montreal became a major fur trading centre. Trappers and traders set out to explore the great lakes and a few men, like Pierre Radisson, actually went by canoe into Hudson's Bay.

Dutch influence was small. The Dutch West India Company fortified New Amsterdam, now called New York, in 1614. In 1617 they made a treaty with the Iroquois Indians. To the horror of French and British, the Dutch even traded brandy and guns to the Indians. By the 1640s, however, English settlers were moving into New Amsterdam and in 1664 it became an English colony. This was an event of major importance, for now English colonies covered the whole east coast of North America from Nova Scotia to Carolina.

# 18

# Farming, trade and industry

## The people of England

In April 1676, the Archbishop of Canterbury sent a letter to all Church of England priests in Kent. He wanted to know how many people lived and went to church in each parish. One curate, from the parish of Goodnestone-next-Wingham, replied in very great detail. This table shows what he wrote:

| Status of households | Number of households | Number of people | Number of children | Number of servants |
|---|---|---|---|---|
| Gentry | 3 | 28 | 7 | 16 |
| Yeomen/husbandmen | 12/14 | 151 | 64 | 34 |
| Tradesman | 9 | 35 | 16 | 2 |
| Labourers | 12 | 38 | 15 | 0 |
| Poor | 12 | 25 | 11 | 0 |
| Total | 62 | 277 | 113 | 52 |

Adapted from P. Laslett, *The World We Have Lost*, 1965

What does this table tell us about the people who lived in the English countryside? The largest householder was in the manor-house. The lord of the manor was Edward Hales; with him were his wife, six children and fifteen servants, nine male, six female. Two other couples in the village were also of 'gentle blood'. These people, and the curate, were probably the only people who could read and write. The six female servants probably worked most of the time in the house, cleaning and cooking. The nine male servants would work in gardens and fields.

Twelve households were those of yeomen, farmers with a good area of land. Together they amounted to over a hundred people and perhaps a third of these were servants, mostly men who worked in the fields. Life for the yeomen was comfortable: they ate meat, vegetables, and eggs; their houses had some wooden furniture and the heads of the households often travelled to the nearest towns.

Beneath them there were fourteen families of husbandmen – farmers who rented a small amount of land and had some hired hands to till it. Nine tradesmen lived in the village, including two carpenters, two brickmakers, a weaver, a shoemaker, a tailor and a woman who called herself a grocer. There was no blacksmith. Shepherds and thatchers must be among the husbandmen and labourers. There was also in the village a hospital for the destitute, with one man and three women in it.

The life of a poor man in the village was hard. Born in a labourer's cottage, he became the 'servant' of a husbandman at the age of eleven or twelve. Here he worked in the fields and lived in his master's house. But this was no high living. 'His landlord's horses', wrote one contemporary, 'lie in finer houses than he.' And when the husbandman said his prayers at night, 'The wife is sleeping in one corner, the child in another, the servant in a third.' The servant remained with his master until he married, then he took a cottage of his own and became a labourer. He and his family found what work they could in the fields

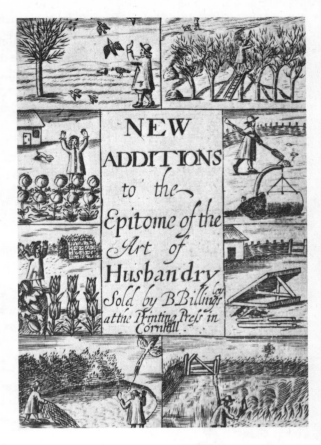

*Scenes from* The Whole Art of Husbandry *printed in Stuart England*

and grew fruit and vegetables in their own cottage garden. His wife spun and perhaps wove cloth, the children scared away birds from the crops and looked after the animals.

> Little boy blue, come blow up your horn,
> The sheep's in the meadow, the cow's in the corn.
> Where is the boy who looks after the sheep?
> He's under the haystack fast asleep.

In seventeenth-century England there were about 5½ million people. Most lived in villages like Goodnestone. It has been suggested that 1½ million were gentlemen farmers, yeomen or husbandmen. Perhaps 1¼ million were labourers, and a further 1½ million were destitute or very poor. The needs of these people were food, housing, clothing and fuel: all could be met from the land. Nearly all of these people lived in small village settlements, like Goodnestone, which ranged from 100 to perhaps 600 inhabitants.

Fewer than one person in ten lived in bigger settlements or towns. London was easily the biggest city. By the end of the century, nearly half a million people lived there. Yet from any church tower you could see green fields and farms. Seaports like Bristol and Norwich had 40 000 people, but apart from them there were few big towns.

## People in the towns

In 1619 the London bakers tried to get the price of bread increased. To do this they wrote down a description of a bakery and a list of its weekly costs. They sent the information to the city authorities to support their claim. There were perhaps 100 000 traders, craftsmen and shopkeepers in England. The bakers were among them and their record tells us about them.

In one bakery there were fourteen people: the master baker, his wife and four children, four paid journeymen, two apprentices, and two maidservants. The following table shows how much money the baker spent in a week:

|  | £ | s | d |
|---|---|---|---|
| *Wages* | | | |
| Journeymen 2s 6d each | | 10 | 0 |
| Maids 10d each | | 1 | 8 |
| *Food* | | | |
| Baker & wife 5s each | | 10 | 0 |
| Children 2s each | | 8 | 0 |
| Others 4s each | 1 | 12 | 0 |
| *School fees* for the children | | | |
| 6d each | | 2 | 0 |
| *Other expenses* include clothes for all fourteen, fuel for the bakery and the house, raw materials for making bread, etc. | 3 | 6 | 4 |
| *Total expenses* | 6 | 10 | 0 |

The baker's house was home and workshop. Little bread was sold on the premises. It was taken to the open-air market and sold on stalls. Behind the house was a 'garner'. The baker paid 2s a week rent for this, and he kept coal, wheat and salt in it. The whole household ate in the house, and all but the four journeymen slept there.

The apprentices lived in the house for seven years. Each agreed to obey the master:

Taverns and alehouses he shall not haunt, dice, cards or any other unlawful games he shall not use, marriage with any woman he shall not contract. He shall not absent himself by night or day without his master's leave, but be a true and faithful servant.

The master, for his part, agreed to teach the apprentices the skills of baking,

Finding and allowing (them) meat, drink, apparel, washing, lodging and all other things during the said term of seven years.

## Changes in farming and industry

In 1587 William Harrison wrote his *Description of England*.

The pasture of this island is according to the nature and bounty of the soil, whereby in most places it is plentiful, very fine, and such as either fatteth our cattle with speed or yieldeth great abundance of milk and cream whereof the

*Two engravings by Wenceslas Hollar, 1640*

yellowest butter and finest cheese are made. . . .

The yield of our corn-ground is also much after this rate following. Throughout the land (if you please to make an estimate thereof by the acre [0.4 hectare]) in mean and indifferent years, wherein each acre of rye or wheat, well tilled and dressed, will yield commonly sixteen or twenty bushels [600–700 litres]. An acre of barley six-and-thirty bushels [2300 litres], of oats and suchlike four or five quarters [1100–1500 litres], which proportion is notwithstanding oft abated toward the north, as it is oftentimes surmounted in the south. Of mixed corn, as peas and beans sown together . . . their yield is nevertheless much after this proportion. . . .

Of late years also we have found and taken up a great trade in planting of hops, whereof our moory hitherto and unprofitable grounds do yield such plenty and increase that there are few farmers or occupiers in the country which have not gardens and hops growing of their own, and these far better than do come from Flanders unto us. . . .

The cattle which we breed are commonly such as for greatness of bone, sweetness of flesh, and other benefits to be reaped by the same, give place unto none other; as may appear first by our oxen, whose largeness, height, weight, tallow, hides and horns are such as none of any other nation do commonly or may easily exceed them. Our sheep likewise, for good taste of flesh, quantity of limbs, fineness of fleece, give no place unto any, more than do our goats . . . and our deer not come behind. As for our cronies [rabbits], I have seen them so fat with some soils . . . that the grease of one being weighed hath very near six or seven ounces (0.2 kg). . . .

I touch in this place one benefit which our nation wanteth, and that is wine, the fault whereof is not in our soil, but the negligence of our countrymen. . . . I muse not a little wherefore the planting of vines should be neglected in England.

Now our soil either will not, or at the leastwise may not, bear either woad or madder [a dye]. . . . The like I may say of flax, which by law ought to be sown in every country town in England, more or less. . . .

Glass also hath been made here in great plenty before, and in the time of the Romans, and the said stuff also, beside fine scissors, shears, collars of gold and silver for women's necks, cruises and cups of amber, were a parcel of the tribute which Augustus in his days laid upon this island. . . .

Of coal mines we have such plenty in the north and western parts of our island as may suffice for all the realm of England, and so must they do hereafter indeed, if wood be not better cherished than it is at this present. . . . Besides our coal mines, we have pits in like sort of white plaster and of fat and white and

*Brewing*

*Farming implements*

other coloured marl.... We have saltpetre for our ordinance and salt soda for our glass....

Tin and lead ... are very plentiful with us, the one in Cornwall, Devonshire and elsewhere in the north, the other in Derbyshire, Weredale and sundry places of this island.

Copper is lately not found, but rather restored again to light....

As for our steel, it is not so good for edge-tools as that of Cologne, and yet the one is often sold for the other.

1 Make a list of the products which Harrison says are better in England than elsewhere.
2 What evidence does he give for his view?
3 How much of this evidence is Harrison's opinion?

For the tenant farmer and husbandman, life and work changed little in the seventeenth century. Two hundred thousand hectares of forest, swamp, fen and moor were reclaimed and put to pasture and arable. More land was enclosed, particularly in the Midlands, where farmers gained great profit by changing over to pasture, rearing sheep and selling the wool. Turnips, clover and other new crops were introduced from Holland by men like Sir Richard Weston, and Barnaby Googe. Now, instead of being left fallow every third year to recover its goodness, the land was planted with root crops: these added goodness, like nitrogen, to the soil and at the same time provided winter fodder for cattle. Fewer cattle were killed in the autumn and more land was naturally manured. Other fertilisers, especially lime and marl, were also used more and more.

But these new ideas spread slowly. Most farmers were reluctant to change their ways and try new ideas. The same was true in industry. There were one or two important inventions, like Thomas Savery's steam engine to pump water from the depths of tin and coal mines. The Bank of England was set up by King William III in 1694, and many local banks soon followed. Money was now to be available for men who wanted to start up in industry. These developments played an important part in the Industrial Revolution of the eighteenth century. But they affected few people in the seventeenth century.

## The growth of overseas trade

The fifty years between 1580 and 1630 were a time of great excitement. New lands all over the world were being discovered. New routes were being found. Brave and adventurous captains were mounting expeditions, setting up trading stations and bringing back new goods.

Their main aim was to find a new route to the East, to the spices and wealth of Cathay (China) and the spice islands. They wanted a route which was quicker and less dangerous than the Spanish and Portuguese routes. The Muscovy Company had been formed in 1555 to find a way. Some explorers lost their lives in the search. Stephen Burrough and Anthony Jenkinson succeeded only in opening Russia up to English trade.

*Sir Humphrey Gilbert*

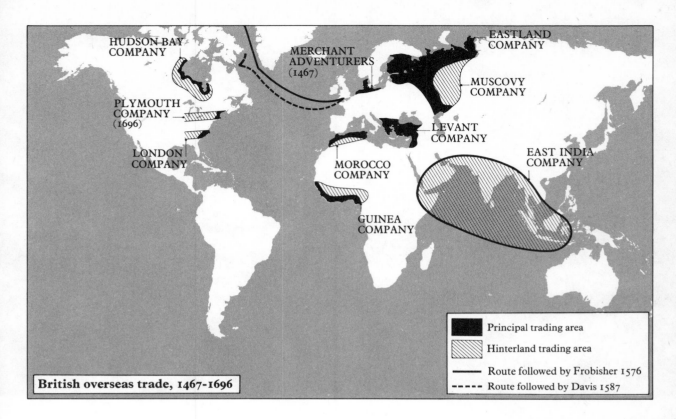

HUDSON BAY
COMPANY

MERCHANT
ADVENTURERS
(1467)

EASTLAND
COMPANY

MUSCOVY
COMPANY

PLYMOUTH
COMPANY
(1696)

LEVANT
COMPANY

EAST INDIA
COMPANY

LONDON
COMPANY

MOROCCO
COMPANY

GUINEA
COMPANY

| | Principal trading area |
| | Hinterland trading area |
| | Route followed by Frobisher 1576 |
| | Route followed by Davis 1587 |

**British overseas trade, 1467–1696**

*Sir Martin Frobisher*

Later explorers tried the other direction. Humphrey Gilbert wrote a
*Discourse to Prove a North-West Passage*. 'There lieth', he wrote, 'a great
sea between America and Cathay, by the which any man of our country
may, with small danger, pass to Cathay, the Molucca, India and all the
other places in the East, in a much shorter time than the Spaniard or
Portugal doeth.' In 1576 Martin Frobisher tried to find the route. He
became lost in Labrador and returned home with nothing, though a
rumour spread that some black stones he had found contained gold.
Many rushed to start mining on the coast of Canada. But then the stones
were found to be worthless.

In 1585 John Davis made an attempt to find the North-West Passage.
After two years of searching he found the Davis Strait, 'finding all the
sea open, and forty leagues [256 kilometres] between land and land,
wherefore the passage is most probable'. But thick pack-ice forced him
to return and no route was ever found.

Exploration was a dangerous affair. In 1591 John Davis returned from
another voyage. This time he had tried to sail through the Straits of
Magellan. He was beaten back by storms which destroyed his anchors and
most of his cable. The rigging rotted, and food, nails and other tackle were
washed overboard. When the storm subsided, the crew put out to land and
were said to have caught and salted 14 000 penguins.

Then the ships sailed north for home. Unfortunately, in the heat of
the tropics the penguins rotted, and a plague of worms infested the ship.

*An East Indiaman sets sail from England*

They crawled over the men while they slept, and ate the ship's timbers. The ship put into Patagonia for help, but some of the crew were caught and killed by cannibal Indians. Later, more were killed by Portuguese pirates off Rio de Janeiro, and others died of scurvy.

At last just sixteen were left, but only five could move. Davis himself steered the ship across the Atlantic, and, when they finally put into Bantry Bay in Ireland, local people thought that it was a ghost ship and all the crew were dead.

Following the footsteps of men like Gilbert, Frobisher and Davis, merchants and traders set out to make their fortunes. They pursued an overland route to the East (the Levant Company was set up in 1581) and they built trading posts in North America and India. They felt that North America would buy English goods, particularly cloth. 'The kingdom hath continued the making of a great store of excellent cloth', wrote John Stow, 'which all nations have always desired for their general use.'

Throughout the seventeenth century, settlements grew, especially in North America. One writer records the start of the Hudson Bay Company in 1670:

At Rupert's river the English built their first fort, which they called Charles Fort. They never had any town or plantations here, and probably never will. They live within their forts in little houses or huts, wherein the builders consider nothing but to defend them from the cold and rains, though they are not so much disturbed by the latter as by the former....

The commodities for trade here are guns, powder, shot, cloth, hatchets, kettles, tobacco, etc., which the English exchange with the Indians for furs, beavers, marten, fox, moose, and other peltry.

By 1714 much of North America was recognised as British.

## The growth of the navy

In Queen Elizabeth's reign, William Harrison wrote in 1587 a description of the navy, 'that for strength, assurance, nimbleness and swiftness of sailing, there are no vessels in the world to be compared with ours'. The following year that strength and swiftness defeated the might of Spain's Armada. Thereafter the navy had a vital role in defending the realm and increasing its wealth.

Perhaps the biggest job was the chasing of privateers. The pirate flag was flown by Scottish, Irish and French ships, eager to capture the wealth of English merchantmen, and even by some Englishmen themselves. One English captain, annoyed that King James I had made peace with Spain, proclaimed himself King of Lundy Island and preyed on all shipping that came out of the port of Bristol. In addition the Barbary corsairs from North Africa were notorious. In just seven years in the early seventeenth century they captured 466 British ships and their crews. They raided the villages of the south coast and took the inhabitants away into slavery. The English navy was ever on the lookout for

*The* Sovereign of the Seas, *built in 1637*

*The Dutch admirals Tromp and De Ruyter attack English ships in the River Medway, 1667*

pirates. In 1620 eighteen ships spent six months attacking North African ports, but with little success. They visited Algiers three times: the first time just forty British slaves were released; with the second, heavy rain put out the blaze of their fire ships; and on the third occasion, the pirate ruler had put a guarded boom across the harbour mouth.

The navy also guarded the seas against ships from rival countries. The English Channel was particularly important against the Dutch. Ships passing Dover Castle were supposed to lower their national ensigns in salute. When the Dutch admiral, van Tromp, refused to do this in 1652, it was used as a cause for war between the two countries.

The war lasted, on and off, between 1652 and 1674. The two navies were well-matched. The English enjoyed some success, for example with the capture of New Amsterdam, which was renamed New York. But in the English Channel there was deadlock. In 1666 the Duke of Albemarle fought De Ruyter, in the 'Four Days' Battle'.

The battle was fought by short-range artillery. On the first day the Dutch, with greater numbers, had the better of it. At night fighting stopped: Albemarle called his captains together and made a famous speech. 'To be overcome', he said, 'is one of the fortunes of war; but to fly is the fashion of cowards.' On the second day, both sides fought bravely. The English, with just forty-four ships to the Dutch eighty, began to retreat. On the third day the Dutch brought up reinforcements. The English plight seemed desperate. But on the fourth day English reinforcements arrived. Now the battle swung the other way.

But towards evening on the fourth day fog came down and the battle ended. Two months later it was started again off the coast of Kent. This time the Dutch retreated and the English plundered the Dutch coast. But then the following year De Ruyter sailed up the River Medway and burned many of the king's ships riding at anchor. Thus the war ended indecisively. But during it, the English navy was divided into two parts: the Royal Navy with ships built for speed and strength, and the Merchant Navy, with ships built for cargo.

It was indeed cargo that gave the navy a job. All through the century, convoys sailed to East and West to bring back goods, particularly pepper and cloves from the East, tobacco, timber, potatoes and other vegetables and later cotton from the West. Indeed, in 1660 Parliament passed a Navigation Act. This included the following provisions:

1 No goods or commodities ... shall be imported into or exported out of any lands ... to His Majesty belonging ... but in such ships and vessels as do truly belong only to the people of England or Ireland and dominion of Wales. ... Whereof the master and at least three-fourths of the mariners at least are English.
2 No goods or commodities that are of foreign growth or manufacture, which are brought into England ... shall be shipped but only from those countries of their growth or manufacture.

Can you suggest why this Act was passed?

In addition, the navy was used in the search for knowledge. In 1700 Dr Edmund Halley commanded a ship into the Atlantic Ocean to observe the stars. Halley was an astronomer, who had seen and named the famous comet in 1682. Now he was studying the magnetic north pole and making a huge chart of the Atlantic. He was away for two years. He sailed from the Antarctic to Newfoundland and charted the whole ocean. Later Halley became Astronomer Royal and he and others continued to use the ships of the navy in their research.

*Edmund Halley, Astronomer Royal*

## Using the evidence:
## Royal Naval convoys in the reign of Queen Anne

The following letter was written on 22 March 1710 to the naval commissioners at Chatham Docks. It was written by one of the crew of the ship *Unity* anchored off Margate:

(1) Hon'ble Sir, I have made bold to write to you to acquaint you of this mischance because I think there is none can give you a truer account than I can. We came to anchor in Westgate Bay the 21st. At one in the morning there came this dogger [a deep-sea fishing vessel]. Our master and one man were on watch. We hailed him, and he answered, 'From Dover.' He had in boat astern ten men and as he came up on us we discharged our pieces. Nevertheless that did not prevail. ... The dogger went about ship and let drive four great guns and a volley of small shot. We discharged our pieces three times, and fired three hand grenades, but it would not do. We cut the cable and made sail. Then they fell a little astern.

As soon as they recovered the wind, they shot up alongside. They entered forty men, and then came shot from their barrels and killed three men and our captain. I heard the men say they made themselves masters of us and they took us in tow and steered away north-east. But merchantmen passed the word along so that the man-of-war *Medway Prize* did see it (and gave chase). The Frenchman cut us adrift. The master and all are gone to Calais (as prisoners). We are all wounded, but them that are gone are worse. I beg your pardon for writing so bad, but my hand being cut I could write no better.

I remain your obliging servant to command,

Richard Reynolds.

(Queen Anne's Navy, Naval Records Society, 1961)

1 What can you tell about the ship that attacked the *Unity*?
2 How was she captured?
3 How did the *Unity* get free?

The next letter was written on 30 December 1704 by the masters or captains of six merchant ships from Dover to the navy's Victualling Board:

(2) Hon'ble Sirs, We whose names are subscribed, being masters of vessels now in Dover harbour, being forced to put in here by reason of stress of weather from the Downs, being laden with provisions for Her Majesty's use, bound for Portsmouth. But, by reason of the many French privateers that are upon the coast, we dare not venture out of this harbour for fear of being taken. For just yesterday, five French privateers stood in and was like to oppose the merchant fleet then coming out of the Downs, had not the captain of the *Burlington* taken great care. The French privateers were from ten to thirty guns apiece, and came within gunshot of Dover Castle. . . . Therefore we thought it proper to acquaint Your Honours therewith, that care may be taken for a sufficient convoy for us, for the preservation of our vessels and Her Majesty's provisions.

4 What cargoes are the six ships carrying?
5 Why are their masters writing the letter?
6 What sort of ship was the *Burlington*?
7 What evidence do the writers give to support their request?
8 Is any of this evidence possibly exaggerated?

Since Britain and France were at war for much of Queen Anne's reign, French raiders were a constant problem. Many attempts were made to check them. This letter was written on 12 December 1709 by the Secretary of the Admiralty to the Navy Board:

(3) Gentlemen, Sir John Norris, Admiral of the Blue Squadron of Her Majesty's fleet, having represented to the Admiralty that, as the manner of the French cruising is with small vessels on our coast, to intercept the trade passing in the Channel, they fall into our fleets in the night, unseen by the men-of-war. They board our small vessels, and carry them without firing. The said vessels make no signal to their convoys of their being surprised.

And this was the case of the last convoy from the Downs, out of which two vessels were taken. This notwithstanding that there is an article in their sailing instructions that . . . they should cut their jeers to prevent their being carried off. [Jeers were the tackle by which lower yards were hoisted: if they were cut, the ship could not sail.]

*A model of a French warship of the seventeenth century*

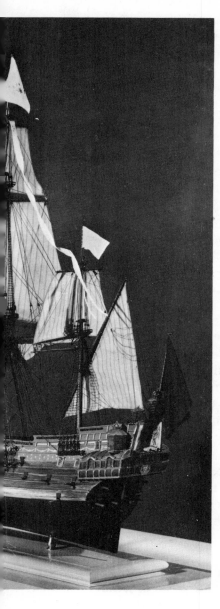

And Admiral Norris offers it as his opinion, in order to prevent the same for the future, that the masters of ships should be ordered to make signals to the men-of-war when a strange ship comes among them.

The next letter is on the same theme. After the commissioner at Chatham had received Richard Reynolds' letter, he immediately wrote to the Navy Board:

(4) And, on this occasion, give me leave to offer what I think would be a great service . . . which is that some careful trusty persons be appointed in the coastal counties of England to keep a good lookout all along the sea coast. And when they discover an enemy, to make a signal by setting afire some wet straw, the smoke of which will be seen a great way off at sea. . . . And the merchantmen, knowing the meaning thereof, may . . . alter their course. It will also be intelligence to our men of war where the enemy is.

Indeed Parliament was so worried about French raiders that in 1708 it passed the Cruisers and Convoys Act:

(5) It is necessary for the better securing the trade of this kingdom that a sufficient number of ships to cruise be appointed in proper stations to protect the merchant ships, outward bound and in their return home. Therefore, over and above the ships of war for the line of battle and for convoys to remote parts, at least forty-three ships of war be employed as cruisers in proper stations. . . . And twelve of these ships of war shall be appointed to cruise the north-east and north-west coasts. . . .

For the better and more effectual encouragement of the Naval Service, proceeds of the sale of captured enemy ships shall go to the captors as prize money. Besides, a bounty of £5 will be paid for every man on board an enemy ship taken as prize.

## Questions and further work

1 Which of these Documents is
   (a) a law which has to be obeyed;
   (b) a description of an event written by an eye-witness;
   (c) an urgent request for help?
2 Which of the Documents was written by a man of little education? How can you tell?
3 Documents 3, 4 and 5 are attempts to improve the protection of British shipping. Which is
   (a) a reasoned suggestion which has been well thought-out;
   (b) an attempt to provide a full service for ships;
   (c) a wild idea?
   In each of the above, say why you think so.
4 What are the possible advantages and disadvantages of the bounty in Document 5?
5 Imagine you are a captain of a navy ship in 1708. Write a letter to the Navy Board to urge changes and improvements in the navy. Say what changes are necessary and why they are needed.

# 19

# Man and the universe

In the picture opposite King Louis XIV is visiting the French Royal Academy of Sciences in 1671. Can you find some, or all, of the following:

1 two items which would help scientists to understand the human body;
2 two items which would help them to understand the stars and the universe;
3 one item which would help them to understand how to conquer a city;
4 two items which would help them to understand plant life;
5 two items which would help them to understand the working of machines;
6 two items which would help them to construct complex buildings?
7 Which of the people in the picture is the king? How do you know?

## The working of the human body

The human body, like that of all animals, lives and grows, decays and dies. It takes in food (digestion) and expels waste matter (excretion). It moves and it breathes in oxygen. The one aspect, however, which fascinated scientists in the seventeenth century was the heart and the blood.

Aristotle had taught that the body contained four 'humours': blood, phlegm, black bile, and choler or yellow bile. Each of these elements influenced character: high spirits, phlegma, melancholy, and bad temper. Illness was caused when the patient had too much of any one 'humour'. Treatment then removed it. Aristotle's teachings survived in Europe, especially through the ideas of the Greek writer, Galen.

Galen's view of the body was that man has life from the vital spirits which travel from the left ventricle of the heart to all parts of the body, including the brain.

By the seventeenth century, however, several men had found mistakes in Galen's system. They did this by cutting open dead bodies. Now it is very easy to take a machine to pieces, but often it is still not clear how it works. So with the human body. In addition, the Church would not let doctors cut open bodies of men just dead. So it was very difficult to find out the cause of death.

Andreas Vesalius was a teacher of anatomy in Padua and, unusually for those days, he cut bodies open himself instead of letting unskilled barber-surgeons do it. One day he closely examined the heart of a dead man: he noticed how thick the septum, the wall between left and right ventricles, was. Blood could not pass through here. Yet this was crucial to Galen's system. All Vesalius' discoveries were written down in 1543 in a book called *The Structure of the Human Body*. And in this book also were many very careful and detailed drawings.

## The work of William Harvey (1578–1657)

William Harvey was born at Folkestone, the eldest of seven sons. His father later became mayor of the town. He received a good education at Canterbury and Cambridge, and at the medical school of Padua. In 1602 he returned to London and five years later he was made a Fellow of

*William Harvey. The drawing*
*shows the heart and blood vessels*

the Royal College of Physicians. After much research he developed in 1616 his own theory of how the blood moves round the body.

'The movement of the blood', he wrote, 'is constantly in a circle, and (this) is brought about by the beat of the heart.' Yet he did not publish his view until 1628 because he wanted to check every detailed aspect of it by experiment.

For example he studied the veins and arteries. He noticed that blood in the veins always flows towards the heart, and that in the arteries away from it. He also examined the heart. He found it a hollow muscle which has a regular spasm. It jerks in, then gently expands. This expansion pushes the blood, via the arteries, to the lungs and other parts of the body.

Harvey's investigations left one main question unanswered. How were veins and arteries linked for the blood to go round in circles? A Dutch scientist, Leeuwenhoek, produced his own microscope. Through it he observed the tiny capillaries, the vessels which join veins and arteries. He also saw the red corpuscles in the blood and the blood itself moving round the body.

The system of Aristotle and Galen had been disproved by observation and experiment.

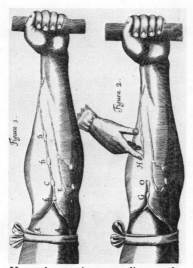

*Harvey's experiments to discover the function of valves in the veins*

## Using the evidence:
## Understanding and preventing disease

### The problem

In 1665, a great plague hit London. People died in their thousands. Fever, vomiting, headaches, were the first symptoms. Then large swellings came under the arms and in the groin. Finally, small rings of red spots ('Ring a ring o' roses') appeared. The victim died within a few days. Look at the pictures of London during the plague (page 217), and the picture of a plague doctor's overall (page 218). People tried many cures for the plague. Here are some:

wearing charms or writing magic words like *Abracadabra*;
carrying flowers and perfumes ('A pocket full of posies');
smoking tobacco;
drinking a pint of sherry a day;
putting mercury on the sores and placing the victim in an oven;
lighting bonfires in the streets and filling affected houses with smoke.

The mayor and aldermen of the City of London made special rules to fight the plague:

(i) If someone caught the plague, the master of the house had to report it to a medical examiner.

(ii) The Examiner sent in two searchers to check. They were usually old ladies who carried white sticks to warn people to keep away.

(iii) The Examiner put the house into quarantine. No one could go out for forty days.

(iv) The door was marked with a red cross and the words 'Lord have mercy upon us'.

(v) If the patient died, the body was removed after dark. No one from the house could go to the burial. Graves had to be at least six feet (about two metres) deep to stop dogs digging up the body.

1 From the pictures and writing above, what did people at the time think was the cause of the plague?
2 Which of the steps shown in the pictures and writing may have helped to fight the disease? Which would not?

### How doctors tackled diseases

1 Traditional medicines included human and animal blood, sweat, a snake's skin, bird's feathers, woodlice and spiders' webs.

*How men coped with the plague*

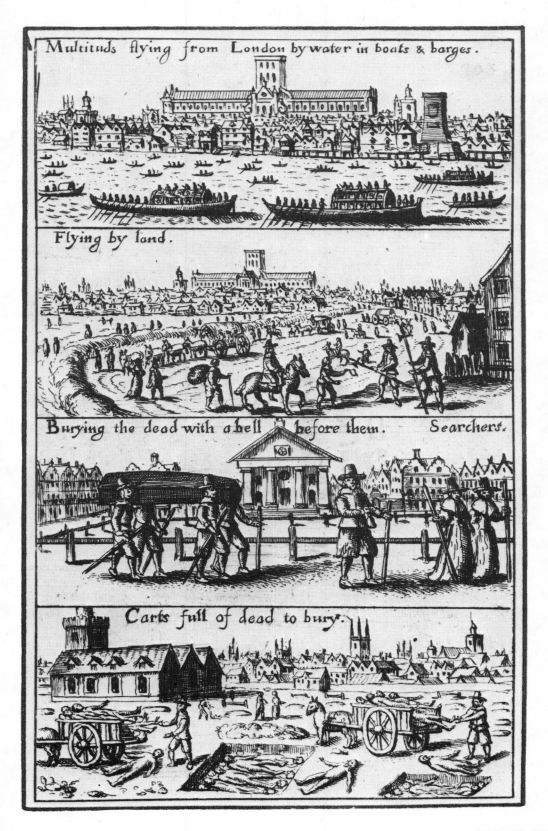

Multituds flying from London by water in boats & barges.

Flying by land.

Burying the dead with a bell before them.    Searchers.

Carts full of dead to bury.

*Write one or two sentences about this picture*

2 Traditional treatment included bloodletting, and touching by a king, an archbishop, or even a famous 'personality'.

3 Anyone could be a doctor and treat people. Operations were performed by barbers. Most men thought that the body was made up of four parts: blood, phlegm, black bile and yellow bile. It was healthy if it had the right amount of all four; if not, some had to be drained off. Hence bloodletting. One rich London doctor of the early eighteenth century is supposed to have said:

> When any sick to me apply
> I physics, bleeds, and sweats 'em.
> If, after that, they choose to die,
> Why, verily, I Lettsom.

4 Hospitals were often very poor. The Hospital of la Charité in Paris was run by monks.

An English doctor, Sir William Petty, recorded the number of deaths at the hospital. 'In 1679 there entered into la Charité 3118, of which there died 452, which is above a seventh part.' Other hospitals had worse records!

Which of the above treatments could actually cause and spread disease?

### Dr Thomas Sydenham and Dr Nathaniel Hodges

Thomas Sydenham came from a well-to-do Puritan family, from Dorset. He studied at Oxford, then at the famous medical school of Montpellier. He never became a member of the Royal College of Physicians because he was a supporter of Parliament. But amongst his patients he had many rich and well-known people. As a result his treatments quickly became well known.

Here is Sydenham's decription of children's measles:

(1) On the first day they have cold and shivers. On the second they have a fever in full, a white tongue, thirst and sleepiness. The nose and eyes run continually. The symptoms increase until the fourth day. Then there appear on the face and forehead small red spots like flea-bites, which cluster together, so as to mark the face with large blotches. The spots spread to the trunk. On the eighth day they disappear.

*A doctor's preventive clothing against the plague*

Dr Sydenham observed his patients closely. He became very angry with doctors who never saw their patients and just talked about 'humours'. One day he interrupted a famous botanist by saying:

(2) Anatomy, botany, nonsense! No, go to the bedside; there alone can you learn disease.

He treated disease with fresh air, gentle exercise, and a few simple medicines. He opposed bloodletting and many other remedies which did more harm than good.

Dr Nathaniel Hodges was one of the few doctors to stay in London while the great plague raged. This was his daily round: he rose early, took a short drink, then saw 'crowds of citizens as in a hospital'. He had breakfast before visiting the homes of plague victims. At each house he 'immediately had burnt some proper thing upon coals'. He sucked lozenges of myrrh and cinnamon. Then he went home to dinner. He drank a glass of wine before and after his meal. Then back to his visits, followed by a few glasses of 'my old favourite liquor, which encouraged sleep and easy breathing through the pores all night'.

Like Sydenham he treated disease with fresh air, plenty of rest, a light diet. He also prescribed the burning of resinous wood 'which throws out a clear and healthy smell' and 'plague water' as prescribed by the College of Physicians.

*Galileo*

3 What has Sydenham done in Document 1? Why has he done this?
4 Which of Hodges' treatments were likely to help? Which were not?
5 Why do you think these two men were important in dealing with disease?
6 One writer called Sydenham a 'crusader against hocus-pocus in medicine'. What do you think he meant?

## Astronomy and the story of Galileo

Apart from medicine the main interest of scientists in the seventeenth century concerned the heavens.

Galileo Galilei was born in the Italian city of Pisa, the son of a poor nobleman. At school he was a clever boy, enthusiastic about his work and always coming up with interesting ideas. His father wanted him to study medicine, but Galileo liked mathematics and physics. He used to sit outside the physics lecture rooms and ask students questions about the lectures as they came out. When the lecturer heard of this he arranged for Galileo to attend the classes. At the age of twenty-five, Galileo became a lecturer in mathematics at the University of Pisa.

But Galileo quickly became unpopular with the other scholars. There is a story that one day he stood at the top of the famous leaning tower in Pisa. He looked over the edge and dropped three items, of different weights, to the ground. He observed that all three hit the ground at the same time. Now Aristotle had taught – and most scholars still believed – that bodies of different weight travelled at different speeds.

People like Galileo who think others are wrong are rarely very popular. And Galileo once wrote to another scientist, Kepler: 'My dear Kepler, you would laugh till you cried if you could hear the arguments which the professors of this university use against me.'

Soon Galileo moved to the University of Padua and here he became convinced that the ideas of Copernicus were correct. Copernicus (1473–1543) did not believe that the earth was the centre of the universe: instead the earth moved around the sun.

*John Kepler*

In a letter to a friend, as early as 1597, Galileo wrote:

I have been for many years a follower of Copernicus. He explains many things which seem ridiculous in the commonly-held view. I have collected many arguments to refute the latter, but I dare not publish them.

This opinion was correct. One of Galileo's friends, Giordano Bruno, had been burned at the stake for openly defending Copernicus.

## Galileo's discoveries

At Padua, Galileo made many important finds. In 1609 he made a telescope and was the first man to use one to study the stars. In 1610 he observed that Jupiter had four moons, and he saw many more stars than people had ever imagined existed, 'Which are more than ten times as numerous as those which are visible to the naked eye.' He saw the mountains and valleys of the moon, and observed the dark patches, or sun-spots, which occasionally appear on the sun. In 1613 he could restrain himself no longer: he wrote a book called *Letters on the Sun's Spots*. In it he supported Copernicus against the opinion of Aristotle, and in 1616 he was attacked and criticised by the Catholic church.

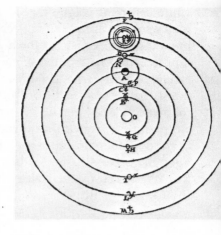

*Galileo's own drawing of the Copernican system of the universe, 1632. Galileo added one of his own discoveries, the four moons of Jupiter*

### *Galileo's later life*

For the next sixteen years Galileo worked in peace, studying and thinking. Eventually, in 1632, he published his great work, *The Dialogue on the Two Chief World Systems*. In this he supported the Copernican view. The book was immediately put on the Index of banned books. Galileo was summoned to Rome to the Inquisition. In June 1633 he was examined and threatened with torture. He recanted (that is, changed his opinion) and was given a penance which lasted three years. In his recantation he stated:

I bow my knee before the Honourable Inquisitor General, I touch the Holy Gospel, and I state that I will always believe that what the Church teaches is true.... I abjure and curse my opinion of the motion of the earth and the station of the sun.

Galileo died in 1642. In that year Isaac Newton was born. And it was Newton who showed the world that Copernicus and Galileo had been right.

## Sir Isaac Newton (1642–1727)

Isaac Newton was born on Christmas Day, 1642 at Woolsthorpe, near Grantham in Lincolnshire. There was probably little rejoicing in the household, because Isaac's father had died just before the birth.

As a child he was delicate, quiet, reserved. He kept himself to himself. He played little with other boys. Yet he grew up to be one of the greatest thinkers in history. At the age of twelve he went to the local grammar school at Grantham. He made models and mechanical toys, and his sundial and water clock still survive. He became head boy of the school and excelled at mathematics.

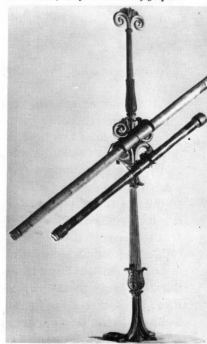

*Galileo's telescope*

In 1661, on the recommendation of an uncle, he went to Trinity College, Cambridge. He made few friends, preferring to work quietly at his studies. After gaining a BA in 1665, he went home for two years because of the plague. But two years later he returned to Cambridge and in 1669 he became Professor of Mathematics.

For the next fifteen years he worked at mathematical problems. Then, in 1684, a young astronomer, Edmund Halley, asked Newton to help him. Halley had read the works of Copernicus, Galileo and others and he saw that the planets had fixed orbits around the sun.

*Newton's telescope*

Halley wanted Newton to work out the orbits mathematically. Newton became interested in why the planets took the same path. He wondered, too, why the moon orbited the earth. For three years Newton gave these problems much thought. And in 1687 he published his *Principia*. He stated the laws of motion and showed the power of the forces of gravity. He proved that the universe worked according to mathematical laws.

In the Middle Ages, priests had taught that they alone could explain how God had created the world, how man and animals should behave, how planets moved, how nature worked. In the sixteenth and seventeenth centuries, scientists questioned this teaching. Men like Galileo and Newton, Leonardo and Harvey, started discussion and argument. The thinking of scientists was starting to change the world.

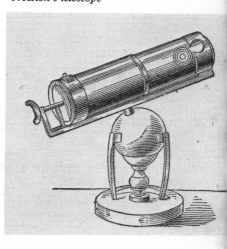

# Index

# Acknowledgements

The author and publishers wish to thank the following who have kindly given permission for the use of copyright material:

Edward Arnold (Publishers) Limited for extracts from *Documents for History Revision* by M. M. Reese and *Renaissance and Reformation* by V. H. H. Green; Associated Book Publishers Limited for extracts from *England under the Tudors* by G. R. Elton, published by Methuen & Company Limited; *Dutch Seaborne Empire* by Boxer, published by Eyre & Spottiswoode (Publishers) Limited and *Cromwell's Master Spy* by D. L. Hobman, published by Chapman & Hall Limited; B. T. Batsford Limited for an extract from *The English Reformation* by A. G. Dickens; Basil Blackwell & Mott Limited for an extract from *Lectures in Foreign History* by J. M. Thompson; Cambridge University Press for an extract from *Europe Finds the World* by T. Cairns; Jonathan Cape Limited on behalf of C. V. Wedgewood for an extract from *William the Silent*; Jonathan Cape Limited on behalf of the Estate of R. W. Chambers for an extract from *Thomas More*; Paul Elek Limited for an extract from *The Discovery of North America*; Victor Gollancz Limited for extracts from *Louis XIV* by J. B. Wolf; Heinemann Educational Books Limited for an extract from *A Man for All Seasons* by R. Bolt; and a short passage from *Britain, Europe and the World* by D. Witcombe; Hodder & Stoughton Limited for extracts from *Here I Stand* by R. Bainton; Hutchinson Publishing Group Limited for extracts from *Portraits and Documents: 16th Century* by J. S. Millward; John Johnson on behalf of H. R. Williamson for an extract from *The Gunpowder Plot*; MacDonald and Jane's Publishers Limited for extracts from *The World of Leonardo Da Vinci* by I. B. Hart; Search Press Limited for extracts from *Ignatius Loyola* by Broderick.

The author and publishers wish to acknowledge the following photograph sources:

Reproduced by Gracious Permission of Her Majesty the Queen pp. 22, 38, 41 bottom, 64, 65;
Reproduced by kind permission of the Archbishop of Canterbury and the Church Commissioners for England. Copyright reserved to the Church Commissioners and to the Courtauld Institute of Art pp. 40 bottom, 147 top;
By kind permission of the Marquess of Tavistock and the Trustees of the Bedford Estates, Woburn Abbey p. 66 top;

American History Picture Library pp. 193, 194, 195, 196, 200, 201;
Ashmolean Museum, Oxford p. 161 top;
Barnabys Picture Library p. 16 right;
Bazzechi-Foto, Firenze p. 220 bottom;
B. T. Batsford Ltd – Dultons 'English Country House' Part title p. 2 bottom right, p. 103;
Biblioteca Ambrosiana, Milan pp. 23, 24, 25;
Bibliotheque Publique et Universitaire de Geneve p. 51;
Bibliothek Der Ryksurniversite p. 125;
Bodleian Library pp. 10, 121 top;
Trustees of British Library pp. 83 (MS 980 c 25 40), 93 top (MS 158 c 27 pF 132), 140/141 top (PB E. 177 (B) 700485), 161 bottom (Shelfmark E 1933);
Trustees of British Museum pp. 29 top, 62 top, 90, 111, 113 top;
Buckinghamshire County Museum p. 141;
Bulloz pp. 74 top, 75, 79, 182, 184, 185, 187;
J. Allan Cash p. 55;
Colchester and Essex Museum p. 155;
Crown Copyright: reproduced with permission of the Controller of Her Majesty's Stationery Office p. 59; 120 bottom;
Documentation Photographique de la Réunion des musées nationaux Part title, p. 2 top, p. 9;
Edinburgh University Library pp. 122, 132, 135;
Mary Evans Picture Library pp. 171, 179;
Folger Shakespeare Library, Washington pp. 53, 66 bottom, 118;
Gabinitto Fotografico Nationale, Firenze p. 29 bottom left;
German National Museum p. 49;
Giraudon pp. 18, 28, 32, 33, 34 top, 40 middle, 46, 63, 72, 73, 74 bottom, 188;
Gorhambury Collection, by permission of The Earl of Verulam p. 147 bottom;
Dean and Chapter of Hereford Cathedral p. 13 left;
Kunsthistorischen Museum p. 41 top;
Editions Robert Laffont p. 174;
Mansell Collection Part title, p. 2 bottom left, 11, 19, 20, 21, 26, 29 bottom right, 31 bottom, 47, 60, 67, 69, 78, 86/87, 92, 108/109, 124/125, 126, 128, 130, 131, 133 top, 136, 138, 139, 144, 148, 151, 152, 157, 159, 164, 165, 178, 178/179, 197, 198, 204, 206, 207, 211, 221;
Magdalen College, Cambridge p. 217;
MAS pp. 80, 81, 82, 84, 87;
Musée Cantonal Des Beaux-Arts p. 77;
Musée de la Marine pp. 212/213;
Museum Boymans-Van-Beuningen, Rotterdam p. 100 top;
National Maritime Museum Part title, pp. 3, 169, 208, 209, 210;
Trustees of the National Gallery pp. 96, 98;
National Portrait Gallery, London pp. 34 bottom, 39, 40 top, 44, 45, 52, 105, 106 bottom, 109, 115, 117, 119, 121 bottom, 142, 154, 156, 167 bottom;
Novosti Press Agency p. 177 top;
Hon. Mrs Clive Pearson p. 110;
Courtesy of the Pilgrim Library p. 199;
Public Records Office pp. 54, 143, 145, 166;
R.T.H.P.L. pp. 13 right, 31 top, 36, 61, 62 bottom, 88, 89, 106 top, 107, 133 bottom, 136/137, 140/141 bottom, 162, 163, 205 top, 219;
Rijksmuseum, Amsterdam pp. 93 bottom, 99, 100 bottom, 101, 102;
Ann Ronan Picture Library p. 220 top;
SCALA pp. 27, 30;
The Scottish National Portrait Gallery pp. 113 bottom, 160;
Snark International pp. 16 top, middle and bottom left, 173 top, 183, 186, 190, 215 left;
Svenska Portrattarkivet National Museum p. 50;
Tate Gallery p. 218 top;
University Library, Cambridge pp. 203, 205 bottom;
Roger Viollet pp. 15, 173 bottom, 175, 176, 189, 191;
Walker Art Gallery, Liverpool p. 37;
Courtesy of the Wellcome Trustees p. 215 right;
Taken from publication 'The Evolution of Russia' by Otto Hortzsch, published by Thames & Hudson p. 177 bottom;
Cover photograph by courtesy of Michael Holford

The publishers have made every effort to trace copyright holders, but if they have inadvertently overlooked any they will be pleased to make the necessary arrangement at the first opportunity.